DASHER

The Kevin Wheatley VC Story

MICHAEL C. MADDEN

Foreword by Keith Payne VC AM KSJ

First published 2021

Big Sky Publishing Pty Ltd
PO Box 303, Newport, NSW 2106, Australia
Phone: 1300 364 611
Fax: (61 2) 9918 2396
Email: info@bigskypublishing.com.au
Web: www.bigskypublishing.com.au

Cover design and typesetting: Think Productions

Title: Dasher The Kevin Wheatley VC Story
ISBN: 9781922488657

A catalogue record for this book is available from the National Library of Australia

DASHER

The Kevin Wheatley VC Story

www.bigskypublishing.com.au

MICHAEL C. MADDEN

Foreword by Keith Payne VC AM KSJ

PRAISE FOR *DASHER*

'The Dasher Wheatley story is one that all Australians should know and be proud of. No one has given us a better example of how we should treat our fellow man. He played hard and he fought hard. A brilliant mate and a perfect soldier. Wheatley's Victoria Cross action was an act of valour and self-sacrifice that surprised none who knew him.'
His Excellency General the Honourable David Hurley AC DSC (Retd General), Governor-General of Australia

'I never met Dasher Wheatley VC, but I would have liked to share a beer with a man whose decision to stay with a dying mate, cost him his life. His compelling courage, that choice, characterise the values that make Australia. It has been an honour to support the family that were left behind. Mrs Wheatley, widowed at age 26 with four young children, has been a tower of strength on the battlefield of life. I salute them both'.
Kerry Stokes AC Chairman Australian War Memorial, donated Dasher Wheatley's Victoria Cross to the AWM

'Dasher loved as hard as he fought and was tactically sound in everything he did. A loyal friend and a dependable leader. Dasher's sacrifice and death affected us all deeply.'
Warrant Officer (retd) Keith Payne VC. AM. KSJ (AATTV Vietnam)

'The Dasher Wheatley story is one all Australians should know and be proud of. His is an example of valour and friendship we should all aspire to.'
Captain (retd) Rambahadur Limbu VC. MVO (British Army Gurkha from Nepal)

'Dasher Wheatley's Victoria Cross action is a perfect example of mateship and tenacity. His actions should be understood and held up as an example of what mates do for each other. Not just in the military, but in all walks of life.'
Senior Sergeant Tim Britten CV (Private 1RAR retd)

'There are rare people who have an aura about them, a fundamental moral and ethical decency that inspires trust, love and a willingness to follow their lead; they exude the very definition of leadership by example. I defy anyone to read Dasher's story in this marvellous book and not shake their head in awe at his selflessness. He earned the VC for one astonishing act of bravery in 1965, but the story I have always found most moving, also told within, was how, early in his tour, he ran through cross-fire to rescue a young Vietnamese girl, using his own body to shield her amidst a hail of fire. The circumstances of his death during the VC action, choosing to stay with a wounded comrade rather than abandon him, are equally astounding. Dasher Wheatley was a warrior who loved.'
Ross Coulthart (Logie winning Investigative Journalist, 5-time Walkley winner, Prime Minister's Literary Award winner)

'Across four nations, some fifty years later, the story of Dasher Wheatley VC, still ricochets around the hallowed halls of the great military institutions. His courage in the face of certain death, stands as an example few will be called to emulate, and most know that they could never replicate. The story of his Victoria Cross and the hunt for Dasher's missing Silver Star are all consuming and a tale well told.'
Chris Hartley LVO

This book is dedicated to the Wheatley family,
and to all Australian Vietnam Veterans.

CONTENTS

Author's Note 1
Foreword 6
Prologue 9
Chapter 1: Heritage 12
Chapter 2: Edna 19
Chapter 3: The Army 25
Chapter 4: Malaya 30
Chapter 5: Football and Mates 41
Chapter 6: The Scungees in PNG 53
Chapter 7: A New Team 61
Chapter 8: Quang Tri City, Vietnam 67
Chapter 9: Ned Kelly 78
Chapter 10: A Jarhead 86
Chapter 11: Valour Denied 92
Chapter 12: One of the Boys 104
Chapter 13: Snipers and the Beach 116
Chapter 14: Howitzers 130
Chapter 15: Blood for Oil 136
Chapter 16: The Frog 142
Chapter 17: Tenacity 147

Chapter 18: The Fort of Death 152
Chapter 19: Torture by Empathy 158
Chapter 20: The A Team 165
Chapter 21: The Final Patrol 174
Chapter 22: Contact 183
Chapter 23: Mateship Personified 194
Chapter 24: Aftermath 204
Chapter 25: Bring Him Home 211
Chapter 26: The Victoria Cross 221
Chapter 27: An Australia Hero 236
Chapter 28: Life Goes On 249
Chapter 29: The Silver Star 256
Epilogue 262

AUTHOR'S NOTE

Although the following is not a work of fiction, it might read like one. Kevin 'Dasher' Wheatley VC was an extraordinary human being. If an author was to create a character like Dasher for a fiction novel and write a story like this one, some people might call it far-fetched and ridiculous. That said, every tale in this book is true and comes from a long list of books, service records, military reports, citations, letters, newspaper articles and interviews.

Kevin Wheatley was a man who commanded respect and led his men by the light of his actions, not his rank. He is widely regarded as one of the finest infantry soldiers Australia has ever produced. By the time, people, who have never heard of Dasher, finish reading this book, they might wonder how it is possible that they had not come across his story before. I certainly hope so.

I could never understand why some other author, more experienced than me, had not already written Dasher's book. He is one of the best-known, most loved and respected Victoria Cross recipients of all time and his story is wildly entertaining. To be honest, I wanted to write it myself for a long time, but was intimidated and frankly, horrified at the idea of taking it on. After all, this is Dasher Wheatley, a man who deserves enormous respect and dignity. I do not think I have ever encountered another person who was more loved by so many people.

While writing this book, I had the absolute pleasure of talking to Dasher's family and many of the men who served with him. People like Warrant Officer (ret) Bill William, Captain (ret) Michael Von Burg MC OAM, Warrant Officer (ret) Ray O'Brien, Lieutenant Colonel (ret) John Sullivan OAM, and more. After talking to these people, and others, it is easy to come away with a good understanding of the awe in which Dasher was held. You can see the emotion on their faces and hear it in their voices when they talk about him. One moment, they are crying and the next, they are laughing their heads off, as they recall the things Dasher used to do. The pain these people suffered, when Dasher died, is obvious. No one suffered his passing as deeply as his family did, however, and it has been a privilege to get to know them.

I first met George Wheatley, Dasher's son, when I was writing my book, *The Victoria Cross – Australia Remembers*, and we have since become good friends. George was the first of the 60 families who would eventually step forward to help me with that book and it was his support that gave me the courage to continue. I can state, with hand on heart, that, without George Wheatley, that book would never have been written and without that book, this one would not have, either. George gave me the encouragement, confidence and will, to begin and after I started, he was the one who kept me going.

Throughout the process of creating this book, George Wheatley tolerated countless phone calls, text messages and emails from me. I constantly pestered him for confirmation of a certain date or name, a long-buried document or photo or simply, for advice and guidance. There were times, when we spoke on the phone every day, for weeks on end and for his part, George never complained. I know it was emotionally difficult for him to continue looking back into his past, but he did it, time and again. The research he did and the work he put in, to find documents, letters and photos, was staggering and will never be forgotten. Thank you for everything, George.

Although there are many people that I should thank, for helping me with this book, I have to say a special thank you to Dasher's widow,

Author's Note

Edna Wheatley. Edna is a wonderful lady and someone I have come to love dearly. In many ways, Edna reminds me of my own mother, their stories are remarkably similar, save for one glaring difference; my mother's husband survived the Vietnam War, Edna's did not. Both Edna, and my mother Shirley, grew up in the same suburbs of Sydney, at about the same time, and even attended the same school. Although, they never met as children, they have now and get along well, which is something that makes me very happy.

Edna Wheatley is easily the second hero of this book. Her life's journey is difficult to fully appreciate and, like so many war widows, she has been the constant rock that has held her family together. The enormity of what she has endured bends the mind. I hope the following pages help give people some idea of what life can be like for the families of servicepeople, especially those who are killed overseas. Adding a Victoria Cross to the mix creates a whole new level of problems for families that are impossible to appreciate, without talking to people like Edna. I know every one of her children, George, Phyllis, Ellen and Leeanne, all adore her and fully appreciate all she endured for them, over their lives. I am very aware of how difficult reliving some of her darkest days was for Edna, as she helped me tell Kevin's story, and I fully appreciate and respect that. The trust and patience she showed me, through the process, was humbling. Thank you, Edna.

Although, there are a lot of stories about Kevin Wheatley in the following pages, this book could have easily been longer. There are many tales about the man that either could not be verified or were simply inappropriate and might cause the family some discomfort, so were left out. This was something I was extremely conscious about, while writing. The Wheatley family has suffered greatly from Kevin's sacrifice and from the nightmarish events that unfolded, after he died. The last thing I wanted to do was to add to that suffering, but I was determined from the outset to write the story, as accurately and honestly as I could. I hope I have achieved this.

It should go without saying that this book is not a glorification of war, nor is it intended to be an open criticism of any government, army or organisation. It is simply the truth, and the simple truth is that Dasher Wheatley was a glorious person. It is my hope that, through this book, many people can learn about him and the crazy and thrilling things he did. Kevin Wheatley should not only be remembered for the way he died and the Victoria Cross he was awarded, but for the man he was and the family he left behind.

When writing my book, *The Victoria Cross – Australia Remembers*, I had the privilege of telling the stories of the then 100 Australians who had been awarded the Victoria Cross. Every one of those stories is an example of outstanding courage and tenacity, but Dasher's stands out to me, as one that speaks clearly to the ideals of valour and humility. In my opinion, the true meaning of Dasher's sacrifice is much deeper than it first appears. His decision to do what he did on 13 November 1965, was considered and deliberate. The consequences for him might well have been orders of magnitude worse than the death he suffered. The Vietcong did not always shoot enemy soldiers, when they had an opportunity to do otherwise. Kevin must have expected to be captured and tortured to death that day, yet, he did not flinch. That took staggering courage.

I have deliberately written this book in a way that makes it easy and enjoyable to read. That meant keeping it shorter than it could have been and presenting it in a novelistic way people can enjoy. I did not want to create an almanac or thesis, filled with dates and citations, but an accurate book, which helps people relate to the characters. To do this, I have taken some liberties with some of the dialogue that characters use. Obviously, I was not there, in person, to record what was said. That aside, I can say that the overwhelming majority of dialogue, used in this book, was provided by people who were there.

I must acknowledge Jim Lowe and his son Dasher Lowe. Jim wrote a wonderful book, called, *A Jarhead's Journey*, and with his son Dasher's blessing, I have relied on that book heavily, in certain chapters. Jim Lowe and Kevin Wheatley worked closely together in Vietnam and became good friends. They were close enough that Jim nicknamed his son after him.

Author's Note

Lastly, I feel obliged to point out that all servicepeople, who go to war, are brave and worthy of national remembrance, not just those who are decorated or those who are killed in action. While this book focuses on Victoria Cross recipient, Kevin Wheatley, it also tells the stories of many other people. To all those people, thank you, we will remember you.

Michael C. Madden

FOREWORD

This book tells the story of a character, unlike any you will ever meet. Dasher Wheatley was an outstanding soldier and about as tough a man as you were ever likely to come across. He left an impression on everyone who met him. His death sent shockwaves through three armies, not just the Australian Army, but the American and South-Vietnamese ones, as well. The man was a legend, well before he was awarded the Victoria Cross.

Kevin 'Dasher' Wheatley was a warrant officer in the Australian Army and a hard-as-nails bloke. He was outstanding, in his own way, because of his complex and multifaceted character. He was many different things to many different people. If you were unlucky enough to come across him on the footy field or in the boxing ring, you would have encountered a lightning-fast and often brutal opponent, who was somehow always three steps ahead of you. If you happened across him at the pub, after you had been giving his mates a hard time, you'd find a savage brawler with fists like lightning. If you were an enemy soldier and found him in the jungles of Vietnam… well, you would just be dead.

On the other hand, if you were an impoverished child in a forgotten hamlet around Quang Tri, you would have seen a gentle man with a milewide grin, who always had food and gifts for you, a loving man who would run into a hail of bullets to cover your little body with his, which is exactly what he did on one occasion. If you were his mate, you would know a man whose courage and leadership were a thing to aspire to. A man who always had your back and never let you down. And if you were Butch Swanton, you would find solace in his presence and know, beyond any shadow of a doubt, that you were not going to die alone.

No one was surprised when Dasher was awarded the Victoria Cross, he was one of those blokes who was bound to earn one, eventually. The Victoria Cross is the Commonwealth's highest decoration for valour, awarded to serving members of the armed forces in wartime. When created by Queen Victoria and her people in 1856, they must have had blokes just like Dasher in mind. Dasher would have been embarrassed, had he lived to receive his award, but I have no doubt he would have worn it with dignity.

To this day, the Victoria Cross remains the most pre-eminent military decoration in the world. From Queen Victoria to Queen Elizabeth II, the monarch has personally reviewed and approved every Victoria Cross ever awarded. The final decision on whether to grant a VC lies with the King or Queen alone, not politicians and generals. This is an obligation the Royal Family carries out with the deepest deliberation and care, and it is a charge that we, who receive the Cross, take extremely seriously. Dasher would have done so, as well.

To date, 101 Australian servicemen have been recognised for their most conspicuous gallantry or daring or pre-eminent act of valour or self-sacrifice or extreme devotion to duty in the presence of the enemy and have, therefore, been recommended for and received the Victoria Cross. The actions of these men represent the finest military practices and resolute courage, displayed by Australian servicemen and women, over the last 100 years.

Dasher's actions on 13 of November 1965 saw him awarded the first Victoria Cross in Vietnam and, at the time, the only VC awarded, without British forces being present, in modern times. It was a test of the institution of the Cross that raised many questions about the legality and indeed, the ethics of granting the award, without the

British being involved. In the end, the quality of Dasher's actions and sacrifice made the decision inevitable. It is my hope that this book helps Australians know and understand who Dasher Wheatley was and what he meant to us, and why the Australian Army still talks about Dasher's actions, to this day. His sacrifice was a perfect example of humility and valour. It was mateship personified.

Lest we forget.
Warrant Officer (ret) Keith Payne VC. AM. KSJ, (AATTV Vietnam)

PROLOGUE

Private Dinh Do huddled behind a tree, the battle raged behind him, bullets zipped through the jungle all around. The young man was a soldier in the Civilian Irregular Defence Group (CIDG) in South Vietnam. He had been out on patrol with his platoon, which was being led by the two Australian soldiers, who were now trapped in the rice paddy behind him. They had been ambushed by an overwhelming Vietcong force, over half an hour before and his platoon had scattered.

Dinh Do had run from the open rice paddy, taking advantage of the cover fire, provided by one of the Australians. Now, in the relative safety of the jungle, to the north of the rice paddy, Private Dinh Do wanted to keep running, the thick jungle beckoned him. He could not will his feet to move, even though he could hear the battle growing behind him. The private had witnessed the two Australian soldiers trying to help each other and those around them, with total disregard for their own safety, as he, Dinh Do, had fled. He was not proud of that.

One of the Australians, the one they called 'Butch', had been shot in the chest and the young private was sure he was dead. But what about the other Australian? What about Warrant Officer Wheatley, or 'Dasher' as they called him? Private Dinh Do stood with his back to the tree, willing himself to turn and investigate the rice paddy, to risk exposing himself, to see if Dasher was still alive. Warrant Officer

Wheatley had remained to help his friend and it was the cover he had laid down that had allowed Dinh Do and the other men to make it to the trees. The Australian had done that, even though they had abandoned him. That had been a staggering act of selflessness and courage and he knew that to flee now would be to betray the honour of those actions.

Private Dinh Do took a deep breath and stepped out from cover, to look for the Australians. To his complete shock, he found both men, almost immediately and what he saw would stay with him for the rest of his life. The two men were only about 20 metres away, still out in the open and being peppered by gunfire. Warrant Officer Kevin 'Dasher' Wheatley was half carrying, half dragging his friend Butch Swanton to safety. Wheatley's rifle was slung over his shoulder, small arms fire was coming from every direction, making the muddy ground around the Australians boil. Ignoring the hundreds of rounds of deadly fire, all aimed at him, Wheatley continued to carry his friend to safety. Private Dinh Do was stunned, but immediately sprang into action.

He ran to Wheatley's side, disregarding the hail of bullets falling around him and helped the Australian drag Swanton to cover. Against almost impossible odds, the two men managed to get the wounded soldier to the safety of the trees but the Vietnamese private saw a dozen or so black- uniformed Vietcong swarming towards them. He did a quick examination of Swanton, amazed that the man was still alive. His breathing was shallow, his face pale and his lips were blue, despite the heat of the day. He was moments from death.

'Still with me, Digger?' Dasher said to his wounded friend.

Swanton nodded and said, 'You need to go, mate.'

Dinh Do could see now that the enemy soldiers were closing in fast. They were about to be overrun. He put his hand on Dasher's shoulder. 'Sir – sir, VC coming, we go now! Your friend die now, we go.'

Dasher, breathing hard from effort, turned to regard him. His dark eyes were wild, but there was no anger in them. Instead, Private Dinh Do saw acceptance and determination. The Australian said, 'Nah, mate, I'm staying with this bloke. You go.'

Prologue

Dinh Do's jaw dropped open. 'Sir, he dead soon, we go now.'

'I'm staying.'

Dinh Do was incredulous. There was no time left, so he said, 'Sir, you have bullets?'

Dasher shook his head. 'Nah, mate, no bullets, just these.' He knelt beside his friend, removed two hand grenades, and pulled the pins on both.

Dinh Do said again, 'Sir, we go!' We die now!'

'It's alright, Private,' Dasher said calmly. 'You take off. I can handle these blokes. The bastards aren't gettin' him.' To Butch, he said, 'It's alright, mate, I'm not going anywhere.'

The private looked quickly towards the clearing, to see VC soldiers charging towards them. He knew what Wheatley was doing. The words, 'I can handle these blokes,' was the warrant officer's way of letting Dinh Do off the hook. Swanton groaned in agony, as Wheatley moved to kneel protectively over him. Reluctantly, Dinh Do nodded and as the enemy closed to within about ten metres, he ran. The last thing the private saw, as he chanced a look back over his shoulder, was the silhouetted figure of the bravest man he had ever met, kneeling over his dying friend. Both of Dasher's arms were outstretched, a live grenade held threateningly in each fist, as enemy soldiers closed in on his front. Private Dinh Do ran for his life.

Chapter 1
HERITAGE

Kevin Arthur Wheatley clung to his mother's neck, as the enormous crowd of people gathered on the dock cheered and waved. The atmosphere was strange. There was a feeling of excitement and fear, a tension which suggested the air around him was about to explode into flowers or flames. He did not know which. All around him, people were crying and singing, as Kevin watched his father march proudly up the gangplank.

Like all the other soldiers, Kevin's dad looked brilliant in his army uniform. His heavy bag was slung over one shoulder and his crisp clean slouch hat was tilted a little to one side. As he reached the top of the gangplank, he turned and waved, then disappeared into the enormous ship. Kevin's mother wiped away tears and they stood together for a long time, as the seemingly endless river of men flowed up the gangplank and disappeared into the vessel. Kevin was amazed by the sheer number of soldiers going aboard and wondered how on earth they were going to fit.

The gigantic metal ship was easily the biggest thing the boy had ever seen, apart from the tall buildings that reached into the sky in the city. But there were so many men going onto the ship that he figured that even if the soldiers were stacked on top of each other, from the front to the back, they still would not fit. It was like watching an army of ants streaming into a hungry steel monster, which devoured them one by one, never able to get enough. He watched, as the huge gangplanks were pulled up and the soldiers crowded onto the decks above, waving down to loved ones. The ship pulled back slowly from the dock, turned, and steamed away.

As he watched, Kevin thought he caught sight of his father, a few times, but it was hard to tell for sure. There were so many men onboard and the crowd of people around him pushed and jostled with each other, trying to get a final glimpse of the soldiers, as they sailed to war. Kevin heard words being repeated by people around him, inspiring words he liked, such as 'heroes', 'brave' and 'adventure'. There were words he did not like, as well, words like 'war', 'dangerous' and worst of all, a phrase he heard repeated a number of times, 'I'll never see him again.'

Eventually, his mother carried Kevin away from the dock and they started the long journey back to their home in McDougall Street, Kensington, in the eastern suburbs of Sydney. As they sat on the train, his mother was quiet, and Kevin noticed a sadness in her eyes he had never seen before. That day was the first time Kevin Wheatley brushed up against the thing the grown-ups called 'war'. At the tender age of about four years old, he could not have possibly understood how much more of it lay ahead for him. Although, the little boy, who huddled safely in his mother's arms that day, could not have comprehended it, in the years to come, war was going to build, direct, and destroy his life.

Kevin Arthur Wheatley had been born on 13 March 1937 in Surry Hills, Sydney. He was the third child of Raymond George Wheatley and Ivy Sarah Ann Wheatley (nee Newman). He had two older siblings, a sister named Florence, and a brother named Raymond, who was known simply as 'Doc'. The long months, while Kevin's father was away at war, were tough on the family, particularly, on his wife Ivy. Ivy was known by most people as 'Poppy' and while her husband was away, the children's grandfather moved in with the family, to lend a hand. He had previously retired but went back to work to help pay the bills. Like most Australian families, during World War II, however, the Wheatleys endured.

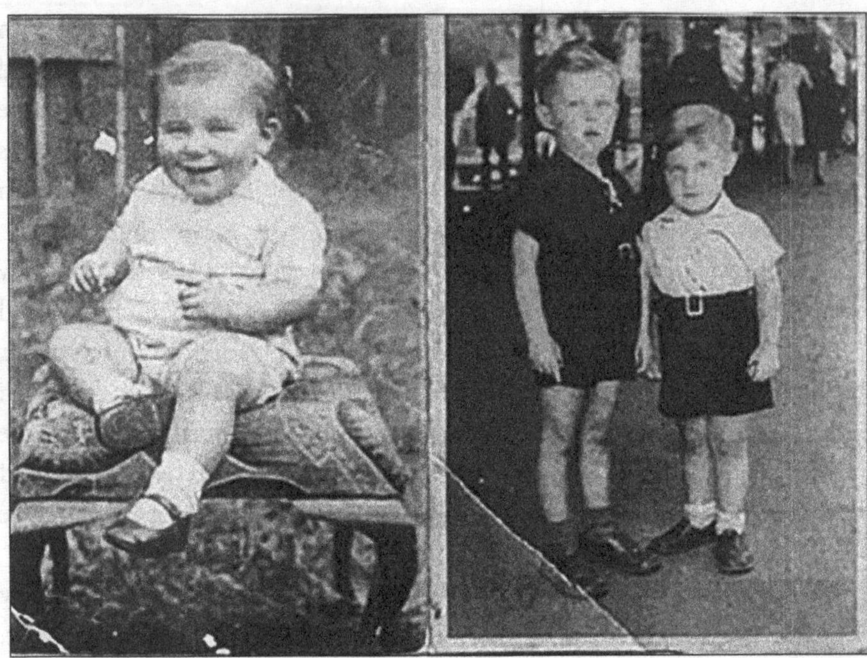

Left - Kevin and Right- Doc and Kevin

After a long tour in Africa, with 2/9 Field Regiment, Kevin's farther returned home. When he came back, however, he was not the same person. There was a distance and anger in him that Kevin was sure had not been there before the war. World War II was devastating to humanity, on a scale that eclipsed any other event in our race's history, besides perhaps World War I, which preceded it. No one who experienced it, in all its devastating power, remained unchanged and people knew little of PTSD and depression, during the 1940s. Men like Kevin's dad carried horrible wounds, both physical and psychological, and it was, all too often, their families who bore the brunt. Something few of them were equipped to do. Raymond Wheatley was discharged from the Army on 27 September 1944 and found work in Sydney.

Young Kevin Wheatley attended primary school at Cleveland Street Public School, but never really enjoyed it. He was close to his brother and sister and although the family struggled financially, they always managed to keep themselves entertained and out of trouble. During his early school years, Kevin picked up the nickname, 'Patches'. As the youngest of three, he was often forced to wear hand-me-down clothes that had been stitched and patched on the knees. He was a quick-thinking and energetic child and always seemed to be on the move. A handsome lad, with dark eyes and messy brown hair, Kevin was smaller than most of the other boys. He had to learn, at a young age, how to defend himself and fight-off bigger kids. Kevin had a knack for finding boyish trouble and his dark features could move quickly from a cheeky grin to a cold stare that could stop even the most determined bully in his tracks. He hated bullies, and if his patented stare did not stop them, his fast fists would.

Doc and Kevin

Life was simple and fun for the Wheatley children. Florence, Doc and Kevin played in their large backyard, which also had a neat and tidy shed at the bottom of the garden. The boys played games, like Cowboys and Indians, with a few of the neighbourhood children and on Friday evenings, their mother would occasionally take them to the five o'clock session at the movies. They would eat dinner in the theatre, whilst watching the film, which, in the 1940s, was a huge treat. There were picnics at the beach on weekends and they would catch a ferry to Manly, just for the ride. During the war years, their mother would take them on short holidays to Ettalong and they would stay at a house, opposite the beach. As soon as the children awoke each morning, they made a beeline for the water and would swim all day.

Ivy with Doc, Kevin and Florence + Raymond Wheatley WW2

When Kevin was about 13 years old, he was given his first bike and rode it everywhere. He absolutely loved that bike and would double-dink his sister Florence, to take her to visit her friends. Florence would go off on picnics to a nearby waterfall with her group of friends and even though Kevin was a little younger, he would sometimes accompany them. Florence still remembers those times fondly and although life could be hard, back then, she and her brothers loved each other and adored their mother. Outside his family, the world Kevin Wheatley grew up in was a complicated one, which was changing faster than anyone could have imagined.

The late 1940s and early 1950s saw Australian suburbia boom. Robert Menzies won the federal election and became the longest-ever serving Australian Prime Minister. Under his governance, a new era was ushered in. It was a time of plentiful employment, a good standard of living and an appreciation of old-fashioned family values. New suburbs were springing up all over the country, as the post-war economy boomed. Homes were being filled with all manner of state-of-the art, labour-saving appliances, like washing machines and vacuum cleaners. Televisions were starting to appear in shop windows, but in the early 1950s, Australia did not have a broadcast service of its own, so they were not to become a part of people's lives until the second half of the decade. For the first time ever, pop and rock music thrilled the young and terrified the elderly.

Migration laws were changed, to encourage non-British settlers to migrate to Australia. This saw an influx of post-war refugees, who hurried to Australia for a piece of freedom and sun. People from Greece, Italy, Poland, Germany and the Nordic regions all established themselves well, setting- up new businesses and contributing to the future of many Australians, yet to be born. It was a time that also saw the beginning of the Cold War and a growing fear and hatred of communism, which seemed to be spreading out of Eastern Europe and slithering its way south through Asia. Tensions arose between the USSR and the USA and fear over the possibility of all-out nuclear war became a reality. In 1951, the Korean War raged, and national service was introduced in Australia. All Australian males, aged 18, had to register for compulsory service.

As the years passed, Kevin's father became increasingly more difficult to live with. Raymond was almost certainly suffering from PTSD, from his experiences, during World War II. Both his temper and the amount he was drinking, slowly increased. As was the case for many veterans of the war, his marriage became strained, but his wife Ivy (Poppy) persisted. After finishing primary school, Kevin attended Maroubra Junction Junior Technical School, however, he disliked school. During these years, his father started a business delivering milk with a horse and cart and his older brother, Raymond (Doc), announced he wanted to drop out of school and join the Army. Although his mother was strongly against the idea, his father approved. Doc was still too young to join the military on his own and needed his parents to sign a form, giving him permission. Despite Poppy's desperate pleas not to, Raymond signed the forms and Doc left home in 1952 and joined the Australian Army. Poppy was furious and this caused an enormous amount of stress on the marriage.

Doc began training at Puckapunyal and, on 31 July 1952, tragedy struck. While on a training exercise, a bullet ricocheted and hit Doc, killing him. Poppy was completely inconsolable. She would never fully recover from the loss of her son and the resentment she felt towards Raymond, for going against her wishes and signing the papers. She blamed her husband for Doc's death and from the moment the bullet had struck, the marriage was over. The young family tried to deal with the crippling grief, but soon, Raymond and Ivy were divorced. These years were dark and tough for the Wheatley family. Doc's death hit them all hard, none more so than his mother.

Kevin's older sister, Florence, helped around the home as much as she could and Kevin, who already hated school, dropped out and started to work with his father delivering milk. Even though his mother and father had divorced, Kevin enjoyed working with his dad. The two worked well together, but it was not all smooth sailing. Raymond's bitterness over his failed marriage and the grief and guilt, he felt over Doc's death, made him even harder to be around. The drinking continued and his temper grew hotter.

Chapter 2
EDNA

In 1953, the Wheatley's milk run took them to a store on Elizabeth Street, Sydney. The milk bar was next door to the popular Prince Edward Theatre, and was owned by a Greek couple named George and Anette. The couple liked Kevin and when he arrived with his horse and cart, full of milk, he always greeted them with a wide smile and cheery disposition. His visits were always welcome. A young girl, by the name of Edna Gimsom (Davis), worked at the store and Kevin took notice of her, immediately.

Edna was an attractive, but quietly spoken girl whose smile lit up the whole world. Kevin decided that the world might be a better place, if only Edna would smile more often, so he did his best to make sure she did. His constant jokes and silly demeanour did not impress Edna, however, and although she thought he was a handsome and pleasant-enough young man, she took him to be a bit of a fool. Edna was still young, but she had an old head on her shoulders. She came from a large family and had already been taken out of school, at just 13 years of age, to help support them. The family would eventually grow to 14 and Edna's support would be needed, for many years to come.

As a student, Edna had attended Strathfield Girls High School and Homebush Ladies College, where she had been a promising pupil.

She had worked part time in a factory as a machine operator making men's underwear. She had been working there on her school holidays, but her father managed to get her exempt from school, so she could start work full time. Edna soon got a job at the milk bar on Elizabeth Street. The store was a much better fit for her than the factory had been, and she enjoyed working there and liked the store owners, George and Anette. Edna's situation was not unusual, many families were finding life difficult during the 1950s and larger families like Edna's could find making ends meet particularly challenging. Many promising academic careers, like Edna's, were cut short during this time, so the student could find work and help the family.

A young Kevin Wheatley

Chapter 2

Kevin was becoming more and more infatuated with Edna, after every visit and soon, the two struck up a friendship. Always the young gentleman, Kevin took it upon himself to start walking Edna to the train station, after work each night. When he had finished work for the day, he would go back to the milk bar and wait for Edna to finish. Every evening, he would walk her to Central Train Station, where he would take the train with her, escorting her safely to her brother in Fairfield. Kevin would see her off, then return by train to Central Station and then, get the tram all the way back home to Kensington. The afternoon walks and train ride gave the couple time to talk and to get to know each other and Edna soon discovered that there was more to Kevin than just a silly jokester. A new friendship blossomed, but Edna still did not see Kevin as a potential partner.

One evening, when Kevin met Edna at the milk bar, to walk her to the station, he finally decided it was time to ask her out on a date. When he did, Edna said 'no', but Kevin was a determined young man and never one to give up easily. Ignoring the people on the crowded street, he hurried over to a light pole and started to climb it, scaling it all the way to the top. As he climbed, he called out, 'Sorry, you're gonna have to say "yes", or I'm not coming down.'

'Kevin!' Edna shouted up at him, 'Come down from there, you'll fall.'

'Maybe, that's up to you. I'm not coming down until you say "yes"!' He shimmied along, until he was hanging from the highest part of the light post.

'You're crazy!' Edna accused and did not know whether to scream or laugh.

He hung there, feet kicking at the air, as he struggled to hang on and shouted, 'Hurry, I can't hang around up here forever!'

Laughing now, Edna finally relented, and Kevin made his way safely back down to the ground. By this stage, a decent-sized group of onlookers had gathered around, and Edna was terribly embarrassed. They hurried away, both laughing, and the two young friends started dating. The relationship grew and, after they had been dating for some time, Edna became pregnant. Still quite young, this was a problem for both Edna's and Kevin's families, especially in 1954. The couple were put under a lot of pressure, to either have an abortion or have the child adopted out, but they refused. Kevin, still young himself, insisted he would marry Edna and do his best to help her raise the baby. Because of Edna's age, she had to get permission from her parents, and with the blessing of both families, the date of 20 July 1954 was picked for the wedding. It would see them married, just one month before Edna's fifteenth birthday; Kevin was seventeen.

Kevin and Edna on their wedding day

Chapter 2

The wedding between Kevin Wheatley and Edna Davis was small and simple, taking place at the local registry office. Edna wore a nice dress, with a pretty hat, long gloves, and violets on her lapel. Kevin's mother and his sister Florence were there, as were Edna's mum and dad and her older brother John. It would turn out to be a busy year for the couple, with the wedding in July and then their firstborn child, George, arriving that December. After the wedding, Kevin moved in with Edna's family and they lived there until 1955, when Kevin's mother moved out of the house in Kensington and the young couple took over the home. It was a busy house. Kevin and Edna lived there with Kevin's sister Florence, his grandfather, and his father.

Life was tough, during this time and Kevin's father was still a difficult man. Raymond had not attended Kevin and Edna's wedding and showed little interest in helping around the house. By December, the following year, Edna would give birth to her second child, a little girl they named Phyllis. Kevin's mother had remarried to a man named Walter Muir, and would have two more boys. Kevin started work in the evenings at a glassworks factory in Crown Street. On one occasion, he came home, after a long shift, to find Edna upset after an altercation she had had with Raymond. Kevin went out to the kitchen to confront his father, and a fight broke out between the two men. During the fight, Raymond stabbed Kevin in the back with a small knife, luckily, Kevin was wearing a very thick and heavy jacket, so was not seriously injured. After that, their relationship became too strained to continue living in the same house, so Edna and Kevin moved out.

Kevin bounced between a few different jobs and work continued to be a problem. He was finding it difficult to decide on a career that would not only provide him with enough money to support his growing family but would also bring enjoyable and challenging work. He needed something that would offer the prospects of a lifelong career, but having left school early, this was proving difficult.

Australia was a complicated place in 1956, the Korean War had finished, but the Cold War was ramping up. Melbourne was set to host the Summer Olympic Games, and by the end of 1956, the country would finally have a working television broadcast network of its own. Television sets were still expensive, however, and seen as an unattainable luxury by most families. The British were conducting nuclear tests at Maralinga in South Australia and military conscription was a matter of great debate around the country but would continue until 1959. One job idea kept coming back to Kevin, he was thinking a lot about joining the Army. He had loved the idea of the Army when his older brother had joined years earlier, but Doc's death had put it out of his mind. Some of Kevin's friends had joined and there was always the possibility that he would be called up for national service anyway, so why not? The Army would be a great way to secure real, grown-up money and he was sure he would enjoy the work.

Kevin and Edna with baby George

Kevin knew his mother would be upset by the idea but could think of no other career path that would give his family the stability he wanted them to have. After some considerable thought, and talks with Edna, Kevin 'Dasher' Wheatley decided to enlist in the Australian Army and on 12 June 1956, signed a three-year contract and began training.

Chapter 3

THE ARMY

In the early months, when Kevin left for his basic training, Edna and her two children did not see much of him. He was almost constantly away, and this meant that Edna had to spend a lot of time alone with the two kids. Life for partners of soldiers is always hard and they can, at times, feel like single parents. During these months, Edna's mother was still having more children of her own and the two women were able to help each other raise, and look after, the children of both households.

Kevin took to his army training with great enthusiasm. He was already a fit young man and had never been afraid of a fight or challenge, so stood out as a talented soldier. He was a relatively short man, at only about five-foot eight, but his demeanour added, at least, another foot. Although, at times, undisciplined and disrespectful to his superiors, Wheatley excelled whenever he applied himself to any given task or new piece of training. He was a natural marksman, gifted at map-reading and orientation, and was becoming well known and well liked, by the men around him. His sense of humour and willingness to take on anything, or anyone, were appreciated by his peers, and it did not take long for his reputation, as a tough and ready fighter, to spread.

After he joined the Army, Kevin took up rugby. He quickly developed a reputation as being one of the hardest and most promising football players around. His speed and ability to read the game quickly saw him pick-up a new nickname, 'Dash' or 'Dasher'. At first, this nickname was only used on the field, but soon stuck and followed him to the pub after the game, where his mates would still use it. Kevin would play for the Army's rugby team in matches against other services teams, which included the New South Wales Police team. He also enjoyed golf and swimming and was showing some promise as a talented boxer.

Kevin with a few of his mates in their boat

In many ways, Kevin Wheatley was more typical of the old-fashioned Australian digger, first brought to infamy during World War I, than the modern soldiers he was training with. Like those men before him, Kevin disliked officers and strict rules that did not seem to make sense. He was always willing to challenge and question things he did not understand and, like so many men from the original AIF, Wheatley would earn himself numerous penalties, over the expanse of his military career. Although, these disciplinary infringements were somewhat frequent, they were never anything serious enough to see him get into real trouble and like the World War I diggers before him, when the chips were down and someone needed to stand up, Dasher was always first to come forward.

Many of the people who trained Wheatley were war-hardened Korean and World War II veterans. They had seen action in places from the Kokoda Track and the deserts of Africa to the Battle of Kapyong. There were still some World War I veterans in the military, mostly elder officers, and NCOs. These people tolerated Dasher's boyish antics and could see the rough and ready soldier, waiting beneath the surface. They had the wherewithal to shape that warrior and bring him out and Wheatley knew he would benefit greatly from their instruction. These men were more inclined to dish out discipline, via way of a fist to the face, than writing a soldier up, and that type of discipline did not bother Kevin in the slightest. He would gladly take a clip across the ear, over a court martial, any day and throughout his training, flirted with both. While he did not like commissioned officers, Kevin respected the warrant officers, sergeants, and corporals, above him and soaked-up the lessons they had to teach, like a dry sponge.

On completing basic training, Kevin was posted to the 4th Battalion, Royal Australian Regiment (4RAR) for more instruction. 4RAR had been raised in 1952 as a training unit whose primary purpose was to train and hold infantrymen for deployment to the Korean War, which had finished, by the time Kevin arrived. After he had concluded this additional training, Wheatley was transferred across to the 3rd Battalion, Royal Australian Regiment (3RAR), which would be his home, for a long time to come. The 3rd Battalion, Royal Australian Regiment, was a mechanised infantry battalion of the Australian Army, which had been initially formed in October 1945 from volunteers from the 3rd, 6th, 7th, and 11th Australian Divisions.

Wheatley's new battalion had a rich history, having been deployed as part of Australia's main land force in the Korean War in late September 1950. They had formed part of the 27th Commonwealth Brigade and took part in the United Nations offensive against North Korea and distinguished themselves at the Battle of Kapyong, receiving a United

States Presidential Unit Citation for their actions there. The battalion fought the Battle of Maryang San, which is widely regarded as one of the Australian Army's greatest accomplishments during the Korean War. They remained in Korea, until the ceasefire in 1953. During the fighting, 3RAR suffered 231 casualties and, after the war, set-up base at Ingleburn and Holsworthy Barracks, New South Wales. It was at Holsworthy that Kevin joined them. The next major conflict, 3RAR was involved in, was one in which Kevin himself would fight, the Malayan Emergency.

The Australian Government first committed troops to Malaya in 1955, however, 3RAR would not arrive until October 1957. Australia had committed troops to assist the British in crushing an uprising from the Malayan Communist Party (MCP). Trouble in Malaya dated back to June 1948, when three European estate managers were murdered by members of the MCP. After the killings, the British Government declared a state of emergency and the conflict, known as the Malayan Emergency, officially began. The Malayan Government was slow to react to the rising threat of the MCP. However, they were forced to take things more seriously, after the assassination of the British High Commissioner in October 1951. This strengthened British resolve to put the threat down and the Malayan Government stepped-up its counterinsurgency measures.

Australia's involvement began in 1950, with the arrival of RAAF aircraft and personnel, in nearby Singapore. By October 1955, the 2nd Battalion, Royal Australian Regiment (2RAR), arrived on Penang Island, to lend a hand on the ground. They did not cross to the mainland, however, until January 1956. Over the next two years, 2RAR's operations consisted mainly of aggressive patrolling and fortifying villages and settlements in the area. Active contacts were rare, but on 25 June 1956, three soldiers were killed. From there, things got worse, and in September 1957, Kevin was told that the Army had decided to deploy 3RAR, who were to begin active operations in November.

Fighting overseas was what he had been training for and the pay, while deployed, would be outstanding, so he was keen to go. It was a real opportunity to make a strong start for his family and a chance to be among the first members of 3RAR to be sent across. He would be going with the advance party and that would provide a challenge he relished. The Australian Army was offering to move Kevin's family to Malaya and set them up in their own home. The wives of soldiers were given an allotment to pay for food and board, but this came out of Kevin's wage.

When Kevin first spoke to his wife about the idea, she was not particularly keen on it. Edna had never even been on a holiday before, let alone, on a jet plane or overseas. The idea of moving her young family to a foreign country, where she did not speak the local language, was frightening. She could see the advantages of the move, however, and decided she would try and look at it as a long-term holiday. Eventually, the idea became exciting, and she broke the news to the rest of the family. Edna's parents did not want her to go, her mother was pregnant, yet again, and told Edna that she needed her at home. This pressure made the decision extremely difficult, as Edna felt that she would be leaving her family, at a time, when she was needed. It was a lot for someone so young to deal with, but Malaya offered an opportunity for Edna to concentrate on her own children and establish her own life. The move would take a lot of work and courage, but once she arrived, Edna knew she would be supported by the Australian Army. She was sure she could make it work but would have to do all the packing and preparation, on her own.

Kevin was training almost constantly, Edna's parents were no help and the Army, short of supplying the air tickets, did not lend a hand, either. It was all up to Edna. She would have to pack-up their lives, on her own and get them ready for a change that was going to be massive, for all of them. She gathered the kids together, along with all the belongings she could take, took her tickets, and set off to the airport, to move their lives to an entirely new country.

Chapter 4

MALAYA

Kevin Wheatley arrived in Malaya with 3RAR in September 1957. While in Malaya, they would be stationed at Minden Barracks, which was nestled in the foothills on the eastern side of Penang Island. Penang Island is the main island off the north-western coast of the Malaysian Peninsula. Kevin and the rest of the men settled in but would spend little time in Minden Barracks. For the first few months, the men trained at Kota Tinggi on the south end of the peninsula and in November, began active patrols. After that, they were almost constantly out in the jungle on operations, which could last for days, or even weeks, at a time.

Edna, George, and Phyllis flew to the city of Butterworth and then, took a ferry across to Penang Island, where they met up with Kevin. For the first few months, the family was housed in the Australian Hostel, on the beach in Penang and were given their own room. This was a huge novelty for Edna and the kids, who had never experienced hotels or holiday resorts, of any type. They took their meals down in the hotel dining room, which would be converted into a movie theatre, later in the day. All their food and entertainment were organised within the hotel, so the family never really left the place, other than to go on trips to the beach. For Edna, this was all a huge culture shock, and the cultural differences were hard for the kids, as well. There were no jars of vegemite, boxes of breakfast cereal or any of the other things they were accustomed to at home.

Edna on the Beach with Phyllis

The Wheatley family in Malaya

During their time in Malaya, Kevin was almost constantly out on patrol or training, so Enda had to manage the children on her own. The Australian Army eventually moved the family to a large two-storey house in Penang. Everything in Penang was run by the English, who still controlled Malaya, during this time. The area, where the house was located, had been taken over by the military, and there were many other Australian, British and New Zealand families staying in houses in the area. The house was clean and spacious and gave the family access to the beach and a swimming pool and life there was much more comfortable and felt more like home. Each house was assigned a maid and the person, sent to look after the Wheatley house, was a Chinese lady named Lily, who spoke particularly good English, which made life much easier. Lily became like family; she had a young son, who often came to stay, when Lily's husband was at work overnight. Lily had living quarters in the house and the woman would sometimes stay with them.

Lilly with Phyllis and one of her beloved dolls

For the kids, George and Phyllis, their time in Malaya would have an everlasting effect on them. Even to this day, Phyllis and George find certain smells, or even particularly hot and humid weather, can trigger a feeling of déjà vu. The family still have photos of Phyllis sitting on the front steps playing with dolls. These photos help her remember pleasant things from her time in Malaya, things she remembers, even now, like the beautiful, cane rocking cradle she had for her dolls. She would spend hours playing with those dolls. As the family adjusted, Kevin continued to train and patrol with his unit.

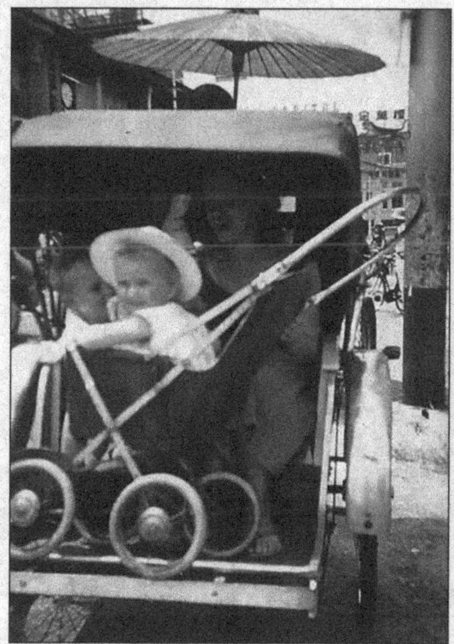

Edna with kids in a Tuk Tuk

George and Phyllis in Malaya

Jungle warfare suited Wheatley and he enjoyed his time in the bush. The men, who had trained him back in Australia, had taught him many valuable lessons, which they had picked up, while fighting the Japanese in the Pacific, during World War II. He used these lessons to his advantage and quickly became a proficient exponent of jungle warfare. However, he found working with the British officers difficult, their attitudes and demeanour seemed arrogant and even insulting. He would clash with these men on a few occasions and was inclined to push back, whenever one of them gave him or his mates an unnecessary order or reprimanded them for not saluting, as they walked by. During his downtime, Dasher took-up boxing, with great success. He was developing a big reputation among the other men of the battalion for being not only a brilliant soldier out in the field, but a skilled fighter in the ring and an enthusiastic and reliable drinking partner, while on leave. The men absolutely loved him.

Kevin boxing a much larger opponent

The Malayan Emergency was no picnic. It is considered today an active or 'warlike' military deployment, not a peacekeeping one. This is a distinction, with a difference. A warlike operation means you literally went to war for your country, while 'non-warlike' means you were sent overseas on another type of operation. To highlight this difference, military personnel are usually awarded campaign medals when they are deployed overseas. These medals are traditionally divided into two categories, active and non-active or warlike and non-warlike.

For non-warlike operations, between the end of World War II and February 1975, Australian servicepeople were to be awarded the Australian Service Medal 45-75. This medal was issued with a nickel-silver clasp stitched onto the ribbon, which showed the name of the theatre entered or the action for which the award was issued. For personnel deployed into 'warlike' or 'active' operations during this time, the Australian Active Service Medal 45-75 would be issued. This also came with a nickel-silver clasp stitched onto the ribbon, showing the theatre or action for which the award was issued. Common deployments normally associated with the Australian Active Service Medal are Korea and Vietnam, but the Malayan Emergency is also recognised and veterans of that campaign, like Kevin Wheatley, were decorated with this medal, with a clasp reading, 'Malaya'.

Patrols, during the Malayan Emergency, were dangerous and contact, although rare, did occur and people were killed on both sides. The Malayan jungle was thick and treacherous, and the men often had to endure torrential rain, which could wash-away trails they were trying to follow and cause all manner of health issues. Staying dry and keeping your weapons and gear clean and operational were art forms and ones Wheatley was extremely good at. He had a knack of moving through the jungle with a quiet economy that made it look easy. His fellow men marvelled at his stamina and his constant ability to push through, even the toughest bush, without slowing down or needing to rest.

Dasher also had an odd way of wearing his equipment loosely on his belt, something that did not escape the notice of his Regimental Sergeant-Major (RSM), a decorated World War II veteran, named Macca McKay. McKay had received the Military Medal for bravery in the field, while fighting the Japanese with the famous 39th Battalion on the Kokoda Track. While out on patrol, one rainy afternoon,

Macca had been walking behind Wheatley for several hours, watching his loosely fitted water canteen and other equipment bouncing off his hips, as he walked. They stopped for a short break and Macca said, 'Dasher, why do you keep your bloody gear so loose on your belt? Doesn't it drive you mad?'

Dasher gave the RSM his toothiest grin and said, 'Nah mate, I like it. The constant slapping on my legs keeps me going.'

Macca laughed and said, 'Whatever works.'

Wheatley had a way of doing things that did not always seem obvious or practical, at first glance. If one took the time to look closer or to ask why he did certain things, however, they would soon discover that there was normally a method to his madness. Macca had seen men like him in the past and recognised his potential, straight away. The two men would work well together for a long time to come and eventually, Dasher would progress through the ranks to outrank the World War II veteran. Something Macca would have been extremely proud to see and no doubt, something he, Macca, could take a great deal of credit for.

While deployed in Malaya, 3RAR took part in several dangerous operations, where they would be forced to work in difficult conditions and in areas where enemy soldiers were known to be, Operations like Shark North and later, Operation Ginger. Operation Ginger began in January 1958 and was designed to disrupt the enemy's food supply, by seeking out and destroying enemy units in an enormous area of around 3,100 square kilometres. The work involved tracking enemy units, searching villages and towns, and setting-up ambushes. These were activities, which taught Dasher valuable skills that he would use to his advantage, later in his career. It was monotonous and frustrating work, however, that rarely yielded significant results. They would often track the enemy for days, only to lose them, as they would cross over the Thai border, something the Australians were not permitted to do.

Part of Kevin's work in Malaya saw him operating as a dog handler. Dogs were used by the Army in Malaya for mine detecting and finding and tracking enemy movement. Kevin kept his dog with him between patrols, bringing the animal home with him. At times, he would bring a member or two from his unit home, usually someone who did not have family in Malaya and was feeling lonely. Kevin's time at home, between patrols, would always be short, but for Enda, these days would be busy. They would regularly have dinner guests and the house would be noisy and full of life, until Kevin would be sent back out on patrol again and things quieted down, once more. On one of Kevin's rest periods at home, he became quite ill. He had drunk some water that was later believed to have been contaminated by rats and broke out with a violent fever. Doctors suspected he had contracted leptospirosis, or 'swamp fever', as it was known, and had to be taken to hospital. However, he recovered fully and resumed normal duties.

While Kevin was out in the bush, Edna stayed in their new home and did her best to make life comfortable and enjoyable for her children. She liked to play beach volleyball but learned that she had to be careful about how she dressed on the beach. Local dress standards were much more conservative than the bikini lifestyle of the Sydney beaches, at home. Edna also took-up badminton and managed to win a few trophies. The Australian families, staying in Penang, were not permitted to go to the shops and markets to buy food. The local water was mostly undrinkable, and the fruit and vegetables sold there were normally contaminated and could prove dangerous for foreigners. This meant they were restricted to eating whatever food was supplied and that meant mostly tinned or powdered goods.

While the family was in Malaya, Edna became pregnant again. This was particularly traumatic, because she was so far from home and family. As it turned out, Edna was not the only one. Many wives of Australian soldiers became pregnant in Malaya, so many, that the Army would bring trucks around the neighbourhood to pick up the pregnant women who would have to climb into the back, so they could be taken to hospital. The hospital was a British Army-run facility at Taiping. The women would be taken there for check-ups and for delivery, when the big day came. For all its centuries of overseas experience, the British Army was not accustomed to dealing with scores of pregnant women or newborn babies. Many of the English staff at the hospital were national servicepeople, who were finishing up their training with the medical unit and were, typically, not very experienced.

Kevin and Edna celebrating New Years Eve

When Edna's big day finally arrived, things did not go to plan. She was taken away to hospital, but the baby breeched. The doctors kept trying to move the baby back into place but could not get it to stay turned. Edna spent several weeks in and out of hospital, and once, when Kevin was out on patrol, had to be rushed into emergency and almost died. She finally gave birth to a healthy little girl, Ellen (Ellie), who was the first C-section in the British Army hospital at Taiting. Without her husband or parents there to support her, the birth was traumatic for Edna. She was sick for several weeks and was struggling to manage, while Kevin continued to patrol, but, in time, regained her strength.

Eventually, the Wheatley family's time in Malaya ended. Kevin was unexpectedly ordered to return to Australia in 1959 and, due to circumstances beyond their control, the family were given next to no time to prepare for departure. For little Phyllis, this was particularly difficult, because she was not allowed to bring her beloved dolls home to Australia. They would not be permitted through quarantine and Phyllis had no time to get used to the idea of leaving them behind. For a three-year-old girl, this was impossible to understand and extremely frustrating. So it was that, Edna Wheatley found herself, once again, hurriedly packing up all the family's belongings and getting the children together for a trip to the airport. The whole experience was something of a whirlwind for the young mother, who was finding out that when the Australian Army wanted you to go somewhere, you went. The little family was taken to the airport and before they had a chance to even catch their breath, they were back in Australia.

6 Platoon returned from a contact in Malaya - Wheatley is in the middle of the front row

They were taken to a boarding house at Potts Point in Sydney, but were soon told they had to move out. Kevin was sent to Liverpool with the Army and Edna was left with the three kids, trying to find a place to live. She did not want to be in the city with the children, while Kevin spent so much time away, so she decided they would have to stay with her parents, for a short time, at their crowded home in Fairfield. The family moved into an old shed in the backyard, for a few months, where they had to use an old kerosene lamp for light. Like the smells of Malaya, the smell of kerosene still brings back memories for all of them, to this day. On one occasion, the kerosene lamp was knocked over and started a fire, which almost destroyed the shed, but luckily, no one was hurt. One thing was clear to Edna, she needed to find a place of their own.

Chapter 5

FOOTBALL AND MATES

The family eventually found their own place at Campbelltown, which was a good fit, as Kevin's mother and sister lived nearby. Life did not improve for the Wheatleys right away, as a soldier's pay, in the late 1950s, was not particularly good. Kevin was working hard and gaining promotions which was helping, he was now a corporal, but money was still tight. During his time on leave from the Army, he picked up work at a local pig farm, to try and supplement the family's income. He was always working, and Edna was almost constantly at home, alone with the kids.

Many other military families took-up residence in the married quarters at Holsworthy Barracks in Sydney, but the Wheatley family never did. While living at Campbelltown, they did not have a car and neither Edna nor Kevin had licences to drive, anyway. Close to Edna's 21st birthday, she became pregnant, once again and gave birth to their third daughter, Leeanne. While Edna was in hospital, Kevin took leave from the Army, to look after the children. He went out and purchased 10 pounds of sausages and a big bag of potatoes and kept the children going on a typical dad diet.

During this period, the entire family contracted chicken pox and became ill. Life, it seemed, was a constant uphill race, throughout the early 1960s, but the family pushed forward. Kevin's hard work was making a difference, soon, Edna was able to purchase their first washing machine, but struggled to keep up the payments to keep it. Kevin worked where he could and continued to play football and was building on his already impressive reputation as a ferocious and talented rugby player. The elder children, George, and Phyllis, started school and Kevin went back and continued to train in the Army, constantly earning new qualifications and skills. He would eventually gain his parachute qualifications and, after moving from 3RAR to 2RAR, for a short time, was transferred to 1RAR. It was here, with the 1st Battalion, Royal Australian Regiment, that Kevin 'Dasher' Wheatley would find his feet and build what would become an immortal reputation, as a natural leader of men, a brilliant rugby player and a bloody good bloke.

His new unit, 1RAR, was a regular motorised infantry battalion, first formed as the 65th Australian Infantry Battalion in 1945 and had been deployed on active or warlike service, during the Korean War and the Malayan Emergency. In later years, 1RAR would fight other active deployments, like the Vietnam War, Somalia, East Timor, the Iraq War, and the Afghanistan War. The battalion has deployed on multiple peacekeeping operations to places, like Japan, Timor Leste, Solomon Islands, Tonga, and the Philippines. Often referred to as First to Fight, 1RAR remains one of the Australian Army's most heavily deployed units and has built and maintained a reputation for being one of Australia's finest. Dasher fell in love with it almost immediately and quickly became a living legend amongst the men.

Even as a corporal, Wheatley had established himself as a steadfast leader in 1RAR. He had a way of getting the men in his unit to do things, simply by being himself. This was a mark of the impressive intelligence, which lay beneath his charming, devil-may-care demeanour. A simple photo of Dasher and his mates, having a beer in 1963, speaks to this. In it, the men are sitting at a table, smiling, and drinking beer. This may not sound unusual, but the men are all wearing high-quality, black suits and drinking from longneck beer bottles, which are cooling in champagne ice buckets. At first glance, it appears that they are attending a wedding or a funeral, but, in fact, there was no special occasion on that day. Dasher had declared that he wanted to take the boys to a pub in Kings Cross for a few beers and that they needed to put on fine black suits, if they wanted to attend.

Kevin taking suit wearing men from 1RAR out for a beer

In 1963, most people did not own suits, let alone, young, low-ranking soldiers of the Australian Army. If they wanted to attend, the men would have to rent or buy a new suit. No one questioned Dasher, they just did as he asked and every one of them turned up, looking a million bucks. This might sound superfluous, but was, in fact, a critical part of what Wheatley was trying to build. It was all part of the character and camaraderie he was attempting to instil in the boys, building respect for themselves and each other. These people were not training to build houses or work in factories, they were being trained to kill people and had to trust each other and know how to follow orders and operate properly, when the bullets started to fly.

In January 1964, Kevin Wheatley was promoted again, this time to sergeant. There was no doubt that everyone loved and respected Dasher, but he could also be a major shit-stirrer, when he put his mind to it. While stationed at Holsworthy Barracks, Wheatley welcomed a new company sergeant major (CSM). The new CSM, a bloke named

Norm, was a straight-down-the-line man, with a calm and measured demeanour. Dasher decided he would welcome Norm to the team, in a way only he knew how. He liked Norm and thought he was a definite improvement on the man he had replaced, but that did not spare the CSM from becoming the butt of one of Wheatley's practical jokes. On the day Kevin was promoted from corporal to sergeant, Norm decided to take him into the sergeant's mess and introduce him to the other sergeants with a few cold beers. The other blokes in the mess already knew who Dasher was and were delighted to have him as a peer.

Dasher at pub with his mates

After a couple of beers, Dasher said to Norm, 'So Sir, did you know the company's got a new nickname for you, already?'

Norm smiled and said, 'Really, what is it?'

Wheatley said, 'They call you "Slacker".'

The smile instantly dropped from the CSM's face. 'What do you mean they call me Slacker? Why?'

'They reckon you're not as firm as the last CSM, you're a bit slack with their training. You don't push them as hard as the last bloke.' This, of course, was a complete lie. The men loved Norm, he was as hard as they came, but was fair and a brilliant CSM.

Chapter 5

Norm said, 'Bloody call me Slack, do they? Thanks, Dash, you're a good bloke. We'll see who's slack.'

Dasher gave him a huge grin and said, 'No worries, Norm, anytime.'

The next day, the men of 1RAR did not know what hit them. Norm was in a thunderous mood and took them all down to the main parade ground, where he drilled them nonstop. Hour after hour, day after day, the CSM put the men through hell. They could not work out what had happened to make their new CSM turn into such a proper prick. He had been an exceptional leader, up until then, but was now inexplicably brutal and cold. After about three weeks of ferocious drilling and constant verbal abuse, the men started to crack and, when Norm was on his way to the mess for lunch one day, a couple of his men stopped him. Unable to stand the abuse, a day longer, one of the blokes asked, 'Sir, how come you're suddenly so tough on us, all this drilling is killing us. We deploying overseas or something?'

Norm looked at them, with cold eyes, and said, 'Why do you think? I know what you blokes call me. I know about the nickname.'

The boys look puzzled and one of them said, 'What nickname?'

Norm scoffed, 'I know you blokes call me, Slacker. You've all been joking about how easy I've been going on you. Did you think I'd just let that slide?'

The boys looked genuinely confused. One of them said, 'Slacker? What are you talking about, we don't call you, Slacker? We did think you were the best CSM we'd ever had, until the last few weeks, anyway.'

Norm said, 'Bullshit!'

Still visibly confused, one of them asked, 'Sir, where did you get this from? I've never heard anyone call you Slacker, we don't even have a nickname for you yet.'

Starting to get a little worried, Norm said, 'Sergeant Wheatley told me all about it. He said you fellas call me Slacker, because I'm so soft.'

The penny dropped with a loud cry of '*Bloody, Dasher*!' The men realised instantly that they had been the butt of another of Wheatley's jokes.

'What?' Norm asked, 'You think he was having me on?'

'Sir,' the men told him, 'You can't listen to Dasher, he's a bloody shit-stirrer. The bastard's gone and set every one of us up!'

Norm started to swear and stormed off, to go and find Sergeant Wheatley.

This type of thing was typical of Dasher, he had a wicked sense of humour and was always finding ways to stir-up his mates, while at the same time, managing to slip in the odd lesson or extra piece of training that he thought might do them good. During his time with 1RAR, Wheatley got to work with, and befriend, some brilliant soldiers and outstanding human beings. They conducted many training operations together and would work in some beautiful places, like the Blue Mountains, The Gap at North Head and Canungra Military Area. Outside of training, the men socialised together, playing rugby, cricket and golf.

They loved a few watering holes around Sydney, but the Civic Hotel in Pitt Street was Kevin's favourite. He built a strong and lasting relationship with the staff at the hotel, none more so than the manager, a woman everyone knew as Ma North. It was in all these places, and on the rugby field, that the name, Kevin 'Dasher' Wheatley, first entered folklore. It was not only the people from 1RAR that knew and fell in love with Dasher, however, but people from other battalions also loved him, as did many civilians. Most of his friends came from the Army and over the years, people, like Ronald 'Butch' Swanton, Reg Hillier, Ray 'Chicago' Ellis, Trevor Adam's, Bill William, Ray O'Brien, Michael Van Burg, John Sullivan, and countless others, would work with Kevin and come away with endless stories and legends about the man.

At the Civic Hotel, Ma North loved Kevin, she greeted him like a son, whenever he entered the place and went to extraordinary lengths to make sure he was well looked after and comfortable. Ma had even set-up a bed for Dasher, behind the piano in one of the corners and let him sleep there, whenever he needed to. It was not uncommon for Ma to close the bar and kick everyone else out, when she thought Kevin, who might have just returned from a long stint of army training, looked tired or drunk and she thought he needed to rest. In return,

Chapter 5

Kevin would often act as surrogate bouncer for Ma, and would happily roll-up his sleeves and throw any troublemakers out, when she needed him to. No one argued with Ma North, and they all knew better than to complain when she rang the bell and declared, 'Dasher's tired and needs sleep. Everyone out!'

The Civic Hotel was a popular drinking hole for the Army men, in and around Sydney. They considered it home turf and did not take kindly to sailors coming by causing trouble. On more than one occasion, Dasher felt obliged to deal with an unruly sailor, who had overstepped the line and was picking fights with his mates. Every one of those men would meet Dasher's lightning-fast fists and find themselves bouncing painfully down the stairs and into the street. Whenever Dasher was about to punch the lights out of some troublemaking sailor, he would shout, 'touché away,' then knock the bloke off his feet. Despite his modest size, Wheatley soon develop an enormous reputation and no one, in their right mind, dared to start trouble at the Civic Hotel.

Outside of the Army, it was on the rugby field that Kevin had the biggest impact. People like John Sullivan, who was a coach in the Riverina rugby competition, got to know Dasher because of his football skills. Like Dasher, fellow soldier Ronald 'Butch' Swanton, was a talented player and he and Dasher became good mates. Butch was with 2RAR at the time, but he played on the same team and drank in the same pubs as Kevin did. Like Dasher, Butch was a well-liked character, who had served in Malaya with 2RAR and loved to socialise with his mates. Both men were life-loving people who enjoyed a cold beer, a quick joke and a good fight. John Sullivan, who would later fight in Vietnam with 2RAR and rise through the ranks to become a lieutenant colonel, describes the two men as simply, 'Easy-going blokes and bloody good soldiers.'

On one particularly long night, in a nightclub in Sydney, Butch and Dasher were drinking into the wee small hours and got into a disagreement. The argument became heated, and Butch said something to Dasher that set him off. Dasher declared at the top of his lungs, 'That's it, I'm gonna kill ya!'

Kevin with mates enjoying a beer

Butch threw his beer away and said, 'You gotta catch me first!'

As a live band played on stage, Wheatley started to chase Butch through the nightclub, knocking people over and sending drinks flying. Both men were laughing hysterically, as they ran through the crowded dancefloor and when Butch jumped up onto the stage, Dasher followed and they sent the startled members of the band scattering. The musicians dropped their instruments and scrambled out of the way, as Butch ran in circles around the stage, Dasher, hot on his heels. Swanton was laughing at the top of his lungs, as he jumped off the stage and disappeared into the crowd on the dancefloor. The band members were hurriedly picking up their instruments and trying to organise themselves to continue playing, as Dasher stood centre stage, trying to see where Swanton had gone.

People were staring up at him in shock and Wheatley suddenly pushed the drummer aside, picked up his drumsticks and started to beat the drums as hard as he could. He hammered a rhythmic tune, as if he was beating war drums and called out, 'I'm coming to get ya, Butch, I'm coming to get ya!'

The crowd went wild and started to cheer and stamp their feet, in time with Dasher's drumming. The band could only watch on and laugh. Unfortunately for Butch and Dasher, they had a football game, the following morning and by the time they arrived, bags in hand, they looked like the walking dead. Their coach, John Sullivan, was furious when he caught sight of his two players. Incredulous, he roared, 'What the bloody hell did you two idiots do, last night? I thought you were going out for one or two quiet ones.'

'We did.' Dasher told him.

'Your idea of one or two must be very bloody different to mine, Wheatley! Get your gear on and get ready.' To Butch, who looked orders of magnitude worse than Dasher, John said, 'And you, you look like you're about to fall over! You're playing reserves, Swanton. Go clean yourself up!'

Butch did not argue. The game got underway, Dasher played at his usually brilliant best, totally unaffected by the previous night's drinking. By half-time, however, the team had suffered two major injuries and there were no reserve players left. Reluctantly, John Sullivan turned to a green-looking Ronald Swanton and said, 'Put your boots on, Butch. You're up.'

Startled, Butch did as he was asked, but was struggling to even tie his laces. 'I'm ready.' He told John.

John looked him up and down, grunted and said, 'Just go stand in the bloody centre, Butch. Try not to fall over, stay onside and don't throw up on yourself.'

Butch nodded and jogged out onto the field. Dasher laughed at the sight of his mate, as he joined him in the middle and the game continued. Butch did what he was asked, he stood in the middle, he did not throw up on himself and he even managed to move enough to stay onside. Eventually, however, the ball came his way, as did a large group of sprinting opposition players. Suddenly, springing to life, Butch charged forward, lowered his shoulder, and laid one of the finest tackles that Dasher, John Sullivan, or any other person present had ever witnessed. It was a perfect, bone-crushing, game-stopping tackle, with but one major flaw. Butch had tackled the referee.

Michael Von Burg, a private rifleman with 1RAR, played a lot of rugby with Dasher. Michael had joined the Army in 1962 and was selected for the Army Inter Services Rugby side and it was here, he first met Wheatley. The team would play against the Navy and Air Force teams, as well as the New South Wales Police Force team. Michael was a flanker or loose forward and Dasher was a prop. From the outset, Dasher made the young private feel at home with other players, like Bobby Sinclair. Both Michael and Bobby had grown up playing hard-tackling country rugby and their big hits would often upset opposition players. Both men were more than capable of looking after themselves, but whenever a punch-up started on the field after one of their trademark big hits, Dasher was always first in to finish the fight.

In Michael's own words, 'Dasher was our guardian angel when we were playing against older, meaner players.'

The standard of the rugby games, in which Dasher took part, was as high as they came. Some of those games, like when Wheatley's army team played the New South Wales Police Force team in 1963, would enter the annals of football lore. That game was a bloodbath, with fights breaking out right around the ground from the opening whistle and Dasher was right in the thick of it. Participating in this 80-odd minutes of complete mayhem, were men like Richard 'Dick' Thornett, who was one of only five Australians to ever represent their country in three different sports. Dick was an Olympic water polo player, before becoming a league and union champion and a triple international rugby player.

During the game, Michael Von Burg was struggling with a much larger opponent, who was giving him a hell of a time. The man kept grabbing his jersey, tripping and punching him, behind play, to try and throw him off his game. At half-time, the team decided to move Dasher, to play just in front of Van Burg, to lend a hand. When the big man moved to drop Michael behind play, there was a sickening crunch and a grunt of pain. Michael turned to see the big man out on his back and Dasher casually sauntering away from him, a grin from ear to ear. There was a huge cheer from the crowd and the big bloke left Von Burg alone after that. The games Dasher played in had a way of always being entertaining. People would go out of their way to come and watch him, especially, his mates from 1RAR who could make up a quarter of the crowd.

Dasher and Michael became good friends, as well as other blokes like Bobby Sinclair, Terry Loftus and Ross Mangano. All these people were helplessly drawn to Dasher. He had a way of lifting those around him and making them smile, like no other person could. He was one of a kind. After their games, he would join the men for post-match beers and for home games, that would be at the Australian Services Canteens Organisation (ASCO) at the barracks, where he would cook dinner for his mates. He loved to put together an elaborate curry, made from army rations he found lying around, all cooked up in a ration tin on a hexamine stove. This feasting and drinking would continue until well past midnight and often ended up with the boys trying to sneak across the battalion parade ground to get back to their rooms for some much-needed sleep. The problem was, they would have to try to sneak past their beloved, but greatly feared, Regimental Sergeant Major, Macca McKay, MM. The World War II veteran would be curled up in his bed in the sergeant's mess, by this time and if they accidently woke Macca, he would come thundering out of his bunk and lock them up for the night.

These years were not all drinking and football. There was plenty of work to do and the men were always sober and clear-headed when they trained. There were other tasks, including guard duty at Victoria Barracks in Paddington and another unique job, the boys of 1RAR were assigned in 1963. In February of that year, Queen Elizabeth II, and her husband Prince Phillip, the Duke of Edinburgh, travelled to Australia to help celebrate the Jubilee Year of the city of Canberra. While Down Under, the Queen visited Parliament House and members from B Company 1RAR were hand-picked to go there and act as her guards. This was considered a high honour.

Prince Phillip inspected the guard each night and Dasher's men would patrol, outside the building, where they were staying. As they marched across the concrete, however, their boots were making a lot of noise and, at one stage, one of the Queen's personal bodyguards came marching out of the building. The man was wearing the traditional red coat and three-foot-high black hat. He stopped in front of the diggers and said in a posh English accent, which set the men's teeth on edge, 'You men are keeping Her Majesty awake with your loud marching. We must insist you go across the road and tell the rest of the guard, there will be no more marching in front of this building, tonight.'

They watched the man turn and stomp away and Ray O'Brien said, 'Well, shit, we can't be keeping Liz awake, can we? Best do as we're told.'

The rest of the men laughed, and they quietly moved away, to guard the building from a more appropriate distance. Guarding the Queen turned out to be a lot of fun and lasted for about one week. While there, the men knew their presence was more for show than for any real need to defend the monarch, they only carried rifles with fixed bayonets and did not have any ammunition, but it had been a good experience. The parading had given them an opportunity to brush up on old parade-ground skills. The experience had helped them bond, which would prove vital in the dangerous years which lay ahead and soon enough, 1RAR would be deployed overseas, again.

Chapter 6

THE SCUNGEES IN PNG

Sergeant Wheatley was finally put in charge of his own unit, becoming platoon sergeant of 6 platoon, B Company, 1RAR. This would become Dasher's own unit and the men under him had a kind of awed respect for Sergeant Wheatley that is still spoken about to this day. People in this platoon, like David Munday, would come to remember him with great reverence. Munday once said that, 'Dasher was an extraordinary man's man who had a way with the guys. When he walked into a room, his presence instantly drew your attention.' Under Wheatley's guidance and his keen eye for spotting leadership talent, Munday soon found himself promoted to lance corporal.

Wheatley pushed his men hard. He forced them to go for long periods without bathing and changing clothes, and once famously claimed that, 'Some day, you will have to do it real hard and real dirty.' This would prove to be correct when 1RAR would later deploy to PNG and eventually, to Vietnam. As a result of the extra drilling and the constant smell of his unwashed men, 6 Platoon became known as 'the Scungees'. This would be a nickname they carried with pride.

During the 1960s, the Australia Army underwent some significant changes. Between 1960 and 1965, the Australian Army adopted a structure known as the Pentropic Organisation. Before Pentropic, the Australian Army had been functioning under a system, known as Tropic. Pentropic was an American system adopted from a desire to modernise the Australian Army and ensure that its units could work alongside those from the United States. The Australian version of Pentropic allowed the Army to be portable by air, capable of fighting on the ground in Pacific theatres and able to conduct anti-guerrilla operations. The idea was to form five battalions, an infantry battalion, a field artillery regiment, an engineer field squadron and other combat and logistic elements, including armoured and aviation units, as required. This was a change from Tropic, where there had been three or four battalions, at most.

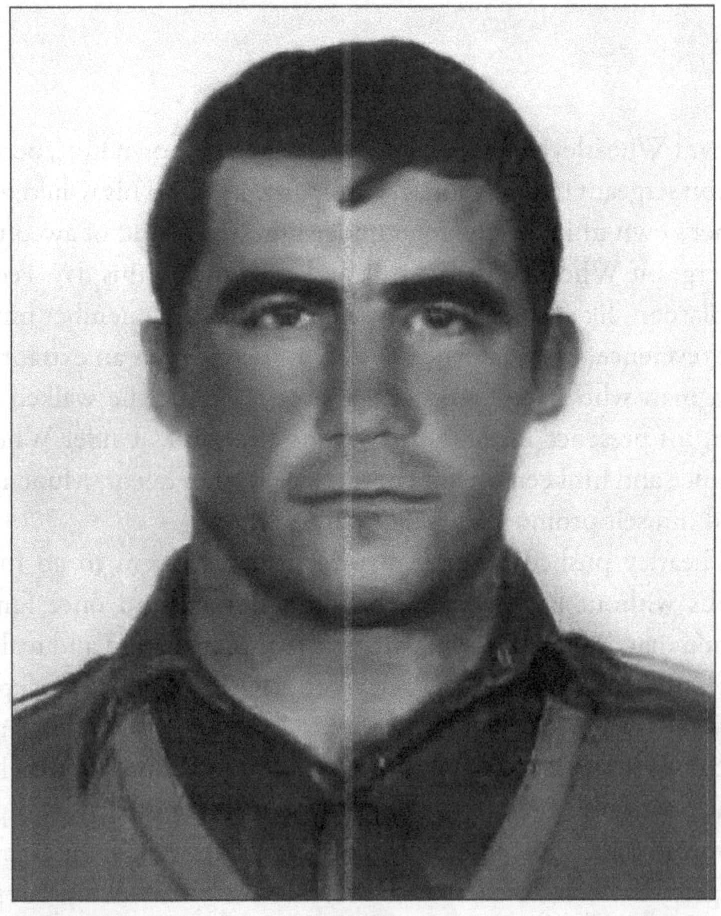

Army photo of a maturing Kevin Wheatley

Chapter 6

As part of this reorganisation, the Army replaced its outdated weapons with more modern ones. It underwent many training operations, which were designed to try out this new structure in various, simulated operations, to see how well it functioned. There were a lot of bugs to iron out, so men, like Wheatley, spent enormous amounts of time away from home, training. The experience gained from these exercises led to Australia abandoning Pentropic in 1964. In the meantime, Dasher Wheatley, and others like him, were going to be terribly busy and word soon came through that they were going to be deployed on a peacekeeping operation to Papua New Guinea (PNG).

Edna Wheatley took this news in her stride. Her husband spent a lot of time away training and she decided that this would be no different. He would simply be working in a different location and the deployment was not going to be a long one, only about two weeks. She knew little of what was going on in PNG and had more than enough confidence in Kevin's abilities to believe he would stay safe and return to her in one piece.

Soldiers cooking in jungle on a training mission

DASHER

Australian troops were commonly sent to PNG before that country's independence in 1975. These troops were primarily used as peacekeepers whose main purpose was to show support for PNG and to discourage neighbouring Indonesia from invading from the west. In 1964, Papua New Guinea was set to hold its first real democratic elections and tensions in the country were high. These elections were the first step towards independence for the people of PNG. Dasher and his men would be going with a full company from 1RAR which would be made up of three platoons, plus its company headquarters and a medical unit. There was about 110 people, in total. This deployment was known as Operation Sprinkler One.

Sprinkler One was a way for Australia to show support to the PNG Government. With its contingent of medical staff, 1RAR would offer free medical care and dental services for the local people. For the infantry troops, part of their role would be to move across to the border and make sure they were seen by the Indonesians, on the other side. It was to be a clear show of force, but one which would not include fighting. This was Wheatley's first overseas deployment as platoon sergeant, and he was excited about the coming challenge.

The platoon flew into Port Moresby, where it trained for several days, before moving out to a place called Vanimo on the northern coast. Before arriving, many of the men had never even seen a jungle before, so acclimatising to the humid weather and tough terrain took some doing. Once they moved out, Dasher's task was to patrol along the border and make sure the Indonesian soldiers, on the opposite side, knew they were there. Although they were not permitted to engage, the men carried live rounds and regularly caught sight of Indonesian troops. As the heavily armed Australians moved through the countryside, many of the local people panicked and fled, when they saw them. For most of the locals, these were the first white faces they had seen since World War II, if ever. This caused no end of problems, and the men were forced to hand out leaflets, written in the local language, so they could explain to the people why they were there and that they had come in peace.

Getting through the jungle to the Indonesian border was challenging, but on more than one occasion, Dasher was able to lead his men along the bank of a border river and get them close enough that they could stop and wave to the Indonesian troops, on the other side. Although, this deployment was non-warlike and the platoon never had to actively engage an enemy force, the experience, gained in PNG, was the final piece of the puzzle that would prepare 1RAR for the horrors of Vietnam that were to come.

Surviving members of 1RAR, who fought in Vietnam and were with Dasher in PNG, talk about that trip and Wheatley's leadership as being critical for their future survival. People, like Bill William, who would eventually become a warrant officer and fight as forward scout in Vietnam with 1RAR. When reflecting on that short trip to Papua New Guinea, Bill says, 'There were two different Dashers. There's Dasher the larrikin and then, there was Dasher the military perfectionist. In the bush, he was a military perfectionist. As platoon sergeant, he was like a father to us. We all knew he had seen action in Malaya and that he had important things to teach us. He was excellent at helping you understand what you had to do and making you feel part of the team.'

By 1964, Kevin Wheatley had established a reputation as being a father figure and an experienced campaigner, but he was still only 27 years old. Despite his modest age, there were critical skills and experiences that he passed down to the men. These were not only lessons that he himself had learned in the field, but those handed down to him firsthand from the people who had fought in World War I, World War II and Korea. Veterans from all three wars were still serving in the military, when Kevin joined, and it was their torch he was passing down. He taught the men critical lessons, like how to stay dry in the jungle, how to set-up an ambush and to never leave evidence of your movements behind.

Unlike soldiers from the United States, who had more of a smash-and-burn technique, when Australian troops were on patrol, they would leave nothing behind. They carried everything away, so there was no indication that they had ever been in the area and Dasher was brilliant at teaching this sort of thing. One lesson he instilled in the men became a wonderful metaphor for how they should operate in all situations. In many jungles of South-East Asia, there are sharply edged vines which grow in thick, blanketing patches. These vines will cut a person to pieces and cause horrific infections, if one tries to simply push through them. Dasher showed the men that if you take the vine in hand, move it aside and hand it to the next man behind you, it is harmless. That soldier then hands the vine to the bloke behind him, and the platoon gets through unscathed, but only, if they work as a team.

There was a multitude of lessons, like this, that Wheatley handed down, things the men would never have thought about, without experience. For instance, wild pigs move through the jungle at night, so the men had to learn that not all noises are the enemy moving around. Opening fire on a small family of pigs was a good way to waste ammunition and give away your position to enemy forces who, otherwise, may not have known you were there. Jungle warfare is difficult and dangerous work and if you get something wrong, your mates might be killed. The weather in northern PNG was a lot like what the men would experience in South Vietnam. This gave them skills that would prove vital, trying to stay dry and keep your gear clean was extremely difficult, but Dasher was a master at this.

One hot afternoon in PNG, when the platoon had returned from a long patrol, Dasher guided the men back to base and a few of the blokes decided they would go out for a few beers. There were a good number of pubs to pick from and as the men walked through town, Dasher saw a huge sign hanging out the front of one of the bars. The sign read, *No Whites Allowed*. Dasher laughed and turned to Ray O'Brien and said, 'That's the pub for me. Let's go in.'

Ray said, 'Piss off, Dash. I'm not going in there.'

The other men agreed with Ray, but Dasher said, 'I'm going in. What are they gonna do, anyway?'

'Beat the shit out of you, for one thing.' Ray told him.

'We'll see.' Dasher said with a grin. 'You blokes coming or not?'

The other men refused to enter, so Wheatley squared his shoulders and walked straight through the front door. Like a scene from an old western movie, everyone inside the bar stopped talking and turned to look, as the Australian stepped inside. His was clearly the only white face in the room, but this meant nothing to Dasher. He strolled up to the bartender, dropped some change in front of him and said, 'How are ya? Beer thanks, mate.'

The bartender looked at him for a moment, then gave him a beer. Dasher made some new mates, that day and when he returned to camp, a few hours later, he was a little wobbly on his feet and wearing a native decorative headpiece. The other men laughed at the sight of him and demanded to know what had happened. He shrugged and said, 'Had a great time, boys, you should have come in. I was the only white boy in there, they were a good bunch of blokes.'

After around fourteen days in PNG, 1RAR finished its deployment and was sent home to Australia, far richer for the experience. The lessons they picked up in PNG proved to be so critical for the years ahead, that some of the blokes would later theorise that the Australian Government had done it on purpose. That 1RAR had secretly been sent to PNG to get them battle ready, because they had already decided to send them to Vietnam and PNG would be a perfect training ground. Whatever the case, the experience was an important one, and gave the men a break from the constant routine of training and drinking, they had been struggling with, at home. It was a circuit- breaker from the comforts of Australian life and jolted them into shape, before the far more deadly deployment to Vietnam, which lay ahead.

Edna and the children were thrilled to have Kevin home, but whispers were starting to spread through the Army about a far-off place called Vietnam. Some special forces people had already been sent to Vietnam, as part of a new unit, called the Australian Army Training Team Vietnam (AATTV), also known simply as 'The Team'. This was only a small number of people, but the unit was already gaining notoriety as it worked with American Special Forces. The AATTV's role was to train and advise the South-Vietnamese Army and help them hold-back communist forces from North Vietnam. From what Kevin was seeing on television and reading in the papers, the Americans were significantly ramping-up operations and it looked like this was only going to continue.

On his trip to Papua New Guinea, Wheatley had proven himself as a reliable and efficient leader and now had two deployments into jungle terrain. His was a unique skill set which, as it would turn out, was desperately needed by the Australian Army and the AATTV in Vietnam. It was not long before Dasher was offered another promotion to warrant officer second class, and a position on this new and highly prestigious Australian Army Training Team Vietnam. He now had a serious choice to make, transfer and be almost guaranteed deployment to Vietnam, or stay with his beloved 1RAR and hope they would soon be sent, as well.

This was an extremely difficult decision for Dasher to make, because, as it turned out, 1RAR was the only battalion in the Australian Army that was considered battle ready, at the time. While other units had to go to places like Canungra Training Barracks in South East Queensland, 1RAR had learned everything they needed to know in their recent deployment to PNG. This made it highly likely that they would be the first regular Australian battalion to go. But the AATTV offered better pay and special forces work was a challenge Kevin wanted to take on, so, in the end, he made the decision to leave 1RAR and join the AATTV. His new training began and before he knew it, he was Warrant Officer Kevin 'Dasher' Wheatley, AATTV, and getting ready to deploy overseas, once more.

For their deployment to PNG that year, the people of 1RAR might have received the Australian Service Medal 45-75 with PNG clasp, but their stay was not long enough. The eligibility criteria for that award suggests one must have been deployed to Papua New Guinea, between 3 September 1945 and 16 September 1975, for a period of 30 days. Unfortunately, 1RAR were only in country for a period of 14 days, so did not qualify.

Chapter 7

A NEW TEAM

For Edna, the idea of her husband going to Vietnam was no big deal. To her, it was just another overseas deployment, like Malaya and PNG had been. It was still early in the war and Edna, like many other Australians, knew little about it. Life in Sydney, with a young family, was hard and in early 1965, the war was not the big news story it would later become. As far as Edna was concerned, her husband was going to Vietnam to train soldiers in jungle warfare, and she knew he was exceptionally good at that.

A few days before he left, the family went on an outing into Sydney. They took the ferry over to Manly and Kevin pointed out Port Denison and other landmarks to the kids. They went to the Liverpool Hotel for lunch and the children enjoyed glasses of cold lemonade, with little umbrellas in them. That would be the family's last outing together, before Kevin deployed and for Edna and the kids, the last they would ever have with him. In the final days, before he deployed, Wheatley was busy training with the other men from the AATTV. When he arrived at his new unit, Dasher was joined by people he had worked with before, good mates, like Butch Swanton and others, he was proud to be training with. Like Dasher, Butch had served in Malaya and been promoted to warrant officer second class and even though, the two mates would initially be sent to different parts of Vietnam, Kevin was thrilled to be training with him.

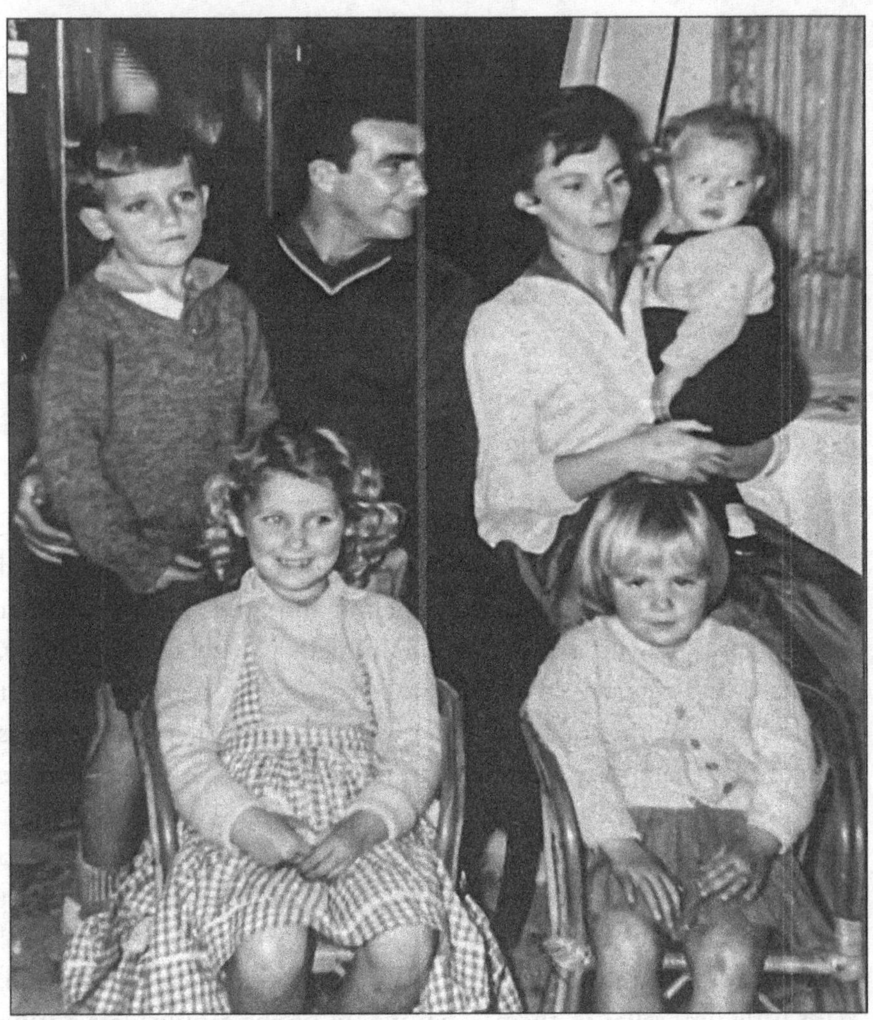

A rare photo of the whole Wheatley family together

When the Australian Army Training Team had been formed, they had wanted mainly warrant officers and higher ranked people, although a few sergeants and corporals would join. Kevin was beginning to suspect that this might have been one of the reasons he had been promoted to Warrant Officer so quickly. They needed people like him, men who had served in Malaya and were good at

Chapter 7

jungle warfare and leading other men. The 1960s were something of a golden age for people in the Australian military. Many of them would find promotions and new jobs within the services, as it quickly expanded and brought in more people to help it deal with the perceived threat of communism, coming from the north, and its growing commitment in South Vietnam. In November 1964, the Australian Government reintroduced military conscription for 20-year-old men, despite strong opposition from within the Army and many sections of the community.

The Vietnam War had been building for a long time and became the climax of the Cold War between the USSR and the USA. Even though the then communist USSR did not fight in Vietnam, it was believed that it was using it, as a proxy, to push communism south through Asia and attack the West. It was a way to do this without starting all-out war and the inevitable nuclear holocaust which would ensue. The Americans, for their part, were all too willing to oblige and sprang at the opportunity to fight the Russians, even if it was by proxy. The American military's understanding of the people, they would be making war against, must have been limited, however, as they initially did not appear to treat the Vietnamese like the lethal opponent they were. Indeed, the US military seemed to almost dismiss their enemy's ability to fight and persist and, as a result, many early engagements against the North Vietnamese forces did not go well.

Vietnam is an ancient country that has a long and complicated history of almost continuous war. Accounts of Vietnam being invaded by foreign nations date back thousands of years. In 258 BC the country was first established as Au Lac and its capital, a place called Co Loa, was situated just north of present-day Hanoi. The country was invaded by China in 207 BC and a 2000-year struggle for independence began. This history shaped the Vietnamese into a nation of hardened and resilient people who knew how to fight, especially, in the jungle.

In AD 40, the famous Trung sisters, two Vietnamese ladies of noble birth, who proclaimed themselves joint queens of Vietnam, led the first major rebellion against the powerful Chinese occupation. For the next thousand years, Vietnam saw almost constant war against the Chinese and a string of legendary kings emerged, from a man called Lac Long Quan or 'Dragon Lord of Lac', who is widely considered to be the first legitimate Vietnamese king. China never managed to fully consume Vietnam, the people were simply too resilient and were always willing to fight. In AD 938, Vietnam decisively defeated the Chinese at the Battle of the Bach Dang River and reasserted their independence, after almost 1000 years of struggle.

The Vietnamese people, hemmed in by the Chinese to the north and by the treacherous mountains to the west, began to expand southwards. They even defeated the mighty Mongols at the Second Battle of the Bach Dang River in 1279 and in 1428, yet another Chinese invasion was defeated. By the beginning of the 16th century, everything seemed to be going well, until the Portuguese invaded and in 1527 the country was split in two. By the 17th century, the French took over from the Portuguese and struggled to enforce Catholicism. By 1757, the Vietnamese fought back and conquered the Mekong Delta, and Saigon was eventually established. Vietnam reassumed full control over its territories, for a time, until in 1858, when France seized both Danang and Saigon. The Vietnamese people fought on, however, and the French paid highly in the fighting which continued over the coming years. In 1890, Ho Chi Minh, the future leader of Vietnam's struggle for independence, was born.

When World War II broke out, the French moved out and the Japanese had a turn at invading. The Japanese occupation ended in 1945 and in September, that year, Ho Chi Minh declared Vietnamese independence in Hanoi. The French were furious and decided they wanted their old country back, and in 1946, the First Indochina War began. France sought to reimpose colonial rule, but suffered a crushing defeat at the hands of Vietnamese general, Vo Nguyen Giap, at the battle of Dien Bien Phu. The French were totally obliterated and packed their bags, finally leaving Vietnam forever.

In the North, Ho Chi Minh declared he wanted to install communism as the governing model. This was met with great resistance from the people of the south who wanted a democratic state and

Chapter 7

Vietnam was subsequently divided at the 17th parallel, into North Vietnam and South Vietnam. In April 1954, US President Dwight D. Eisenhower claimed that the fall of North Vietnam to communists could create a 'domino' effect in South-East Asia, which would see communism spread all the way to Australia. In 1956, the Geneva Accords imposed a deadline of July that year for the governments of the two Vietnams to hold elections, but they both failed to meet the deadline. Sighting this as the catalyst for the southerly spread of communism, the United States decided to go to Vietnam and help the South-Vietnamese Government resist the North. The idea, that they might not be able to do what other superpowers had failed to do for more than 2000 years, never occurred to the Americans, and the modern Vietnam War began. By 1965, the Americans were neck-deep in the war and sinking fast. The US reacted to this the only way it knew how, by spending more money, more lives and ramping up the war.

Like the United States, Australia's involvement in the Vietnam War was driven largely by the fear of communism spreading through South-East Asia. Up until late 1964, Australia had no more than 200 military personnel in South Vietnam, but was determined to send more. The number of AATTV members, being sent to South Vietnam, was increased and, on 29 April 1965, Australian Prime Minister, Robert Menzies, announced that the 1st Battalion, Royal Australian Regiment (1RAR) was going to be deployed. By this time, however, Wheatley would already be in Vietnam, fighting with the AATTV. He did not regret his decision to join The Team, however, as it was a special unit with a unique heritage.

The Australian Army Training Team Vietnam had been raised in 1962 and initially sent 30 officers and warrant officers to South Vietnam as advisers. When Wheatley joined in 1965, under the command of Colonel Francis Serong, who would later become Brigadier Serong DSO OBE, the AATTV increased its members from 30 to 100 and spread them out from the Mekong Delta in the south to the Demilitarised Zone (DMZ) at the northern border. The work carried out by the AATTV members or advisers, as they were known, was as unique as it was dangerous. They would mostly be sent to advise local troops and train them, usually working with no more than one or two other advisers in the field.

The AATTV was the first Australian unit into Vietnam and would be the last out. By the end of the war, The Team's 1000 advisers would earn four Victoria Crosses, two Distinguished Service Orders, six Military Crosses, 20 Distinguished Conduct Medals, 16 Military Medals and a whole lot more. This made it one of the most decorated Australian military units in history and it would suffer casualties of 33 killed in action and 122 wounded in action. They were among the finest group of Australian soldiers, ever put together and Dasher fitted right in.

Chapter 8

QUANG TRI CITY, VIETNAM

Warrant Officer Wheatley arrived in Vietnam as an adviser for the 1st Division of the South- Vietnamese 1 Corps (1/1). He was stationed at the Military Assistance Command Vietnam (MACV) headquarters in Quang Tri City. Quang Tri was a small market city and the capital of the Quang Tri Province, the most northerly province in South Vietnam. The city was situated on the busy road, known as Route One and was surrounded by rice paddies and farms. It was about 10 kilometres inland from the South China Sea and sat on the eastern bank of the Thach Han River, about 25 kilometres south of the Demilitarised Zone.

In 1965, Quang Tri was a small municipality of about 10,000 people. Due to its location and layout, it was considered exposed and vulnerable to attack from the north. It was seen as a powerful symbol of South-Vietnamese defiance, and quickly became a popular target for the Vietcong, as well as the People's Army of Vietnam (PAVN). The PAVN were the regular army of North Vietnam and far more deadly than the Vietcong, who were mostly made up of militia fighters, who often cameoed as farmers during the day. Quang Tri would become the scene of some major battles, in later years, including a particularly deadly clash, during the 1968 Tet Offensive.

Warrant Officer Wheatley in South Vietnam

Chapter 8

There were about a dozen other Australian advisers in Quang Tri, when Dasher Wheatley arrived. As was the norm with the Australian Army Training Team Vietnam, they were mostly warrant officers and highly skilled fighters. Many of the men had gained valuable experience in guerrilla warfare, while serving in places like PNG, Borneo and Malaya. Like Kevin, most of them had been trained by people who had, in turn, gained their experiences of jungle warfare in the South Pacific, during World War II. These advisers were a vital part of the Australian Army and, quite literally, irreplaceable.

Over their time at Quang Tri, the AATTV advisers became close and, as normally happens when Aussie men work together, developed ironic nicknames for each other. There was a bloke they called 'Tiny', who was a giant, hard-as-nails man of about 130 kilograms. Tiny was a drover from Western Australia and had grown up on his father's outback cattle farm. The other blokes joked that he would have had to have ridden a draught horse on the farm, as no other horse would have been able to carry him. Then there was 'Curly', a young man who was so totally bald that he even lacked eyebrows and eyelashes. Another digger, named Ted Wade, was known as 'Bucket Arse'. Ted was about five-feet two-inches tall and weighed in at about 55 kilograms, dripping wet. The bloke had no discernible posterior whatsoever, hence, the nickname, Bucket Arse.

'Roger the Lodger', was a former 1RAR digger who had a habit of disappearing for weeks at a time, when on leave. He would show up, completely unannounced, at a mate's home, bags in hand and asking to stay. Another adviser, by the name of Herbert Beazley, was affectionately known as 'Limey' or 'Henry the Eighth'. Herb was a big, friendly man who had migrated to Australia from England as a kid. The Diggers called him Limey or Henry the Eighth, because he would sing the old song, 'Henry the Eighth', into the wee, small hours, during the men's drinking sessions at the Quang Tri bar.

These men had to rely on each other in ways other soldiers might not, because they were usually deployed with only a few other Australians. Normal infantry battalions, like 1RAR, would be in country and working alongside hundreds of their mates, while AATTV advisers would be lucky to have two or three other Australians with them when out on patrol. Most AATTV members did not have a full command of the local language and therefore, needed to communicate with most of their teammates via translator. There were Americans with them of course, but it was still not the same thing. Because of this isolation, life could be lonelier and more stressful for an AATTV soldier than for others. The people they were forced to rely on, to keep them alive, were mostly foreigners and often broke their trust. The local soldiers regularly abandoned them, when the fighting became intense and at times, even turned out to be enemy infiltrators who just outright turned on them.

Wheatley with Australian and American advisors

As for Dasher's new home, Quang Tri was a pleasant-enough city. It had stores, shops and open markets throughout, all of which serviced the local area, including the surrounding farms and hamlets. The French had left their mark on the place, during their many years fighting in Vietnam, their presence shaping local architecture and, to the delight of Dasher Wheatley and the other Australians, French bakeries. The smell of hot bread cooking was a welcome reminder of home and always boosted a man's appetite. Besides the many shops and markets, the most prominent buildings in the small city were the Catholic church, the school, the hospital, and of course, the MACV compound, which Dasher would call home, during his first few months in South Vietnam.

The MACV compound was an old French barracks, located on the eastern edge of the city, adjacent to a public school. The school's soccer field served as a heliport, whenever needed. Like most military encampments, the headquarters was surrounded by chain link fencing, sandbags, barbed wire and minefields. The compound had several machine-gun bunkers, and a single gate gave entry to the base from the main street. The gate was policed by a guard hut, which was staffed by local Vietnamese police known by the Australians as 'White Mice'. They called them this because of their size and the white uniforms they wore. They were not trusted by the Australian and American troops who dwelled within the camp, and for good reason. Over years of operation there, many were found to be spies or Vietcong operatives. It was common knowledge that intel was regularly leaked to the Vietcong through them, however, there was little the Australians could do about it, other than to watch them carefully. Quang Tri was, after all, a South-Vietnamese city and the Australians were in South Vietnam to help the local population, not to overthrow it.

The MACV compound was well fitted out with numerous offices and had an assembly hall for meetings and showing movies. It had a bar, a radio communications shack and even a spacious dining hall which had a fully cosmopolitan kitchen, staffed by skilled army cooks. There were almost 50 clean and comfortable two-man rooms, which were located within three buildings. The rooms were fitted with simple trundle beds and not much else. The whole facility was maintained by local South-Vietnamese workers, including maids who would be assigned up to four rooms each, to look after. The men even had their laundry cleaned and pressed daily. When the Australians first set up in Quang Tri, not long before Dasher arrived, they managed to build a tennis court in the compound. The tennis court was surrounded by a tall, chain link fence and was constructed in the middle of what had been a minefield. Naturally, the diggers had removed and relocated the mines, setting them up in a location to the east. They even installed a basketball backboard and hoop, complete with chain nets, much to the delight of the Americans.

Military helicopter landing at the Quang Tri school landing zone

It was a smoothly run operation and one of the few places in Vietnam where one could safely drink the water, straight out of the tap. Even the food was outstanding. The Army cooks prepared beef, pork, and chicken dishes, as well as pastries and ice creams. The advisors' compound was comfortable, compared to what many other units had to contend with in South Vietnam, but unfortunately for Dasher and his fellow soldiers, they spent little time there. Most of their days were spent out in the field on dangerous operations, well beyond the wire and in harsh jungle terrain. Out there, they ate a simple diet of rice and fish, with the Vietnamese troops they were working with and had to use water-treatment tablets to be able to drink whatever water they could find. It was a tough and dangerous existence.

What made matters even worse was that these operations were not planned by Wheatley and the other Australians. They were in South Vietnam to advise and assist the 1st Division of the Army of the Republic of Vietnam (ARVN), not to lead it. The 1st Division was part of the South- Vietnamese 1 Corps, which oversaw the northernmost region of South Vietnam. The 1 Corps was one of four corps which made up the Army of the Republic of Vietnam (ARVN), a force which only existed from 1955 to 1975. The 1st Division, Dasher was working with, was based in the old imperial city of Hue, to the south. The province of Quang Tri was one of 1 Division's major areas of operation and deemed critical. Due to the advisory nature of their role, the AATTV advisers could not force South-Vietnamese officers to take a course of action they felt might be necessary, nor could they prevent them from doing something foolish or dangerous. They could only advise and, at times, felt like passengers on a runaway train, winding its way through an extremely dangerous landscape.

Wheatley's battalion within the 1st Division was known as 1/1 and consisted of about 90 men in three companies. Each company had a junior officer and an NCO who often used weapons that dated back to World War II. They, at times, carried outdated weapons like M-1 carbines, BARs, even Thompson submachine guns. The 1st Division was commanded by Captain Dai Cy Hahn, a young South-Vietnamese man with a big reputation. Hahn would later be promoted to major and spoke English and French fluently. He could quote Shakespeare, as well as many verses from the Bible, at will. He was no fool, but could be erratic and unpredictable and at times, appeared unmotivated. He was talkative and extroverted and had something of a reputation for sleeping with officers' and politicians' wives. Some people believed that might have been how he ended up at Quang Tri, in the first place.

Reporting directly to Hahn was US Army Captain Harvey Hougen, a tough, smart, and dedicated Korean War vet. Dasher liked Hougen and the two men worked well together. If he or another of the Australians needed to convey something of importance to Hahn, they normally did it through Hougen, letting the American deal with the man, rather than having NCOs, like Dasher, confronting him constantly. With time and experience in the field, Dasher's company, 1/1, became an effective unit that was more than capable of bringing the fight to the enemy which, over the coming months, they would do far more than Wheatley had ever expected. He would quickly learn that this war in Vietnam was not at all like his deployments to PNG or even Malaya. It would be dangerous, demanding, and violent in the extreme.

Life for Edna and the family at home continued, as normal. During 1965, the soldiers did not have mobile phones or social media. There were no telephones in most of the places the Australians stayed in South Vietnam, so Kevin was unable to call home. Even if he did have a phone, Edna did not own one in their house, so it would have been impossible to call her, anyway. The only way to communicate was by mail and due to the postal strike back in Australia, even that was difficult. Although strikes were not as common in 1965, as they were in later years, many anti-war protests involved union members at wharfs declining to load cargo, which was intended for the Australian soldiers in Vietnam, and sometimes, even postmen refused to deliver mail.

Mail for the men in country was a huge deal. It was their only real means of communicating with their family back home and a way for mothers to send gifts to the sons they were so desperately missing. The mail would come in with resupply on trucks and helicopters they called 'Hueys', and the men would be beside themselves with excitement, when they heard the Hueys flying in. Although the sound of Hueys was something the soldiers loved in Vietnam, it would haunt many later in life. Huey was the nickname given to the HU-1 Iroquois helicopter, which was the workhorse of the American Army, during the Vietnam War.

Helicopters were a major part of the American military strategy in South Vietnam, the war would have been almost impossible without them, and no helicopter is more iconic than the HU-1 Iroquois or Huey. They were used in 'dust-off' or medical evacuation missions and to fly troops in and out of remote, and otherwise, inaccessible areas. The Americans and Australians used the multiple variations of the Huey for many different roles, to both directly engage the enemy as gunships and as transport. The thudding sound of the choppers approaching could mean mail, resupply, medivac or air support, although, during the deepest parts of the mail strike, back in Australia, it often meant disappointment. For Dasher Wheatley, as for most Australians in Vietnam, communication with family was rare. Later in the war, the protests would ramp up and all sorts of strikes and embargoes were forced upon the Australian troops, serving in South Vietnam. At times, with devastating results, both to morale, due to the lack of mail and news from home, and by the blocking of desperately needed ammunition and supplies.

Wheatley and another advisor in Quang Tri

As he settled into life in Vietnam, Dasher was finding that his reputation had preceded him. Many of the Australian men, he was serving with, already knew who he was, and the Americans at Quang Tri were quickly finding out. One afternoon, Wheatley overheard one of the Australians complaining about a large American marine who had been giving him and a few of the other boys a hard time.

'Where is this dickhead?' Dasher asked, and when the soldier told him the man was drinking in the bar, Dasher nodded, rolled up his sleeves and said, 'Right, I'll go sort him out. Won't take long.'

The other men jumped up and followed Dasher who immediately sought the big marine out and demanded that he come out of the bar to fight him. The marine did and when Dasher saw the enormous size of the man, he grinned and said, 'Alright, dickhead, I hear you like bullying blokes smaller than you. I'm about the smallest fella here, so give it a crack.'

The American laughed, opened his mouth to say something, but before he could, Dasher sprang forward and punched the American hard on the jaw. The big marine staggered backwards, swearing as he held his face. The fight, which ensued, became a thing of legend. Even though the American was double Wheatley's size, Dasher more than held his own. The marine managed to knock Kevin down a few times, but each time he would spring back up and unleash a string of quick blows into the American's face and the big marine was quickly becoming exhausted and was struggling for breath. He managed to knock Dasher down again and said, 'For God's sake, man, stay down. I need to catch my breath.'

Dasher was on his feet again, in an instant and said with a huge grin, 'What do you think I'm doing? A few more minutes of this and you won't be able to lift your hands.'

Dasher flashed forward and unloaded a flurry of blows on the big man, dropping him to the dirt. Groaning and panting, the marine wiped blood away from his mouth and said, between huge gasps for air, 'I've had enough.' He held up his big hands, to signal he surrendered.

Dasher nodded, 'Good idea, and stay away from my mates. You touch another Australian soldier and I'll be back.'

The American never bothered the diggers again and Dasher went back to his room with a cold beer. The rest of the Americans, stunned to have seen their toughest fighter bested by one of the smallest Australians at the base, could only look on in awe. This incident quickly established something of a truce at the MACV Compound, between the Australians and Americans, who originally were not getting along. Dasher's keenness to fight, and his otherwise cheerful and fun-loving demeanour, made getting along easy, although the men from both nations mostly kept to themselves.

Chapter 8

Back home, the war was starting to get more coverage on TV, but Edna Wheatley still did not pay much attention to it. She had never entertained the idea that her husband could be killed, she thought he was simply too tough. The few letters that were exchanged with the family, when he was overseas, were normally short and simple. Kevin could never say much about what he was doing, as he was now a special forces soldier. He would ask about the kids' schooling and always let them know he was doing fine and staying safe, but otherwise, he could not convey much about what he was experiencing. After Kevin had been away for a while, however, Edna noticed that the tone of his letters was starting to change a little bit. He was writing to his son George in a way that suggested he was now the man of the house and she noticed that some of his usually jovial light-heartedness was less obvious. Kevin's mother sent him a cake and, in a later letter, asked if he received it. The letters were normally like that, simple and short, trying to deflect the worry families really felt.

Chapter 9

NED KELLY

It did not take long for Dasher Wheatley to distinguish himself in the field and show those around him that he was among the best they had. Captain Dai Cy Hahn organised several patrols into the surrounding countryside and both, the American advisors and the South-Vietnamese troops, soon took notice of how the Australian operated. Dasher always moved to the front, working on point whenever they patrolled.

The men who worked 'on point' of any unit, were always most at risk when moving through the jungle in Vietnam. Known as forward scouts, those working at the front of a moving platoon, were usually the first to trigger mines, walk into booby traps or bear the brunt of an ambush. It was a dangerous and stressful role, so Dasher, who would never ask another man to do something he himself would not do, led by example, by continuously and purposely going forward and working with the men on point. From there, he would guide them through the jungle and make an example of himself. His navigation skills were awe-inspiring. Not only could Wheatley find safe and effective routes through the confusing landscape, but he was also able to instruct those around him on how to do the same. He taught them valuable skills for surviving in the bush.

Chapter 9

Dasher working in South Vietnam village

Dasher also had a huge reputation with the local kids in South Vietnam. Whenever he was out on patrol, Wheatley would make sure his pockets were filled with treats and soap. He would hand them out to the dozens of adoring children, who would flock around him, whenever he passed by their homes. This was something Wheatley took seriously and put a lot of energy into. He would often sell cigarettes and even military supplies he had 'found' along his travels and used the money raised, to buy treats to give away. Whenever the Australian entered a hamlet, village, or even a particularly poor section of Quang Tri city, he would call out to the kids in his ever-improving Vietnamese and tell them to gather around. He told them to call him, 'Ned Kelly', and they did. Invoking the name of the legendary Australian outlaw was something Dasher found funny and cool. So, whenever they saw Wheatley lead his long line of soldiers into their local village, hamlet or neighbourhood, the children would rush out and gather around him, singing out a resounding chorus of, 'Ned Kelly, Ned Kelly, Ned Kelly!' They adored him.

Wheatley's courage and love of children was made apparent, during one patrol, which began in late May. Captain Hahn had ordered his men out, to track down an enemy battalion that had been spotted in the area. Dasher and his unit had not gone out alone, another 1st Division company of ARVN soldiers had headed out ahead of them. On 28 May 1965, after a few days of searching, word came in over the radio that the other ARVN company had found the enemy battalion and was pursuing it. Captain Hougen gave Wheatley the coordinates he had been fed, over the radio and Dasher pulled out his map. 'Here,' he said, showing the American a place, just to the north of a small hamlet, marked on the map. 'They're pushing them south, towards this hamlet. If we hurry, we can dig in on the track before they get there and act as a blocking force. They'll be trapped between us and the other company.'

'Good,' said Captain Hougen, 'take us there.'

Dasher quickly worked out his best route and led his company through the jungle. The going was tough and as they drew closer to the location Dasher had picked. The incoming radio reports and the sound of distant gunfire told Wheatley that the VC battalion was moving faster than he could. He realised that he would not be able to intercept them, before they reached the hamlet. As it turned out, by the time they broke through the jungle, the Vietcong battalion had already reached the hamlet. Captain Hahn had no choice, but to set up on the south side of the hamlet and block the enemy battalion from there. The situation was far from ideal. They knew there would be civilians trapped inside the hamlet, so Captain Hougen sent men forward, to lead them out. Dasher helped Hahn, Captain Hougen and the other advisors set-up the men of 1/1, behind a dirt embankment, beside a road on the edge of the small village. As soon as they had effectively dug in, the VC battalion, still being pressed ever-southward by the ARVN, fell back, and started to scatter around the huts.

Dasher stood up at the front and started firing at the retreating enemy soldiers, who were totally taken off guard. The second ARVN company who had been pursuing the VC, trapped them from the other side of the hamlet. The plan had worked and as the rest of Dasher's men joined the shooting, the Vietcong started to scatter around the huts, looking for cover. Dasher could see their fellow ARVN company on the far side of the village and swore, as he watched them set up a 50-calibre machine gun and start firing it into the small village. They were obviously trying to destroy Vietcong trapped there, but Dasher's 1/1 company was directly down range. It takes a lot to stop a 50-calibre bullet, more than wooden huts and human flesh. Wheatley shouted to his men to get down, as a second ARVN 50-calibre machine gun also opened fire. All hell broke loose, as the rounds flew through the hamlet and fell directly into Wheatley's position.

The machine gun, used by the ARVN in 1965, was the Browning .50 calibre. It was an updated version of the heavy machine gun, which had been designed toward the end of World War I, by John Browning. The Browning was so powerful, it was commonly strapped to vehicles and fired its huge, thumb-sized rounds at an astonishing velocity of almost 900 metres per second. It was extremely effective, up to around two kilometres and each round could reach as far as seven kilometres. It fired as many as 500 of these lethal bullets, every minute, and right at that moment, rounds from at least two of these 50-calibre machine guns were hammering Dasher's position.

Between the terrifying waves of incoming friendly fire, Dasher had to risk sticking his head over the top of the embankment, to watch for retreating VC soldiers. The last thing he needed was for the enemy to inadvertently overrun his position. Dasher and Captain Hougen had to work hard to convince the men that they needed to keep getting up and firing at the enemy. It was critical they kill any Vietcong soldiers who were running towards them. A wave of 50-calibre rounds swept the dirt embankment in front of him, and Dasher ducked low and let it pass. As he rose again, he saw that a terrified South-Vietnamese woman had become trapped, out in the open. She was obviously one of the unfortunate residents of the hamlet, who had not been able to get out in time and she had three small children with her.

Vietcong soldiers were running past the woman, firing their AK-47s and dying, as the ARVN fire withered them. Dasher's heart sank, as he saw the terrified little face of one of the children trapped in the open with her mother. She was a small girl, no more than three years old. Wheatley shouted at the woman, waving desperately and gesturing for her to run towards him. Somehow, the woman saw him and quickly gathered her children. The terrified family started running towards Dasher, but as they drew closer, machine-gun fire swept the ground in front of them and the smallest of the children, the terrified-looking three-year-old girl, screamed and stopped in the middle of the road. The mother did not notice and made it safely to Wheatley's position, behind the embankment.

The small girl, who had stopped in the road directly between Dasher's men and the horrific battle behind her, covered her face with her little hands and started to scream. Bullets shrieked past her. They were coming from both directions now, as Wheatley's 1/1 company fired at the Vietcong in the village. Dozens of 50-calibre bullets ripped at the dirt road around the girl and she screamed and fled, running as fast as her little legs would carry her, straight back into the village and towards the rattling machine guns. The mother wailed in horror and desperation and Dasher Wheatley decided he had seen enough.

The Australian jumped up from cover, SLR in hand, and ran directly into the hail of bullets. He dashed across the battlefield as fast as he could, rounds zinging past his ears and tearing at the ground around his feet. He ignored all of it and ran the girl down, bending low to scoop her up in his arms. He dropped to his knees, folding himself around her and protecting her little body with his own, as hundreds of rounds rained down around him. In that moment, huddled over the child in the middle of the road, Dasher thought of his own kids and what it would do to him, if anything like this were to ever happen to them. It did not bear thinking about.

There was a brief break in the gunfire, so Dasher, slinging his SLR over one shoulder and holding the girl in his arms, sprinted back towards cover. Bullets fell about him again, but he, somehow, made it back safely and, to his complete astonishment, the little girl was completely unharmed. Her mother was beside herself. Wheatley handed the girl over and re-joined the fight, continuing to do his job, as if nothing had happened.

Dasher's actions, that day, were witnessed by every man in 1/1. It was an act of such stunning bravery and compassion that it made a profound impression on all of them. Word spread and by the time the unit returned to the advisors' headquarters at the MACV compound, it was all anyone was talking about. The Australian Army decided it wanted to acknowledge Dasher's heroic actions from that day. He was told he was to be recommended for a Mentioned in Dispatches. It was the first decoration Dasher would be recommended for, but by no means the last.

A Mentioned in Dispatches (MiD) was considered a tier-four award (tier one being the Victoria Cross). It was a British award for members of the armed forces who displayed gallant or meritorious actions. It is so named because a person awarded a MiD would have their name appear in an official report, written by a superior officer and sent through to the high command. No medal was awarded for a MiD, but rather, one would receive a certificate and wear an oak leaf known as a 'device' on the ribbon of the appropriate campaign medal. Their name and actions would traditionally be published in the London Gazette, for all to see. This award is no longer available to Australians and has since been replaced by Australian awards, such as the Commendation for Gallantry, the Commendation for Brave Conduct, and the Commendation for Distinguished Service.

Despite being told about his MiD, and even later, writing home to tell his sister Florence that he had been put up for several awards, it was never issued. Dasher's actions, that day, are mentioned in a document from the AATTV archives, dated December 1966. That document clearly states that '…the member was recommended for the award of the MiD because of his efforts…'. Unfortunately, the award was never followed up on, until it finally appeared in his original Victoria Cross citation. It was later removed, however, as it was deemed unrelated to the incident for which he would later receive the VC. It is now believed that the confusion and mix-up with the original Victoria Cross citation played a large role in seeing that the MiD was forgotten about.

There were, in fact, two actions that appeared in Wheatley's original VC citation, which were later removed, before the Cross was awarded. The first being for saving the girl in May 1965 and the second was for an action in August, that year. It appears that, as both were written into his original VC citation and then removed, they were forgotten about and were never followed up. At the time of writing this book, Kevin Wheatley has still not received his MiD, nor has he received the award for his actions, which followed in August 1965. There were other Kevin Wheatley actions of note, events which are recorded in books, written by the people who served with him, where he clearly should have been decorated. Those actions are detailed in this book.

Sadly, being overlooked for decorations was common for Australians, during the Vietnam war. As each year passed, the war became more and more unpopular and decorating servicepeople was considered politically dangerous, so was discouraged. Dasher's missing awards, however, particularly, the two which appeared in his original Victoria Cross citation, could be retrospectively awarded by the Australian Government, should they choose to do so. Unissued gallantry and distinguished service decorations, including those from the Vietnam war, are often awarded retrospectively. The Australian Government could, even now, award him the modern equivalent of a MiD, which would be a Commendation for Gallantry. One only needs to consider his actions on that day, however, to realised that Wheatley should have received something much higher than a Mentioned in Dispatches. To receive nothing at all is a total outrage, which can and should be rectified, as soon as possible.

Chapter 10

A JARHEAD

Dasher first met US marine, Lieutenant Jim Lowe, at a small airfield, outside of Hue. Like Dasher, Jim had been assigned as an adviser to the 1st Division of ARVN and expected to be there, for a period of about seven months. Jim Lowe was coming to replace a marine who had been killed in a hand-grenade accident, just a few days earlier. Dasher had been told little about the new addition to his team, other than he was a good soldier and a former maths major from the University of Notre Dame. The two men were to become good friends and form the backbone of a team, which would see a lot of action.

Along with Lowe, there was a tall, black Marine Corps gunnery sergeant, named Jim Sharp. 'Gunny Sharp', as he was known, was a Korean War veteran who had lied about his age, to get into that war and had been a battalion sniper. Sharp had been awarded an American Silver Star, before he had even turned 18 years old. Jim Lowe and Jim Sharp both liked Dasher, from the moment they met him, but, at first, struggled to know what to make of the wild man from Down Under. In Jim Lowe's book, *A Jarhead's Journey*, Jim described his first meeting with Dasher at the airfield, that day.

> Dasher was built like a fire hydrant, about 5'8" and 160LBS (but he would give you his weight in stone) with no body fat.

His body was covered with tattoos from his thick neck down to his ankles. He never stopped laughing and smiling. Everything was 'bloody this' or 'bloody that' and nothing seemed serious or sacred to him. Dash was about 28 in 1965 and was already a revered legend among the Aussies. They told me the squat, hard-headed fellow had also been one of the best Rugby players in Australia, as well as an accomplished boxer. His exploits in Malaya gave him an aura of invincibility, which I believed he himself believed. He certainly feared nothing.

> We worked closely together for nearly six months in the field, staying up on point with the lead company on each 1/1 operation. Working in the field with Dash was a learning experience that neither Quantico nor Fort Bragg, could provide. He was the ultimate soldier. He was also the master instructor. One thing that impressed me about Dash, as soon as we began working together, was his skill in communicating with the Vietnamese. He would sit down with the locals and share jokes, in Vietnamese, since only Major Hahn spoke any English. I asked Dasher where he went to language school. He said he had not, yet within three months in country he was speaking the language with ease, while I was struggling fiercely after four months in language school. When I asked him his secret he said, 'I reckoned it was easy, Skipper, because there are little blokes this high (gesturing to his knee) that are speaking it.' He just willed himself to do it, that simple.

The Team had another unofficial member, a man known simply as Tam. Tam was a friendly Vietnamese soldier who was the unit's driver. There was some distrust of Tam, so Captain Hougen pulled Lowe and Sharp aside, to quietly warn them to be careful speaking around Tam. The Vietnamese driver appeared to speak no English, but the men believed he probably understood more of the language than he let on. Although they had no direct evidence that Tam was himself a Vietcong, they believed he was probably an informant or even a double agent. It had not escaped Dasher's attention that, in all the time Tam had driven them around in South Vietnam, they had never once come close to hitting a landmine or booby trap. He seemed to have an uncanny ability to avoid danger.

Before The Team moved back to Quang Tri, they needed to wait at the airfield in Hue for some supplies, which were being flown up from Da Nang. These were items Dasher and Captain Hougen had purchased on the black market, items they could use to improve the defences, back at base. One reliable source of supplies, during the Vietnam War, was illegal barter with local businesses, and smart operators like Wheatley and Hougen knew how to work the system. Dasher and the other advisors would trade captured Vietcong weapons for concrete and barbed wire, whenever they could. This was used to increase security, back at headquarters. Most of the weapons they captured were Chinese and Russian-made and totally untraceable. Whenever The Team found themselves in a situation, where the number of guns captured was greater than the number of dead bodies or prisoners they had taken, it was easy to slip a few aside to use for trade later.

Kevin Wheatley and Jim Lowe

Chapter 10

While awaiting the supplies, Dasher overheard a call on the radio which came in from a South-Vietnamese officer, who was asking for a dust-off (medical evacuation). From what Dasher could figure, the bloke was only a short distance to the south-west of the airfield. It seemed the ARVN company had been ambushed by group of Vietcong who had been waiting in a cave and tunnel network. To Dasher's disgust, as soon as the Vietnamese helicopter pilots who were within earshot of the radio heard the call, they opened the front engine compartments of their two helicopters and pretended to carry-out maintenance inspections. The men totally ignored their dying countrymen, who were probably bleeding to death, just a few kilometres away. Men they might well have known and whom, with a little courage and grit, they could have extracted and taken to hospital, in a matter of minutes.

Jim Lowe asked Captain Hougen, 'How do we help here, Sir? Why aren't these pilots doing something?'

The captain grunted, 'We can't do a thing. These pilots don't give a shit, Lowe. If they don't want to fly into an LZ to pick up their own wounded, then I'm sure as hell not going to risk your life doing it for them. If it was you, Dash, or one of our people out there, we'd be moving already, but you'll soon learn, this is a very different war. American and Australian pilots will fly through a hail of lead and shit, to pick up anyone who needs it, be it their own people or anyone else, but the locals won't do the same. Sorry Lowe, we can't do anything.'

Jim nodded, and Dasher could see that the American was frustrated. Wheatley figured it was a good sign that this new American had shown a willingness to help, but appeared to have the common sense not to argue with Captain Hougen when he had been told 'no'. Hougen was a career officer in his mid-thirties, who had been in country about nine months and knew what he was doing. He had established himself as a respected leader in the field, during his time at Quang Tri and Wheatley had seen enough of the man to be willing to follow him. He continued to listen to the two Americans talk and looked south-west, to where he thought the desperate ARVN men were, even then, fighting for their lives. He felt powerless and frustrated. He had to keep reminding himself that the local people's experience of this war was vastly different and more complicated than his own.

The Vietnamese people had been fighting this war, and others like it, for thousands of years and had seen little to no improvement to their lives, as a result. All things considered, it was hard to imagine why they would risk their lives rushing out to kill an enemy, who were, in reality, their fellow countrymen. In some cases, they might be fighting their own neighbours and even, other family members. It was the Americans, Australians, New Zealanders, and other nationalities who were the foreigners here, not the Vietcong, nor the armies from the North. To Dasher, a simple man from the suburbs of Sydney, it all seemed overly complicated. He was starting to wonder if winning this war was even possible. Without unconditional support and even a little desperation from the local population, it was difficult to see how it could be.

Dasher and another advisor navigating through the jungle

Eventually, the supplies arrived, and The Team loaded up and headed north to Quang Tri. Dasher sat beside Jim Lowe in the back of the jeep and Tam was driving, with Captain Hougen in the front. The trip was about 50 kilometres along Route One. That part of the highway was known by the Americans as 'The Street Without Joy'. It ran through fishing villages, just east of the foothills, which led to the infamous, Ho Chi Minh Trail. Most of the local population lived within a kilometre or so of the road, as did the Vietcong. There were little villages and hamlets along the highway, each had stores and shops, which sat almost directly on the road. There were schools and churches, as well, many of which had been built by western, Christian churches and missionaries. Despite all the death and carnage of the war, there was some good work being done here, and these structures were proof of that.

As they headed north, toward Quang Tri, Captain Hougen said to Jim Lowe, 'Don't try to win this war by yourself or try to do it in one day. Guys who do, drive down this road sitting up in a jeep and go back the other direction in body bags. Do not trust anyone, except the people in this team. Not even young Tam here.' He ruffled the driver's hair playfully and continued, 'Don't even trust the people you meet at the compound. Your predecessor was killed by a grenade that exploded in the back seat of this very jeep, right where Dasher is sitting now.' He poked a thumb over his shoulder towards Dasher. I believe it was sabotage. Again, don't trust anyone, but the people on this team.'

Jim swallowed and said, 'I understand.'

They made their way back to headquarters and the new American advisors settled in, getting familiar with the base and finding their place among those already stationed there. It was not long before Jim Lowe and Jim Sharp found themselves in the bush with Dasher and the rest of the company. As they were to find out, the Australian way of fighting the war was vastly different to what they were used to. Both Jim Lowe and Jim Sharp were smart enough to take good advice and recognise strong leadership, when they saw it. They quickly figured out that these 'blokes from Down Under' had learned a thing or two, during their time in the jungles of South Asia, during World War II, Malaya and Borneo. The lessons they taught the Americans would be long-lasting and lifesaving.

Chapter 11

VALOUR DENIED

Operation Lam Son 90 was an operation where the ARVN 1st Division decided to attack a suspected concentration of Vietcong in an area, west of a village, called Boa Cam. This was far from the first operation Jim Lowe and Jim Sharp had been on with Dasher and the others, but it was to prove to be the most dangerous, so far. Boa Cam village was near the Laos border, about 25 km west of Quang Tri. It sat deep in the jungle, along the bank of Quang Tri River. The attack would be carried out, after heading west, then turning to the north, near the river. Dasher had his work cut out for him on this one. Safely navigating the men there was going to de difficult and the idea Hahn had come up with, to attack the Vietcong, was not a good one.

Captain Hahn wanted to set-up what was a typical ARVN pincher movement. A move that Dasher had watched Hahn try, several times, in the past and that had proven to be consistently unsuccessful. Ignoring the advice from his US and Australian advisors, however, Hahn was determined to proceed with the plan. Working with a poor strategy was only part of the challenge, the operational briefing for the patrol took place on the Monday afternoon and the unit would not move out, until 0500 the following morning. This was how things were normally done, out of MACV headquarters, much to Dasher's consistent frustration. It was well known that Vietcong spies were often present at these briefings, whether in the guise of compound staff, police, or other contractors. The briefings were never as secure as Wheatley wanted them to be and no matter how many times he, Captain Hougen, or any of the other advisers, told Hahn not to have the briefings, until the moment they were ready to head out, the man refused to change the way he did things. As a result, the Vietcong were consistently warned about these operations and might have as much as 12 hours to prepare for the coming assault.

Hahn and the other South-Vietnamese planners simply did not care about this. They believed that any tip-off would allow the Vietcong to flee west, towards Laos and heavy casualties would, therefore, be avoided. Unfortunately, and perhaps predictably, the VC would simply leave behind snipers and booby traps to catch the ARVN, who would inevitably walk straight into them. The Australian and American advisors did the best they could to deal with the situation and for Dasher, one of the most effective ways, he could handle it, was to always stay with the blokes on point. If anyone was going to be out front, when snipers and booby traps were inevitable, it was going to be him. It was not that he did not think anyone else in the 1/1 was capable, rather, that he knew it was the most difficult place to be and putting the most experienced people in that position was only logical.

At 0500, the truck convoy rolled out in a line of blazing horns, flashing lights, and rarely implemented radio silence, which infuriated Wheatley. If there were any Vietcong spies in the area, they could not possibly have missed the fact that the patrol had begun. They drove west, through the foothills and then, in the afternoon, moved out, on foot, into the jungle. They set-up camp for the night and after dinner, Captain Hahn pulled out a flask of bourbon and offered it to Dasher. Dasher shook his head. 'Not out here, mate.' He said firmly, then settled in to get some sleep.

The next morning, Wheatley awoke, soaked to the bone. Early morning dew ghosted about the tree canopy above. He sat up and turned to a sleeping Jim Lowe. The American marine had several 20-centimetre-long leeches latched to each of his nostrils and one particularly fat one, which hung from one of his ear lobes. The creatures were thick and deep purple in colour and were a regular part of life in the Vietnamese jungle. Dasher kicked the American and said, 'Skipper, wake up.' He tossed the drowsy American a packet of salt and nodded at his leech-covered face.

Dasher getting some rest on a long patrol

Chapter 11

Lowe put his hands to his nose and ears, rolled his eyes and took the salt from Wheatley. He used it to remove the enormous blood suckers and handed it back, with a short, 'Thanks, Dash.'

When the unit headed out, that morning, Dasher and Jim Lowe moved up to the front. Wheatley had been pleased that, over the last few patrols, Jim Lowe had picked up the habit of staying on point with him. The two men were always leading their company, walking side by side in concentrated silence, as they studied the terrain ahead for snipers and booby traps. Lowe was proving to be a skilled and a welcome addition to the team and Dasher was beginning to enjoy the man's company. Captain Hougen and Jim Sharp travelled about halfway back in the group, where they could keep an eye on Captain Hahn. This was the formation the unit most used and, like Wheatley and Lowe, Sharp and Hougen worked well together.

Dasher was now using updated maps that had been generated by the American Air Force. These had replaced the old, and often dangerously inaccurate, French maps he had been using in the past. He had been thrilled by this, but even with the new maps, finding his way through the hills, was difficult and slow going. On the evening of the second day, Lowe and Wheatley stopped Captain Hougen and suggested they change direction and take a pass, a little further to the west and south. This would see them come down the west side of a ridgeline and get better access to water from springs shown on the map. Lowe explained that, although this would take them a couple kilometres out of the way, they would be able to move faster, give them access to fresh water and give them a better chance of catching the enemy off guard.

Captain Hougen agreed to the idea and went away to try and convince Hahn to accept the advice. 'It'll be easier sledding and we'd have a better chance of catching the VC off guard.' he explained to Hahn, pointing to the map.

Hahn frowned and asked in his thick, Vietnamese accent, 'Easier sledding? What mean?'

Hougen said, 'I mean there are easier trails to follow. Trails made by game that won't be so steep. There should be plenty of cover, but no heavy brush to cut through and plenty of fresh water.'

'You preach to choir, Hougen', Hahn said, with a nod. 'Let's go.'

The unit made the turn and headed north toward the river, just after midday. As they moved, Dasher could hear Captain Hougen talking on the radio to the communications shack, back at Quang Tri. He was able to keep the Air Force spotters up to date on their position and ensure they would be able to find them quickly, as needed. It had been an unusually quiet operation, up to that point, and Dasher knew that was likely to change. So far, they had not even been fired on by a single sniper, not even as they had crossed the westernmost rice paddies and foothills, on the first day out. Dasher hated snipers, with a passion, but their absence troubled him.

By mid-afternoon on 18 August 1965, the third day out on patrol, Dasher and Lowe were moving at the front of the column with their radio operator placed thoughtfully between them. They were about one kilometre from a river that Dasher had been leading them towards, when one of the ARVN soldiers, ahead of Dasher, stopped suddenly and ducked low, signalling that he had spotted something. Dasher put up a hand signal to stop and get down, which was passed, quickly and quietly, back down the line. As Wheatley squinted against sunlight falling on him through a gap in the trees above, he saw movement through the jungle and heard voices. He hurried towards the forwardmost point man and crouched beside him. The soldier pointed and Dasher saw the man had found an enemy supply depot that had been set up in a small village. Dasher could clearly see, at least, two dozen VC soldiers moving around, in plain sight. Fortunately, Dasher and his men had not been seen. Jim Lowe moved up beside him and whistled softly. He sent word back to Captain Hougen and the unit silently went about setting up, to assault the village.

They quietly moved to half surround the place and set up their heavy machine guns, before Hahn gave the order to attack. The ARVN soldiers began the assault, by lobbing a volley of hand grenades into the village and then, opened fire, as those grenades started to explode amongst the enemy. They had successfully launched the raid, before being detected, which had given them a massive advantage and knocked out two unmanned machine-gun emplacements, before the enemy had a chance to use them. Multiple VC soldiers died, before they had even fired a shot. War is not a sport. One does not go into battle looking for a fair fight or one dies beside his mates. This is how battles are won or lost.

The team moved in, firing, as the demoralised Vietcong retreated into the surrounding jungle. The men searched the village and started to look for supplies, munitions, caves, and bunkers. It turned out that the village had been converted into a serious supply depot. They found a large cache of weapons, ammunition and food that would have been extremely valuable to the VC and Dasher was certain they would not give it up without a fight. He quickly started to move around the perimeter, looking for any place from which the enemy might want to launch a counterattack. There was a steep ridgeline, above and behind the village, which Wheatley decided would be the most likely place. As he moved towards it, he spotted a group of black-pyjama-wearing men, moving across the ridgeline. This was the counterattack he had feared, and it was clearly going to come at them from high ground.

Wheatley swore and called for Hahn, instructing the officer to organise a platoon, to move into a blocking position and attack the ridge, before the inevitable counterattack began. Hahn looked up, but he could see no sign of the enemy. His face was uncertain, and Dasher could tell he was not convinced. Rather than wasting time arguing with the officer, Wheatley fixed his bayonet to the front of his rifle and took off at a run. He sprinted up the ridgeline, SLR in hand and jaw set, as he prepared to assault whatever force was waiting for him up there. He knew that hesitating would allow the enemy time to set up and that would lead to disaster. The only way to stop them was to get in amongst them and disrupt their plans, any way he could. Behind him, Jim Lowe had managed to convince Hahn to take the threat seriously and had taken off behind Dasher, with a group of about fifteen ARVN soldiers.

As Dasher neared to top of the ridge, he ran into a barrage of small arms fire. He could hear rounds zip past his head and the enemy started to lob grenades at him. The hand grenades exploded to his left and right and the ground thudded beneath his boots, as he charged.

He continued to run at the enemy, through the maelstrom and soon saw that there were, at least, twenty Vietcong soldiers on top of the ridge. Continuing forward, Dasher began to fire his SLR, as he ran, first dropping one enemy, then another. Jim Lowe and the other ARVN soldiers followed behind, shooting past Wheatley and the enemy began to fall back. Dasher shot another enemy and three more suddenly rose from tall grass to his left, but Wheatley dropped two of them and Lowe killed the third. The Vietcong scattered, startled by the ferocity of the Australia's assault.

He finally reached the top of the ridge, panting hard and encountered another handful of men, who were still trying to hold their ground. Wheatley, who now had Lowe and his group of ARVN soldiers behind him, pushed them back into the jungle and killed those who were not fast enough to get out of the way. Dasher took a moment to reload and as he was swapping-out magazines, another Vietcong fighter rose from the long grass, to his left, just metres away. The man raised his weapon, not at Dasher, but at Jim Lowe.

The big marine saw him and pulled the trigger on his M-2 Carbine, only to hear the single most-feared sound a soldier can hear, in such a situation. The unmistakable 'click' of an empty weapon trying to fire. Dasher, knowing he could not reload in time to save Jim, leapt forward and smashed the butt of his rifle Hollywood-style into the side of the VC soldier's head, as hard as he could. The sound of the man's skull cracking was like two rocks being crashed together. He fell sideways, dropping to the grass instantly dead. Wheatley's fast thinking and lightning-quick hands had saved Lowe's life. In that moment, Jim knew he was about to die and describes it in his book, *A Jarhead's Journey*.

> I pulled my trigger and heard the loudest click in my life. I had used up the whole banana clip in my carbine and he had me bore-sighted. Why he hesitated, I do not know. I heard a loud smack after my click. His head tilted sideways, and he fell from a horizontal butt stroke from Dash's SLR. The VC had me bore sighted but hesitated for a fraction of a second and was dead instead of me.

Chapter 11

Dasher hurried to Lowe's side and the two found some cover behind a tree, as the rest of their men hurried past, chasing the remaining Vietcong into the jungle. Lowe inserted a new magazine, while Dasher was breathing heavily and doing the same. The Australian had a sly grin on his face, as he considered the marine, 'What?' Lowe asked.

Dasher muttered and said, with a smile, 'Notre Dame maths major, my arse. Ya'd think a bloke would be able to count a few bloody bullets.'

Lowe tried for a witty retort, but found none. He was still shocked and frankly, too surprised that he was still alive, to be able to think of anything clever to say. Instead, he burst out laughing and said, 'Thanks, Dash. I'll go get some security up here.'

'Yeah, you do that.' Dasher said, with a wink and set out to check that the enemy had, in fact, fled the field, this time. Once he had satisfied himself that they were really gone, he started to count the dead.

On the afternoon of 18 August 1965, Warrant Officer Second Class Kevin Wheatley had managed to attack and route an entire platoon of Vietcong soldiers up hill. The enemy had held the upper ground and might have outnumbered him, as much as twenty to one, yet Dasher had prevailed and stopped what could have been a costly counterattack. It is, perhaps, fitting that this action took place on 18 August 1965, exactly one year, to the day, before 108 men of 6th Battalion, Royal Australian Regiment (6RAR) would find themselves outnumbered by about the same ratio as Dasher had. Those men would find themselves fighting for their lives, in what would become known as the Battle of Long Tan. A fight where the diggers had been ambushed by a force, vastly superior in size and had, somehow, managed to win out. Because of the battle of Long Tan, 18 August is recognised as Vietnam Veteran's Day in Australia.

When Captain Hougen made it up the ridge, he was thrilled to see that his best fighter was still alive. The American captain was positively ecstatic, a huge smile split his normally serious face, as he looked around at the many dead Vietcong. He said, 'Shit, nice job, Dash!'

'We aren't done yet.' Jim Lowe said, his face dark. 'Can I call in a Bird Dog? Those bastards are still out there.'

Hougen nodded and as Lowe called in a Bird Dog, or US Air Force spotter plane, Dasher had his men place markers, at the north and south edges of their position, so that they would be visible from above the tree canopy. The Bird Dogs were small Cessna aircrafts, designed to be able to fly low and slow. They could land and take off on short runways and had incredibly low stall speeds, which meant the pilots had a better chance of finding targets in the jungle below. It also made them easy pickings for enemy infantry in the jungle, so flying the small Cessna in Vietnam was highly dangerous work. Once a Bird Dog had confirmed a target, the pilots would radio the coordinates to fast moving jets, which would scream past and drop napalm or explosives on the designated position. Dasher and the rest of the infantry loved the Bird Dog pilots. During their time in Vietnam, the Bird Dogs were vital in assault and rescue operations and saved countless lives. Although the Bird Dog never operated in RAAF service, around 30 Australian pilots flew them, 15 of whom were awarded the Distinguished Flying Cross.

Dasher soon heard the low drone of a single engine Cessna and the pilots easily picked up his markers. Using those markers, they were able to work out where to tell the jet pilots to drop the napalm. Lieutenant Lowe had instructed them to aim for an area, 200 metres south-west of the markers. The Marine hoped this would seal-off any escape route the VC might be trying to use. Jim contacted the Bird Dog pilot on the radio and said, 'You're clear to go, if you have the juice.'

'Roger that' came the simple reply and soon, US Air Force jets were screaming low above the trees, setting fire to everything and everyone below, with liquid fire. The strike had come in exactly where Lowe had wanted it. Dasher watched with admiration the American direct the airstrike, impressed with his professionalism. From that moment forward, Dasher and the rest of the Australians called him 'Lowe', rather than just 'Dasher's Lieutenant', as they had been.

As was their want, the Americans were very keen to produce a body count and kill sheet, to feed to the massive media machine, which was constantly snapping at their heels. The count from the assault on the village, plus Dasher's charge and the following napalm strike, were what the Americans would call 'impressive'. The graphic and gruesome job of counting all those bodies and tallying up the captured weapons and supplies were all part of job and one the men hated. War is much more than just, 'Days of boredom punctuated with seconds of terror,' as Winston Churchill had once, so famously, proclaimed. Every contact resulted in an inevitable clean-up, which was never pleasant, but simply had to be done.

Wheatley in a South Vietnamese hamlet

After another week in the field, the tired 1/1 finally returned to Quang Tri, from what had been a phenomenally successful operation, which had produced one of the largest ARVN victories, to date. A parade was held, as well as a military ceremony, in which Lieutenant Jim Lowe was awarded his second South-Vietnamese Cross of Gallantry for helping Dasher in his bayonet charge. Wheatley was told he was to be awarded a Knight of the Republic of Vietnam National Order Medal. It was the highest award that existed in South Vietnam and had been modelled on the French Legion of Honour. It was given to military members and civilians for exceptional service, valour, or otherwise outstanding feats.

The American officer, Captain Hougen, was deeply impressed with Wheatley's one-man bayonet charge up the slope, and the USA announced that they were going to award him a Silver Star. The Silver Star is the United States' third-highest award for valour, in the face of the enemy. Dasher complained to Jim Lowe that all of this was unnecessary and that he disliked awards and medals. He could not understand the point of creating so much fuss, over a bloke just doing his job. He need not have worried, however, because, as was the case with his Mentioned in Dispatches, he would never see the Silver Star, nor the South-Vietnamese Knighthood.

During the Vietnam War, the Australian Government had a bizarre policy of denying foreign awards to serving members of its military. This meant that, no matter what a person did, nor how eager a foreign government might be to acknowledge them, the Australian Government would not permit it. This policy made as little sense then, as it does now, but has since been abandoned. Today, any service person, who was offered a foreign award, while this policy was in place, can now accept and wear it.

Wheatley's Knight of the Republic of Vietnam National Order Medal would eventually be sent to his family, but at the time of writing, his Silver Star is yet to be presented. Despite multiple attempts by Dasher's family and friends, not to mention countless letters from the American Government who had tried multiple times to hand the star over, the Australian Government blocked it, time and time again. Even as late as 2020, long after the policy of not accepting foreign awards had been abolished, Australian officials and bureaucrats continued to thwart attempts by the family to receive the Silver Star.

Wheatley's actions on 18 August 1965 were recognised by the Australian Army and he was told, once again, that he would receive a gallantry award for what he had done that day. Even today, it is mentioned on the Australian War Memorial website and many other places, that Lieutenant Colonel Clarence Bishop, Infantry Deputy Senior Adviser, announced that Wheatley was to be recommended for an 'appropriate Australian Medal for heroism' for his actions on 18 August 1965.

Chapter 11

Dasher's charge up the ridge was the second of the two actions, mentioned in his original Victoria Cross citation, which were later removed. The first being where he saved the little girl in May. As stated in an earlier chapter, both actions were removed from the citation and subsequently forgotten about. As with his MiD from May, at the time of writing this book, Kevin Wheatley has still not received any Australian award for his deeds on 18 August 1965. Once again, this is a mistake which can be corrected, at any time, with just a little bit of courage.

Chapter 12

ONE OF THE BOYS

It did not take Jim Lowe and the other Americans long, to work out that Dasher loved to party. When the team returned from operations, Dasher would head to the local bars in Quang Tri and paint the town red. He was always careful to make sure he returned to base by curfew and at times, he would spend the remainder of the night at the headquarters bar, drinking with mates. Among those mates, was a young local, by the name of Herbert.

Wheatley had become extremely fond of Herbert, who suddenly appeared on the base, one day, and proceeded to waddle around, as if he owned the place. A few of the other blokes had decided to poke a bit of fun at Herbert, who was not only extremely short, but appeared to be almost naively friendly. A youngster, like Herbert, was taking an enormous risk, walking around with so many robust and often hungry soldiers looming over him. He seemed totally oblivious to the fact that he could have been snatched away and eaten, at any moment. If not for Dasher warning the other solders to back off and leave him alone, Herbert would have almost certainly been killed and consumed. He would have made a fine meal, because Herbert was a duck.

On more than one occasion, Wheatley was heard to say, 'If any of you bastards harm one feather on Herbert's head, you'll have me to deal with.' That was enough to quell any ideas the men may have had about enjoying a roast duck dinner. One could say that Herbert became untouchable after that, because no one dared lay a finger on him. Most nights, when Dasher would be drinking in the bar, Herbert would be right at his side. In between songs and jokes, Dasher would gently push the duck's bill into his drink and hold it there until the duck had a good gulp. After doing this a few times, Herbert would be wobbling all over the bar, to the raucous laughter of all present. Eventually, Herbert would decide he had had enough and quietly retire under a table in a corner, to sleep it off.

Dasher would always find the duck, whenever he returned to base, or the duck would find him. It was not unusual for Herbert to disappear while Dasher was out on patrol, but the duck seemed to know when he returned and would come waddling back onto base, in search of his mate. It is hard to overstate the importance of distractions and niceties, like Herbert, in a war zone. Patrols were long and dangerous and when the men returned, they were often exhausted and highly stressed. Making life at the base as comfortable as possible, played a vital part in keeping the soldiers sane and healthy.

An example of how stressful life could be in the jungle, even when you were not in a direct firefight, was one particularly poorly planned operation, where the unit walked directly into a Vietcong 82-mm mortar barrage. As usual, Dasher and Jim Lowe were at the front, helping the men who were unlucky enough to be taking point. When the barrage started, they found themselves trapped. Moving forward, to attack the mortars, would likely see them walk into a machine-gun ambush and the bulk of the shells were falling at their rear, so they could not fall back, either. The earth shuddered and shook, as explosions tore through the jungle and it was impossible to know where the next round was going to land. A bloke did not know whether he should sit still or try to move out of the way. Either decision was equally likely to get you killed, so the only real choice was to try and find whatever cover was at hand and wait it out.

Kevin with his good mate, Herbert the duck

Searching around, Dasher found his men shelter, by moving close to a nearby canyon wall. His South-Vietnamese colleagues would not move, however, they were frozen by fear and indecision. As far as they knew, taking one step to the left, or one step to the right, might put them directly under a falling mortar round. But then again, so might standing still. These attacks were always highly stressful and extremely dangerous situations and, more likely than not, they would not so much as lay eyes on a single enemy soldier, from start to finish.

Chapter 12

This was one such occasion. Dasher and the other advisers went to work, trying to encourage the men to stay calm and move to the cover Dasher had found them. Eventually, the men moved, and they settled in to wait out the deadly barrage.

As was the norm, for that time of day in South Vietnam, the skies opened and rain started hammering down. Lightning lit up the sky, sending bright flashes and booming thunder crashing through the trees, as if competing with the exploding mortar rounds, to see which could terrorise the soldiers more. The plan to move close to the ridge had worked, as most of the shells were landing back up the trail they had just vacated. The danger, now, was that the enemy would have a spotter, out somewhere, who might find them and have the Vietcong adjust fire to their new location. There was nothing to do, except lay low in the miserable wet and wait.

That day, Jim Lowe was finding the situation particularly stressful. He was doing his best to keep a cool head, but not knowing where to stand, combined with the stress of trying to look through the pouring rain for any enemy spotters who might give their position away, was starting to wear him down. He was scared, cold, wet, frustrated and becoming extremely irritable. A bad combination for an infantryman in Vietnam. So, as he considered Dasher a mentor in the field, Lowe turned to see what the Australian was doing. To Jim's complete shock, Dasher was not only as cool as a cucumber, but he was smiling and laughing. Wheatley was laying down behind some large rocks, about five metres away. He had made himself comfortable, on his back, in a patch of muddy, red clay and was playing with a night crawler. Night crawlers are 20-centimetre-long worms, found throughout the jungles of South-East Asia.

Seemingly oblivious to the deadly mortar shells exploding around him, Dasher would carefully pull the long worm out of its hole and then, let it go and watch it crawl back in. Just before the animal could completely disappear beneath the earth, he would pull it gently back out again. He just lay there, in the miserable, pouring rain, not a trouble in the world and chuckled, as he repeated this process, over and over. Determined to find out just what the mad Australian was doing, and half thinking his friend had finally lost his mind, Lowe hurried over to Dasher and hunkered down beside him. 'What on earth are you doing?' he asked. 'Aren't you worried about these mortars?'

Dasher did not even look up from the game with the worm. He smiled and said, 'The VC think they are bothering me with this random shelling, don't they, mate? That's nothing compared to the way I'm messing with this bloody worm's mind.' He smiled and looked up at his friend, as a particularly close mortar exploded behind them, sending a spray of mud and foliage into the air. Many of the soldiers, nearby, shouted in alarm and Jim jolted with shock. Dasher did even flinch. 'I'm not a bloody worm, though, am I?' he said, with a chuckle and went back to his game with the worm.

Lowe had to take a moment, to let that sink in. He knew there was always method to any of Dasher's apparent madness and he had no doubt this was no exception. But playing with a worm and laughing in the middle of being mortared? He watched silently for a while and finally understood the message that was there for him. There was nothing any of them could do, except wait until the VC gave up or ran out of rounds. Like the worm, they were completely powerless to change their situation and had no choice, but to stay low and ride it out. They could wriggle abound the jungle, like confused and panicked worms, jumping from one position to another, in hope of getting out from under a mortar round they would never know was coming. They could not see the incoming shells, nor did they have any way to predict where they were going to land, so why worry about it? If the rounds were not getting any closer, and apart for the one that had recently exploded close by, they were not, then, there was nothing to do except to endure.

Jim smiled and did his best to relax and watch Dasher's worm game, as the mortars hammered the earth and the thunder continued to rumble along with it. The learning process, he decided, was never boring when you were with Dasher Wheatley. The man was always thinking of other people and doing everything he could, not just to keep his men safe, but to educate them and make their lives better. Case in point was an incident the following day, when they had stopped by a creek to refill their water supply. Lowe watched Dasher carefully refill his canteen from the stream and then add the required treatment tablets they used to kill-off any bugs that might be living in the water. He hooked the full canteen back on his belt and, as they started to move out, cupped his hands together and started to drink the water, directly from the stream.

Incredulous, Jim said, 'You stupid Aussie! What are you doing drinking that, when you have a canteen of treated water on your hip?'

Dasher smiled and said, 'Don't worry about me, Skipper, I never get sick. I can stomach the water. This,' he said, tapping his water canteen with one hand, 'is for you, when you run out of water or get hurt. I'm not wasting the tablets on me.'

After the patrol had ended and they had all return to Quang Tri, Dasher was walking through the city with the Vietnamese driver, Tam. He found a store which sold all types of musical instruments and remembered Jim Lowe talking about how he loved to play the guitar back home. So, he purchased one for his new mate and brought it back to base. Lowe was thrilled. He played long into the night, strumming out countless folk songs and even belted out 'Waltzing Matilda', whenever the Australians pressed him.

Life at the Quang Tri headquarters was as comfortable and liveable, as its inhabitants could make it, but Dasher was starting to feel the isolation that came with special forces work. He missed being part of a much larger team and although, there were plenty of good people at the base with him, most of them were South-Vietnamese. There were a few Australians and Americans mixed in and while they were all fine people, Dasher missed the mateship that came from playing football and working in an army battalion. Life for AATTV soldiers in Vietnam was stressful and lonely. They were forced to work in small groups and with people who mostly did not speak the same language, it was vastly different to what he had experienced in Malaya. He was lonely and starting to miss his family and his old mates, particularly, the blokes from 1RAR. So, Wheatley would try and keep that loneliness at bay, as best he could, and he did it the only way he knew how.

Dasher spent a lot of time drinking and socialising, whenever he was not on patrol. One night, Wheatley and his mates decided that the guitar-playing American, Jim Lowe, had retired too early. They needed some music to help them continue drinking and singing into the wee, small hours. Dasher, pair of chopsticks in hand, made his way over to Jim's room, bashed on the door and let himself in. Jim's roommate, at the time, was out on patrol, so the Lieutenant had been enjoying the rare quiet and privacy that had afforded him.

'Skipper, you awake?' The question was a joke. If Jim had been asleep, he no longer would be. 'Skipper, I finally worked out how to use these bloody things.' Dasher held up the chopsticks, a goofy grin on his face. 'Wanna see?'

'Dash! It's midnight!'

'Sure is, Skipper, the night's still young. Look what I did.' He stepped to the side of Lowe's bed and poked the end of one of the chopsticks at him, almost taking out one of the American's eyes. 'See, I sharpened the end of this one to a point. Now I can throw the other one away and use it like a fork.' He laughed and held out a hand. 'Get your guitar, Skipper, the blokes want you to play 'Waltzing Matilda'. They wanna buy you a beer, come on.'

Knowing resistance was futile, Jim reluctantly took Dasher's hand and let him pull him to his feet. He grumbled something about crazy Aussies, as he pulled on his boots and grabbed his guitar. On the way out the door, he said, 'You dammed Aussies never actually sing 'Waltzing Matilda', when you're at home, do you? I'm convinced the whole thing's a joke.'

Dasher frowned, 'Joke?'

'Level with me, Dash, it's a joke you guys play on the rest of us, right? It's a horrible song, you only sing it when you travel abroad, to drive the rest of the world crazy.'

Dasher laughed and led Jim back to the bar and the marine reluctantly led a chorus of 'Waltzing Matilda', followed by the normal string of country and folk songs they loved to hear. The night was going well, Herbert the duck was staggering up and down the bar, seeming to bob his little head in time with the music. The men were singing loudly, and everyone was in good spirits, but eventually, a US colonel decided to stop by. The officer had a group of Bird Dog pilots with him and, as they entered the bar, the singing stopped abruptly and Jim ceased playing, as all eyes turned to regard the new arrivals.

Lowe stood and saluted the colonel, but the Australians turned their backs and started singing again. The colonel had only been at Quang Tri for a short while, he was the new Section Commander. So far, the man had not received a warm welcome from the Australians. He had made some unwelcome changes, since taking over and had an airy, almost superior, demeanour about him, which had done little to endear him to the men. Australian soldiers are always a very tight-knit bunch of people, something Jim Lowe and Jim Sharp had learned. One does not simply walk into an Australian unit, of any design and expect to receive respect and admiration, simply because of the pips you wear on your shoulders. You had to earn that respect, as Lowe had done at Dasher's side. This is a simple fact that hundreds of officers, from many a country's armies, have had to learn, the hard way. From the British officers, during World War I, to General MacArthur, during World War II, the diggers did not care for foreign commanders and these American officers were struggling to learn the same lesson.

The Aussies' singing was getting louder by the second, so the colonel waved for Jim to continue playing his guitar. Most of the American Bird Dog pilots joined in with the Australians and were welcomed warmly enough. The diggers loved those blokes. The colonel moved to the bar and watched curiously, as Herbert the duck came waddling down the bar and stopped in front of him. The partly intoxicated duck cocked its head sideways and stared at the man with one bloodshot eye. The American officer was wearing a perfectly pressed, tan summer service uniform, and regarded the duck seriously. He had, no doubt, heard about Herbert the duck and that he had become something of a mascot for the Australians. Trying to look unsurprised by the sight of the animal, and perhaps, wanting to come across as one of the guys, the colonel picked Herbert up and started patting him. As if reading the minds of every Australian in the room, Herbert promptly shat all over the colonel's immaculate uniform.

Jim Lowe saw this happen and desperately tried not to laugh. He pretended not to have noticed and kept playing his guitar. The American pilots did likewise, but Dasher, and the rest of the Australians, let out a huge cheer and laughed audaciously. The mortified colonel put the duck back on the bar and, with as much dignity as he could muster, beat a quick retreat out of the bar and returned to his private quarters. In one short moment, Herbert, the duck, had accomplished exactly what the Aussies had wanted to do, since the colonel had taken over the Quang Tri MACV command base, shit down the front of his impeccably kept uniform.

Life continued, as it was, at Quang Tri MACV command base, for a time. The Australians generally kept to themselves at mealtimes and recreation, but managed to build a very friendly rapport with the local South-Vietnamese troops. It was a relationship that was often tested with serious trust issues, but one the Diggers did a particularly good job at maintaining. It seemed to come easy to them. Their relationship with the Americans, however, although always courteous, pragmatic, and professional, was at times strained. The Aussies ate at a large round table, by themselves, while the American NCOs ate in a common area in the hall, separated from everyone. It was like everyone gravitated to their closest colleagues and those with whom they felt most comfortable. Even Jim Lowe usually ate with the Air Force Bird Dog pilots, rather than with his digger mates.

In his book, *A Jarhead's Journey*, Jim states that this was mainly because he felt they were his link to air support, should he ever need it, out in the field. It was in his interest, and the interest of his unit, to keep a strong and well-greased relationship with the pilots. After all, if one required fast air support, medivac, resupply or pretty much anything else, it was less likely to come from the Australians, New Zealanders, or South-Vietnamese than from his fellow countrymen, the very airmen with whom he shared a meal every night. Sound thinking.

One day, before dinner in the compound, Dasher invited Jim to join him and the rest of the diggers, at their table. There was an empty seat at the usually full Australian table. Jim was happy to join them, but was a little stand-offish at the unusual invitation. He was all too aware of how tight the Australians were and how prone to practical jokes they could be. Jim got his food and the tumbler of ice, issued at each meal, before heading over. The tumbler of ice was for the fruit juice, served with dinner every night. Something they had all come to call, 'panther piss'. Dasher saw the American crossing the room and stood up and shouted at him to come and sit down. Jim did.

Dasher having a beer at Quang Tri

Fearing the Aussies were up to something, the big marine arranged his place and started to eat. He quickly noticed, with some alarm, that none of the usually talkative Aussies were speaking. They were all looking silently at their plates, eating quietly, like a group of monks, who had taken a vow of silence. Feeling more than a little uncomfortable, Lowe said to Dasher, 'Pass the pepper, please, Dash.'

Even though the pepper shaker was directly in front of him, Dasher ignored the request and continued to eat in silence. He wiped his mouth and started to butter his dinner roll, an intense look of concentration on his face, as if the task at hand was one of the most complicated jobs he had ever undertaken. Beginning to get a little annoyed, Lowe stared at Dasher, but refused to ask for the pepper again. Whatever game the boys were playing, the American was determined to not let them get the better of him. Much to his frustration, however, Dasher kept his eyes down and continued piling butter on his dinner roll, until there was almost no bread visible at all. Jim knew his Australian comrades were up to something, so decided to stay silent and sneak a peek around the table.

To Lowe's left sat the huge man they ironically called Tiny. Beside Tiny sat the totally bald younger digger they naturally called Curly and beside him, was the tiny and arseless bloke, they called Bucket Arse. Roger the Lodger was at the table, as was Herbert Beazley, the man Dasher had named his famous duck after. It was a vastly diverse collection of Australian characters that must have been an immense novelty to Jim Lowe, who now sat stewing in their uncomfortable silence, wishing he had declined Dasher's invitation to join them. Eventually, after growing rather frustrated, Jim said in a louder and clearer voice, 'Can someone please pass the salt and pepper.'

It was Tiny who finally spoke first. 'No.' The enormous man rumbled, without looking up from his plate.

Jim sat, flabbergasted, trying to work out what on earth this group of normally friendly and talkative men were doing. He knew he was the butt of some weird prank or practical joke, but could not, for the life of him, work out what that might have been. Whatever was going on, he was determined not to let it get to him. After some deep consideration, and refusing to give in, Lowe finally said, 'Thank you.' He got up, walked over to an empty table, grabbed the salt and pepper shakers from that table and placed them next to his plate. He grasped the back of his chair, smiled, and said, 'Before I sit down, eat my dinner and retire to my quarters, is there anything I can get for any of you gentlemen, while I am up?'

The whole table broke out in a roar of laughter and the Australians started passing money back and forth, as if they were settling bets of some kind. As it turned out, Wheatley had been bragging to his mates that he had gotten to know his new lieutenant so well that he could anticipate every move he would make, under any circumstance. The invitation to join them for dinner, followed by the silent treatment, was something of an acid test. Dasher had bet that the marine would not get upset by the rude treatment, but that he would remain at the table and finish his dinner politely. Furthermore, Dasher had stated that Jim would not complain about the treatment, but that he would find a way to calmly let them all know that he was not going to just sit there and tolerate their disrespect. Dasher had won the bet and announced he had taken around 50,000 piasters or about $350US. A huge sum of money for a warrant officer in 1965.

'Thanks, Skipper, now we're loaded, mate.' Dasher said with a wide grin. 'Let's go party.'

'You go party, Dash, I have things to do.' The marine said, returning the grin.

Dasher nodded his understanding. The two men had an unspoken agreement that, while they worked together very closely outside the wire, when they returned to base, they would keep a comfortable and disciplined distance. After all, Lowe was technically Dasher's boss. Wheatley headed out to enjoy the spoils of his victory, while Jim finished his meal and went back to his quarters alone.

Chapter 13

SNIPERS AND THE BEACH

Dasher Wheatley remained at Quang Tri, as an ARVN adviser and continued to work closely with Lieutenant Jim Lowe. The two men persisted at staying on point, whenever they went out. Their trusty company commander, Captain Hougen, who had finished his tour of duty, returned to the United States. He was replaced by a South-Vietnamese officer, named Lieutenant Lon. Dasher would miss Hougen, although he thought this new company commander was a decent-enough bloke. At least, his English was sound, and he was keen to help the advisers keep now *Major* Tieu Ta Hahn in check. Hahn had somehow received a promotion and now, had even more authority.

Within a few days of Lieutenant Lon's arrival, they set out on their next patrol. This one was a four-day operation that began with Dasher travelling in a truck southward along Route One. The company was told to exit the trucks somewhere between Quang Tri and Hue and then, walk east to the coast. They had orders to track down and trap a large group of Vietcong, who had been staying in a nearby fishing village. If the VC were not found in that area, the plan was to move west, through the foothills, to try and trap them in the nearby hamlets along the Ho Chi Minh Trail. This was going to be a dangerous mission, with enemy contact, all but guaranteed and the tactics Hahn was using were driving Dasher to the point of exasperation.

As with operation Lam Son 90, the briefing for this patrol had occurred the night before they had set out, giving the enemy plenty of time, to get out of the way and plant snipers and booby traps, along their path. Sure enough, as they disembarked the trucks and headed out on foot, it was not long before they came across hidden hand grenades rigged with trip wires. On one particularly awful day, snipers fired at the team, from first light until about noon. This was especially problematic for Lowe, who, at around six feet tall, was much bigger than Dasher and was a full head taller than the Vietnamese soldiers around him. Worse, he was clearly an American and the Vietcong knew, all too well, that if they managed to put a round in a Yank, they might just cut a unit off from resupply, supporting airstrikes and even bring the whole operation to a halt. Not to mention, the bounty they would collect from their bosses.

Jim Lowe carried an M-2 carbine. The M-2 was a 30-calibre or 7.62 mm, semiautomatic or fully automatic rifle, which had a banana-shaped magazine that could hold 30 rounds. The M-2 was a spin-off of the M-1, which was used by the Americans in World War I. The M-2 was particularly useful to Lowe, as he found that most of his targets tended to be less than 100 metres away, whenever the shooting started. The M-2 fired quickly and reliably and was easy to reload. Its high fire rate and short barrel meant that its range was not great, but it was amazingly effective in the bush. Range did not matter to the American, though, because his mate Dasher carried an SLR and he knew how to use it. Dasher's SLR was always in his hand and constantly kept in immaculate condition. He obsessed over the weapon and, like all good infantryman, treated it as if it was his lifeline, his best and most reliable way to get home alive.

The SLR also fired 7.62-mm rounds but was far more accurate and extremely deadly, up to as far as 500 metres. The L1A1 Self Loading Rifle, or SLR as it was known, was a Belgian-designed, gas- operated, semiautomatic rifle that took 20 or 30 round magazines. Unlike Lowe's M-2 carbine, it had no full auto function, and was a more complicated weapon which required greater maintenance and care. When well maintained and operated, however, it proved incredibly effective and reliable. The SLR functioned, by using a short stroke gas piston, located above the barrel. The SLR was the standard rifle used by the Australian Army, for over 30 years. In the hands of a professional and highly trained marksman, like Wheatley, it could be devastating on the enemy, as it was proving to be on this patrol. Every sniper they encountered, along the way, died from a bullet from Wheatley's SLR. Every single one of them.

About halfway through the day, as Dasher had been methodically and efficiently picking-off enemy snipers, he laughed and said to Lowe, 'It's a bloody good thing all these Vietcong blokes are Vietnamese.'

'Why's that?' the Marine asked.

'Poor eyesight and poor training, mate. They were lousy shots. You should be dead, fifty times over by now.'

The next day, they finally encountered a sniper, with better eyesight and better training than most. He had them pinned down and Dasher was unable to sight him. 'Got me stumped, Skipper.' he said quietly to Lowe, as he searched the jungle with his dark eyes. 'The bugger's out there somewhere, but I can't find him.'

Jim nodded and said, 'I've got an idea.' He turned and signalled for the radio carrier to come across. The young man did, and Lowe took the radio.

'What are you doing?' Dasher asked.

'I intend to take care of this bastard, by other means.' The marine called in a Bird Dog. He had to lie and tell the pilot that it was a full platoon of Vietcong fighters that had them pinned down, not just one sniper, but the pilot did not argue with him.

'A platoon, you say?' the pilot asked doubtfully.

'Swear on my grandmother's grave.' Lowe said, in a perfectly serious voice. Using a US airstrike, to knock one sniper out of a tree, was easily grounds for a court martial, but Jim had decided, a long time ago, he was not going to survive this war by following rules. About half an hour later, the sniper problem was gone, as was a good portion of Vietnamese jungle, to their east. As Dasher watched the smoke rise, Lowe said, 'I don't mind using Uncle Sam's megabucks, if I need to. What do they say, "if you got it, use it"?'

Dasher laughed and clapped his friend on the shoulder, and they moved out. The unit eventually moved into the targeted fishing village, at daybreak the following morning, but no surprise to Dasher, the VC were long gone. He had no doubt this had been part of Major Hahn's plan all along. The man would do anything he could to avoid casualties and Dasher fully understood why. It was all part of the mentality of the South-Vietnamese military. Hahn was in charge here, not Dasher, nor the Americans. If an American or Australian officer had overseen this same operation, they would have moved in far more carefully and, no doubt, found the place full of Vietcong soldiers. They would have attacked this village, killed a couple dozen Vietcong and captured a pile of weapons, but they would have, no doubt, suffered casualties themselves. This would have been regrettable, but understandable.

On the other hand, if Major Hahn had done the same thing, he might have faced court martial. One of the main objectives of the Army of the Republic of Vietnam was to avoid casualties, at all costs, because, unlike the VC, whose numbers appeared to be endless, the ARVN found replacing dead soldiers exceedingly difficult. Such were the challenges that faced the officers of the Army of the Republic of Vietnam. The Vietnam war was complicated and, at times, extremely difficult to fight. Not just for the Americans and their Australian and New Zealand counterparts, but for the ARVN, because, when all was said and done, they were the ones who suffered the most, when things went wrong.

On the day after they had found the abandoned village, 1/1 stopped for lunch on a sandy beach. Lieutenant Lon was poring over a map with Major Hahn. As lead advisor, the ARVN lieutenant was now the person who would do most of the talking with the major. On operations like this one, Dasher mostly handled land navigation, while Lowe took care of air support. The ARVN soldiers were capable enough, but they did not always get navigation right and it was one of Wheatley's strongest traits.

Hahn was pointing to the map, then looking into the distance, gesturing towards some faraway landmark, explaining to Lieutenant Lon that the distant landmark was the same thing he was pointing to on the map. As the major looked away, Dasher took a quick glance at the map and saw, straight away, that Hahn was wrong. While the major was not looking, Dasher showed Lon, where on the map, Hahn should, in fact, be looking. The lieutenant nodded his thanks and, when Major Hahn turned back to the map, Lon smoothy corrected his mistake and helped him understand their position more accurately.

In this way, and with Lieutenant Lon's help, Dasher had made sure the unit avoided getting lost, yet again. The Australian decided, right then and there, that he liked the young ARVN lieutenant very much. Gunny Jim Sharp had worked closely with Lon on this mission and the two men seemed to be getting along well. Dasher liked and trusted Sharp, so that went in the lieutenant's favour. While Lon might not yet be able to fully fill Hougen's shoes, he was on his way to gaining the adviser's confidence.

As the men started to spread out on the beach and relax, Dasher spoke to Sharp and pointed out that Hahn had not yet set-up suitable security, before they had stopped for lunch. They were, after all, out in the open. Sharp nodded and looked up the beach, 'Right, thanks, Dash. I'll let Lieutenant Lon know and get him to talk to Hahn. I might suggest he set-up observation posts in the dunes, up and down the beach.'

Dasher nodded and said, 'Cheers, mate.'

Dasher was relieved Sharp was on the case, but feared the observation posts might be put in place too late. They should have been set up before the rest of them had moved into the open, to keep an eye out for enemy movement. It was well and good to set them up now, but, for all they knew, snipers could be already watching them. Gunny Sharp moved off to talk to the major and check the security to the north, as Dasher and Lowe went south to oversee the setting-up of an outpost in the dunes, in that direction. Once the work was done, they enjoyed their lunch, but Dasher had an uneasy feeling in the pit of his stomach. The troops were tired, it was hot, and he worried they had been too lax when they had moved onto the beach. Had he been the one in charge, they would be long gone from this place, by now. He looked around at the men, his ever- present SLR in hand. They were dispersed around the beach, kicking back under the shade of palm trees and abandoned grass-roofed shelters.

To Dasher's surprise, Major Hahn announced the troops would be allowed to strip down and go for a brief swim, for another hour, before they headed out. The major said to Jim Lowe, 'OK to swim without waiting one hour after lunch, Lowe?' He then laughed and stripped down to his khaki boxer shorts and jumped into an old, abandoned sampan fishing boat. The major put one foot on the bow and hooded his eyes with his right hand. He struck the comical pose of a sea captain exploring the ocean and said, 'Lowe, you take photo.'

Jim grunted, took out his camera and said, 'Look, George Washington crossing the Delaware.' He snapped the photo.

Dasher, who had now stripped down to his underwear, made a comical impression of the major behind his back. Lowe took a photo of Dasher and he and Sharp laughed. Hahn, mistaking the laughter as being meant for him, smiled and looked pleased with himself. Dasher decided he would risk a quick swim and Lowe, Sharp and Lieutenant Lon soon followed. Dasher splashed Lon playfully and told him he was going to drown him for fun. The Australian started chasing the Vietnamese officer around in waist-high water, holding his ever-present SLR over his head, to save it from getting wet. Lieutenant Lon was laughing so hard, Dasher was sure he was going to piss himself. The man's laugh was like that of a small girl and soon, all the other men were laughing as well.

Wheatley decided it would be wise to keep their playtime short and soon, he, Lowe, Sharp and Lieutenant Lon were back on the beach and in uniform. They quickly rechecked their security set-up and sat down to watch, as the other men kept swimming. Dasher was resting on a fallen tree in the shade with Jim Lowe, when Lieutenant Lon came over and joined them. He sat down between the two men and pointed to his map, showing Wheatley the route that he wanted to take to the next village. Before he could finish explaining what he wanted to do, there was a loud smack and he fell abruptly forward. At the same time, Dasher heard the now, all-too-familiar crack of a Chinese carbine sniper rifle.

Dasher, with Jim Sharp, mimicking Major Hahn

Chapter 13

Dasher and Lowe both rolled reflexively away, weapons in hand, as they both lay prone, searching the jungle to the north for the sniper. Dasher looked quickly at Lieutenant Lon. The man had a perfect, 9-mm hole in the back of his head and the Australian did not need to investigate further, to know his new mate was dead. He turned his eyes to the north again and started to swear. Despite his best efforts, Dasher never did find the sniper who killed Lon and no more shots were fired. The sniper had obviously moved on after taking the shot, and Dasher could not help but wonder if the round had been meant for him or Lowe. He privately believed it had been intended for the American, but never gave voice to that belief.

Dasher and Jim Lowe, just before Lon was killed

Jim Sharp radioed a helicopter and they sent Lieutenant Lon's body back to headquarters at Quang Tri. They packed up and moved on out again, heading south and now, in need of yet another lead company commander. By the time they finished and made it back to Quang Tri, the team's mood was low. Operations ceased for the regiment, for a couple days, while they prepared for Lieutenant Lon's funeral. In the short time he had been with them, Lon had made a good impression on the men and was going to be missed. Dasher learned that Lon had been married for a couple years. He had no children, but Wheatley knew his widow would be suffering more than he or any of his men was.

Top - Dasher resting in front of a fallen tree moments before Lieutenant Lon was killed by a sniper - Bottom - (left to right) Jim Sharp - Major Hahn - Jim Lowe - Kevin Wheatley, at the beach

Chapter 13

Lieutenant Lon's wife lived in a village, not far from Quang Tri. She came from a Buddhist family who grew rice and bred cattle, goats and poultry in the area. Dasher did not attend the funeral, but Jim Lowe and Major Hahn did. At the funeral, which was held at one of the family's houses, the body lay in state in a plain, white wooden box. The mourners were all dressed in white, including the widow. Lon's wife was a beautiful young lady. The woman, who was greeting family members, took one look at Jim Lowe and let out a loud shriek. She collapsed to the floor, sobbing and wailing uncontrollably. This alarming display of grief went on for well over two minutes, an eternity, given the circumstances. The American was stunned, and turned to Major Hahn, who was standing beside him. Hahn simply nodded calmly and motioned for him to stay calm and do not move. The big marine clenched his jaw and stood at attention.

He watched the grieving widow, as calmly as he could, and then as abruptly as it had started, Lieutenant Lon's widow stopped wailing, got off the floor, with the help of some family members and straightened her waist-length black hair. She took a moment to collect herself, then said very calmly and in well-rehearsed English, 'Lieutenant Lowe, thank you so much for coming. You were a good friend to my husband. I know you are a long distance from your own family. I thank you.'

Stunned, Lowe simply nodded. Major Hahn said something to the woman in Vietnamese, then took Lowe by the elbow and led him out. Major Hahn told Tam, the driver of his jeep, to get in the back, because he wanted to drive. Jim sat up front, while the major drove them back to Quang Tri. On the way back, he explained that the wailing and carrying on was customary. It was a way for Lon's widow to demonstrate that her grief was genuine and that her marriage had been a good one. The greater the grief, the better the marriage had been. Lowe thought to himself, 'that must have been one happy marriage'.

Back at Quang Tri Headquarters, Dasher was getting worried about Gunny Jim Sharp. He had been watching his American mate and was concerned that Lon's death had affected him more than he was letting on. Even though Sharp and Lon had only worked together for a short time, they had gotten along well and spent many hours talking. Dasher could tell Sharp had been disappointed when he had been told he could not attend Lon's funeral. The American was sitting on a chair, out the front of his room, brooding, as he cleaned his weapon and gear.

'G'day, Gunny.' Dasher said as he approached. 'What ya up to?'

Jim didn't look up from his M-2 Carbine as he continued to clean it. 'Maintaining my weapon, Dash. What does it look like?'

'Yeah, well, you can stop that and come with me.'

Jim looked up, his eyebrows raising. 'Come where?'

'You need a drink, mate, so do I.' Dasher informed his friend. 'Lon was a good bloke and that was bullshit what happened. Let's go tip a few.'

Jim looked like he was about to argue, but instead he stood up and said, 'Yeah, alright. You got beer?'

'Nah, mate, we're gonna hit every boozer from here to the DMZ.'

Jim laughed, 'Really?'

'Yep, pub crawl, Gunny. Let's go.'

Jim shook his head and sat back down, 'Thanks, Dash. I do appreciate it, but you know I can't do that.'

'Why not? Those arms bloody painted on?'

Gunny Sharp's face twisted in an expression Dasher thought was halfway between annoyance and disappointment. 'Look at me, Dash, I'm black. I can't drink in the same bars you do, I'm an American. It's not allowed.'

'Yeah, I know, you come from a country full of dickheads and arseholes, that doesn't mean shit today, mate.'

'Yeah, Dash, it does. They won't let me in.'

'They won't let a black American in, but you're not American today, mate, you're something better.'

'Dash, what are you talking about?'

Wheatley stood to attention and said officially, 'By the powers invested in me, by a nation that's not full of dickheads and arseholes, I, hereby pronounce, you're an Aussie, for the rest of today.'

Jim laughed and stood up. 'Is that right?'

Chapter 13

'Yep,' said Dasher. 'You're as dinkum as meat pies and sandy beaches. Today, you're an Australian Aborigine. Get your shit, we're going.'

Still grinning, Jim said, 'That's mighty honorary of you Dash, but I don't think they'll buy that in the bars around here. At least not the ones run by Americans.'

'Bullshit, if those pricks are too bloody stupid to have a beer with a decorated vet, because he is black, then, they're too bloody stupid to know what type of black you are, as well. Trust me, mate.'

Jim looked doubtful, but the widening grin on his face suggested he liked the idea. Eventually, he said, 'You might be the craziest son of a bitch I've ever met, Dash, but you know what? Let's do it.'

Dasher grinned wide and clapped his friend on the shoulder. 'Good man, just follow my lead and don't say a word to anyone. She'll be right.'

Wheatley led Gunny Sharp to the Quang Tri boozer and told him to take a seat in the corner, while he went to the bar. He said to the bartender, a big American corporal, 'Two beers, mate.'

The corporal looked at Sharp, sitting in the corner and shook his head. 'Sorry, Dash, your friend over there will have to leave. Can't serve negroes in here.'

Dasher pushed down a sudden bolt of anger and forced himself to smile. He looked over his shoulder at Jim, a confused look on his face. 'What, old mate over there? What you talkin' about. He's not black, he's an Australian.'

'Is that right, Dash?' The bartender said. 'Looks black to me.'

'Nah, he's not black.'

The bartender's eyes darkened. 'Dash, I can see the man. He's black.'

Dasher shook his head, 'Really? I can't see it.'

'Seriously?'

Dasher nodded and said, 'Anyway, he's not black, he's a bloody Australian Aborigine.'

'He's still black. Black is black'

'Bullshit, corporal. Your shithouse rules might apply to Americans, but not to Aussies. We drink wherever we want.' He said the last bit with a hint of anger in his voice. The bartender looked like he was about to argue, so Dasher said in a low, conspiratorial tone, 'You ever met an Australian Aborigine?'

The bartender, who was squinting at Jim, as if he thought that might help him better judge his race, said, 'Can't say I have. But I don't think I…'

'I'd stop making eye contact if I were you.' Dasher cut him off. 'They don't like that. Dangerous and proud people and bloody good fighters. I could go over there and tell him you won't serve him, but to be honest he scares the shit out of me.'

That got the bartender's attention. 'He scares *you*?' he asked incredulously.

'Yeah, course he does! You can go and tell him to get out, if you want, I'm not.'

The bartender looked torn, but eventually shook his head and poured two beers. He handed them over and said, 'You'd better not be dicking around, Dash. I'll get my ass kicked.'

Dasher picked up the beers and winked. 'She'll be right. Just make sure everyone leaves him alone and keep the drinks comin'. He doesn't talk much, so just leave him be.'

Dasher and Jim Sharp in Quang Tri

Chapter 13

That set the tone for the rest of the afternoon. Dasher and Jim Sharp moved from bar to bar and repeated their story at each one. Perhaps, because it was Dasher who was with him, or maybe because the Americans actually believed Sharp was an Australian, but Jim was permitted to drink in every bar in Quang Tri, that day. Decades later, Jim Sharp told this story to Dasher's daughter, Phyllis, and told her it was one of the best days of his life. He felt like an equal, a respected and appreciated soldier and totally forgot about the colour of his skin. He also said that it was about the drunkest he had ever been.

Chapter 14

HOWITZERS

The next operation started a couple days after Lieutenant Lon's funeral. They travelled west for four horribly hot days, being sniped at and mortared continuously, as they moved forward. The unit was starting to learn from the Australian and American advisors and was now functioning well. They suffered no casualties and continued to advance, eventually, flushing out the Vietcong force that had been sniping and mortaring them.

They pursued the retreating enemy through the jungle, until finding and following a trail, which took them through a series of small villages. They travelled cautiously, always weary of walking into an ambush and soon came across an ARVN artillery registration point. The friendly registration point was one of several inside the Quang Tri Province. Each had, at least, two 105-mm Howitzer artillery pieces and was designed to extend artillery support for units like 1/1 who were operating further away from Quang Tri. This registration point had a total of four Howitzers, all manned and ready to go.

Dasher approached Gunny Sharp and showed him a point on his map, where he thought the retreating enemy might be located. The location was high, along a ridgeline above them, and Dasher thought it would have made a good place to rest and set-up an ambush. Wheatley said, 'You reckon you can ask Hahn to talk to the artillery commander? See if you can get him to target that location. Saves us running them down and doing it the hard way.'

Warrant Officer Wheatley on patrol in South Vietnam

Sharp nodded and went back to talk to Major Hahn. It only took a little convincing and soon, Hahn had persuaded the commander to fire on the position. The appropriate permission was obtained from headquarters and the Howitzers were moved into position. They were carefully aimed, loaded and fired. The Howitzers boomed and four shells screamed out of the guns and disappeared into the sky. A short time later, Dasher heard the far-off rumble of exploding ordnance. He turned to Jim Lowe, 'You think we got 'em?'

Jim said, 'Let's find out.' The marine got on the radio and asked one of his Bird Dog mates to fly over and take a look at the damage.

As it turned out, Dasher's hunch had been right. The Vietcong they were chasing had been leading them into a trap. They had set-up an ambush, right at the point on the map, where Dasher had thought they would. There was almost a full company of them, at least sixty people. They had set up foxholes and dug in, hoping to destroy 1/1, as it passed. The pilot reported that the first four rounds were right on target and that the VC had been decimated. The pilot said that the few survivors left were gathering the dead and wounded. Lowe ordered another volley and four more rockets boomed into the sky. According to the Bird Dog, the second volley had been even more devastating than the first. Dasher and his men thanked the artillery commander and very cautiously headed towards the site.

ARVN artillery registration point

When they arrived, the scene was an ugly one. Instead of ambushing Wheatley and his men, it looked like this company of VC had been all but annihilated. Even Gunny Sharp, a hardened Korean War veteran, found it hard to stomach. Dasher thought it was like walking onto the set of a horror movie, built into a landscape that would have looked at home on the Western Front, during World War I. As Dasher looked around, thankful he had skipped breakfast, he decided it was possible that not one enemy soldier had escaped the bombardment. There were still dozens of mutilated and badly charred bodies, scattered around the site. Normally, the VC carried their dead and wounded away with great efficiency. They even went to the trouble of removing weapons, to cover up how effective any strike might have been. Dasher figured that to do that, however, they would need a few blokes left alive, to do the carrying. There was no sign of the snipers, nor the mortar teams and no fire was coming in at them from a second position. To Dasher, this meant they must be all dead.

'Poor bastards.' Jim Sharp noted, taking in the carnage.

'Better them than us, Gunny.' Dasher told him. 'I'm just thankful we aren't the ones lying in the mud up here. I reckon this could have gone pear-shaped pretty easily, if we hadn't come across those Howitzers.'

Jim Lowe had the unpleasant task of photographing the scene and verifying the body count. Dasher was delighted with the success. There were more weapons left at the site than bodies, which meant they would be able to put a few aside and trade them for some much-needed concrete and barbed wire. That was not exactly legal, but they desperately needed the supplies, and it was difficult, in the extreme, to obtain them through proper channels. He figured he might also be able to buy the boys a few extra cases of beer. Lowe called in a chopper, and they loaded the Huey with the captured weapons. Just the right amount, to match the body count. Dasher wrapped the extra weapons in his tent canvas and for the price of one case of beer, the Huey pilots agreed to send them to his room, back at the compound. Dasher Wheatley was no fool. He understood that war was a business, however nasty, and if you wanted your side to come out on top, you had to play by the rules of the game.

After the awful mess had been cleaned up, they made their way back to Highway One, the Street Without Joy, and settled in beside the road, to wait for Tam to arrive with their convoy. As usual, Tam would be leading the long line of trucks, so Dasher had confidence it would arrive safely. In the meantime, Major Tieu Ta Hahn was so relieved with the outcome of the day and so pleased by the work of his men, that he found a vendor on the road and bought four beers. One for himself and one each for Dasher, Jim Lowe and Gunny Sharp. Jim Lowe, not keen on the idea of drinking warm beer, found an old lady selling ice. Trying to remember the correct words in the local language, he asked the old lady, as politely and clearly as he could, 'May I have some ice, please, Ma'am?'

The old lady froze, a look of complete horror on her face. Hahn and Dasher both burst into uncontrollable laughter. 'What… What did I say?' Jim asked, his face getting red.

Major Hahn was laughing too hard to answer, so Dasher said, 'You stupid Yank, you just asked this nice old lady if you could have a piece of arse!'

'Oh no,' Jim said, turning apologetically to the woman. 'I'm so sorry, Ma'am, I'm… ahh… Toi xin loi… Toi xin loi' The lady still looked shocked, so Lowe turned back to Dasher, 'Shit, Dasher! Tell her I didn't mean it.'

'Nah, mate, you're all right. Besides, she's not bad looking. Play ya cards right, ya might get lucky.'

'You're an asshole, Wheatley.'

'Yeah, heard that before, Skipper.'

A Cheeky grin from Dasher

It was about then, much to Lowe's relief, that Tam and the trucks finally turned up. Jim hurried inside the first one, Dasher and Hahn followed, still laughing. They headed back to base for some much-needed rest and Dasher went to work, trading his weapons for the supplies he could use, to improve security at Quang Tri headquarters. He also bought his mates a few beers and managed to secure some leave. He decided he would travel to Hong Kong and blow-off some steam.

Dasher took a helicopter to Hue and then, a C123 military aircraft to Da Nang and then a C130 from there to Saigon. He enjoyed a night on the town and stayed at Australia House in Saigon, before flying out to Hong Kong. Once he arrived in Honk Kong, Kevin checked into a nice hotel and enjoyed the good life, for a while. He slept by the pool, during the day, partied at bars, restaurants and nightclubs, at night and revelled in the safe and comfortable environment. While there, he purchased gifts for the family and burnt through no small amount of cash. In the true tradition of so many diggers before him, he even managed to go AWOL for a few days and enjoy an extra couple of days off. He came back in time to avoid any real trouble and returned to the war and the horrors that awaited him there. And await him, they did.

Chapter 15

BLOOD FOR OIL

In an area north of Da Nang, the Vietcong attacked and destroyed an Esso Oil refinery. Uncle Sam is, as most people are aware, rather fond of his oil. He, therefore, demanded retribution in what was, literally, a 'blood for oil' mindset. It did not matter that the attack on the refinery was long over, and the proverbial horse had well and truly bolted, Uncle Sam wanted blood.

Operations in that area of South Vietnam would normally have been taken care of by the Hac Bao Black Panthers, the 1st Division's Strike Company. Those men were a quick-action force, composed of highly trained men, hand-picked from different units throughout the South-Vietnamese military. They had a well-deserved reputation as an effective fighting force, as good as any out there. At that time, however, the Hac Bao Black Panthers were sunning themselves on a beach in Nha Trang, on a week of rest and relaxation (R&R). This meant that Wheatley and the rest of 1/1 were sent south on a search-and-destroy mission.

The plan for Wheatley and the men of 1/1 was simple, as far as search-and-destroy missions went. Find the Vietcong (any Vietcong) and send their location through to headquarters and a second unit would be flown in by helicopter, to help obliterate them. Wheatley's company travelled through Hue, then began the search part of their mission. They methodically probed the jungle, west of the refinery, before moving in closer and sweeping across its northern perimeter. Dasher decided that the Vietcong had done a surprisingly good job on the place. It was a total mess. The refinery had been built on the edge of an industrial area and had jungle and hills to the west. There were other ARVN units involved in the mission, beside Dasher's. One was moving towards the site from the south, and a nearby marine base had just started firing artillery rounds into the jungle to Wheatley's west. The area Wheatley and his men had already cleared.

Dasher was, as always, operating on point with Jim Lowe. The two mates cautiously led the unit from the front, walking about 10 metres apart, with a radio operator between them. Radio operators were a vital part of the team and Dasher always kept one close by. The radio man with him, that day, was a nice young bloke who rarely spoke and always followed orders. Dasher liked that about him. He had worked closely with the man on their last few outings and had found the bloke to be reliable and trustworthy. As they moved, Dasher saw streets to his north and east, jungle to his west and the incoming ARVN artillery was becoming constant. It was gradually getting louder, which could only mean the rounds were coming closer, although, Dasher was not sure what they were firing at. As far as he knew, there was nobody in the jungle they were targeting.

Wheatley walked past an elaborate-looking pagoda that towered above the surrounding buildings. A pagoda is a Chinese-style religious tower, usually, with multiple eaves that were turned up at each corner, like layers on an elaborate wedding cake. Jim Lowe swore, as an artillery round landed no more than 500 metres way. 'I hoped they don't bring them in any closer,' he said. 'That wasn't even half a click away. What are they shooting at? We've cleared that part of the jungle, there's nothing there.'

Dasher shrugged and stopped in front of the pagoda. There was a huge pile of wood, which had been curiously placed midway between the road and the pagoda. 'What a stupid place to put a woodpile,' the Australian remarked, just as an artillery round exploded behind the pagoda. It was loud enough to make Dasher's ears ring and he felt the shockwave of the blast from where he stood. 'Bloody hell,' he roared. 'What the fuck are they doing?'

'Idiots!' Jim shouted back. He motioned that they should move towards the woodpile and use it for cover. They had only taken a couple of steps, when Dasher heard the unmistakable sound of an incoming artillery round. He and Lowe dropped instantly to their stomachs, the radio operator did not. The woodpile in front of them exploded, the shockwave from the blast hammered through the ground and lifted Dasher about half a metre into the air, before slamming him back down and knocking the wind out of him. His ears rang and his world blurred. He shook his head, to clear his vision and forced himself to his feet, as he struggled to get his breath back. The pagoda was peppered with shrapnel holes and huge logs, from the now-gone woodpile, were sticking out of it. He checked Jim and then himself and discovered, with no small amount of amazement, that they were both unharmed.

'Get on the radio!' Dasher shouted at Lowe. 'Make 'em stop!'

Jim nodded and turned to find the young Vietnamese radio operator, but the young man no longer existed. He, and his radio, had been totally obliterated by debris from the blast. Only a bloody pulp remained. Dasher and Jim both swore, as more rounds started to fall around them. Men were running everywhere, a few were being torn to pieces by the explosions. Dasher looked around to find his new company commander, the man who had replaced Lieutenant Lon, but found that he too was dead. Another commander gone! The man had only been walking a few metres behind them. Thankfully, a second radio man was still alive and was scrambling to his feet, in a wild panic. He started to run, taking the radio with him.

'Get him!' Dasher shouted and he and Lowe took off, after the frightened man. Jim got to him first and threw all his considerable weight into the man, driving him down to the ground. The radio operator screamed and struggled to get away, Dasher hurried over and helped Lowe restrain him. 'Lay still, ya bloody idiot!' Dasher barked at the man. 'Calm down!'

Chapter 15

The two men held him down long enough, to get the radio off him, then let him go. He took off toward the jungle, like a rabbit. Lowe got on the radio and dialled the mayday frequencies, quickly reaching the nearby marine outpost that was firing on them. He told the young marine, on the other radio, that they were taking friendly fire and gave him their position, begging him to stop the shelling, as quickly as he could. Within no more than fifteen seconds, the incoming artillery stopped. The young man, whoever he was, had acted quickly and saved countless lives. Dasher let out an explosion of breath and decided that if he ever found out who that young marine was, he would buy him a beer. On the other hand, if he ever found out who had been directing that artillery, he would bloody kill him!

Major Hahn ordered Lieutenant Lowe to call in a medivac and had their dead and wounded removed. They were resupplied, given a new radio and radio operator, then told to move out to an abandoned barracks, at the south end of the Da Nang Air Base runway. When they arrived, their many walking wounded, those who had not been bad enough to have been medivacked out, were treated. Wheatley and Lowe decided to take a quick trip over to see the marines who were stationed near the air base. Jim thought he might be able to get to the bottom of what had happened and make sure the Americans knew there were ARVN operating in the area. The last thing he wanted was a repeat of the friendly fire incident which had just occurred.

Jim drove Dasher to the marine base in a Jeep. When they pulled up to the gate, they were stopped by a sentry, who gave the two men a puzzled look. Even though Jim Lowe was, himself, a marine, at that moment, he was not exactly dressed like one. Both Dasher and Jim were wearing black uniforms, adorned with Vietnamese insignia and had Australian bush hats on. As was normal for most special forces, they wore no dog tags and carried no means of identification. The marine on guard raised his M-14 and pointed it directly at Jim's forehead. 'Woo, wait a minute, pal, I'm a marine,' Jim said, holding up his hands.

'Sure, you are, where's your ID? What's with the uniform and hat?'

'I don't carry ID, not when I'm working with the ARVN!'

Up to that point, Dasher had been trying to contain himself, but as he sat there, he could see the sweat oozing from his friend's pores. He suddenly burst out laughing, 'You're done for now, Skipper.' He roared with a laugh.

'Dasher, you're not helping.' Lowe complained. He said to the sentry. 'Look, I'm Lieutenant Jim Lowe, US Marine 086352. I'm working with this idiot,' he poked a thumb towards Dasher, 'and the ARVN, as an advisor. Half the people here know me, my call sign is 'Hobo'. We're here to see… Dasher, cut it out!'

Wheatley was laughing even harder. 'Don't mind me, *Hobo*, you're doing great. At least, he hasn't shot ya yet.'

Ignoring the Australian, Lowe said, 'We're the ones you idiots hit with eight-inchers, a couple of days ago. I need to make sure your CO knows we're around, so we don't end up getting in a firefight with the marines or getting strafed by our own aircraft.' Dasher was still chuckling, and the guard was starting to relax. Lowe said, 'Look, I've got my radio on the back seat. I can call and verify who I am. Every carrier in the gulf knows who I am, and that I don't carry ID!'

Eventually, the sentry let them through, no thanks to Dasher. Jim parked the jeep, the two men got out. Dasher said, 'I reckon we should go meet the supply sergeant and maybe, the cook, before you talk to the CO. If we really want to find out what's going on around here, they're the ones to talk to. There should be a corporal in the radio shack who probably knows more about how things work here than the CO does.'

Jim nodded. 'You know your armies, Dash.'

'Been in one long enough, Skipper.'

They poked around and found out what they could and were eventually met by the regimental commander. The commander was a serious-looking colonel, Lowe have never met before. Jim saluted the well-dressed officer, who said, 'Lieutenant Lowe, welcome to Da Nang. I understand you gentlemen are down here from Quang Tri.'

'Yes, Sir,' Lowe answered, 'Allow me to introduce my partner, this is Warrant Officer Wheatley of the Royal Australian...'

Before the American could finish his formal introduction, Dasher cut him off and offered the officer his hand. 'Never mind all that,' he said, 'Dasher's the name, Sir. You might have heard of me referred to as the champion box-biter of South-East Asia.'

Jim hissed under his breath, as if he thought they were both about to be locked up. He opened his mouth to apologise for his Australian comrade's abrupt manner, when the colonel took Dasher's hand and said with a smile, 'Nice to meet you, Champ. Are you taking good care of our lieutenant?'

'Yeah, Sir. He's in good hands.'

Dasher and the colonel walked off, talking openly, as if they were a couple of old school mates, who had known each other their whole lives. Jim just stood in mute astonishment and then, followed behind them. As Wheatley would learn from his new colonel mate, the man directing the artillery rounds, which had hit Dasher's men, was a US Army major, who was working as an adviser with the ARVN. He had only arrived in Vietnam, a short while ago, without even attending adviser school, let alone graduating. The major had decided he wanted to try using some big guns, so, ignoring the normal chain of command, called the marines and told them he had a target for them to fire on. He gave them coordinates about 500 metres to the west of Dasher's location, but had been using one of the old, French-made maps they should have stopped using, long ago. The map just happened to have a 500-metre error on it, directly in the vicinity of the oil refinery.

Chapter 16
THE FROG

The unit stayed at their temporary base, at the end of the runway, for about another week. During this time, Jim Lowe contracted a bad case of dengue fever and Dasher and Jim Sharp had to rush him to hospital. While he was away, Dasher continue to lead the ARVN unit on several patrols out of the airfield, but managed to avoid any serious incidents.

On their last night, before returning to Quang Tri, Dasher convinced Lowe, who had now returned from hospital, to go with him to the Da Nang Air Base Officers Club. Wheatley had heard that the food and the venue were first class and he wanted to see for himself. The two friends made their way across to the bar and settled in to enjoy a top-notch meal, which they washed down with a few cold American beers. After dinner, they sat near the bar and talked quietly. Jim was still not feeling well and had not eaten much. Dasher, on the other hand, was in fine form. Always friendly and talkative, he spotted two American Bird Dog pilots at the bar and decided he'd go and say g'day.

He shook each man's hand and said, with a wide grin, 'Thanks, fellas. You blokes are bloody brilliant. You've saved my arse more times than I can count. Let me buy ya a beer.'

Chapter 16

Wheatley taking a cool swim while on patrol

The Americans shook his hand and Dasher bought them each a beer. He had a few drinks with the pilots, then went off to the toilet. While in there, Dasher found a small green frog sitting on the windowsill. He picked it up and brought it back to the table with him. If Lowe was surprised when Dasher sat the frog down on the table beside his beer, he did not show it. The two mates enjoyed a short chat, while Dasher played with the frog on the table. Jim was starting to complain that he was feeling unwell and wanted to retire, when three US Army majors and a lieutenant colonel walked boldly across the bar and stood over their table.

One of the majors, a big and very intoxicated man, pointed at Jim and yelled, 'That's that jarhead from Quang Tri everyone talks about. Thought he'd be bigger.' Wobbling slightly, he turned to Dasher and said, 'And this must be the shit-crazy Aussie who masquerades as an officer. You're not though, are ya, fella? You're just a glorified sergeant major. I hear you people eat insects and take shits in the bush, back home. That right?'

Dasher stood up, a cold smile on his lips. This, he thought, could be fun. Before the Australian could retort, however, Jim put up a hand

and said, 'We are about to retire for the night, Sirs. We're to return to Quang Tri in the morning, so, by your leave, gentleman, please.' Lowe stood up, still a little uneasy on his feet. His bout of dengue fever had taken a lot out of him and Dasher could see that he wanted nothing more than to go to bed, get a good night's sleep and return to Quang Tri, without being court martialled for brawling with superior officers. Dasher, on the other hand, had no such concerns. He was more than ready to meet the challenge, head-on. Another major stepped in front of Dasher and produced a grasshopper from his pocket.

'There you go, Aussie,' the major said, 'Show us how you lot from Down Under eat grasshoppers.'

Dasher squared up and gave the American a cool stare. He figured these idiots must have put some thought into this little ambush, otherwise, why would an army major be walking around with a grasshopper in his pocket. These blokes were clearly bullies and Dasher hated bullies. He said, 'How do we deal with insects, Sir? You really want me to show ya?'

Lowe, who apparently wanted to avoid a fight, about as much as Dasher wanted to have one, snatched the grasshopper from the major's hand and said, 'You eat them like this, Sir. Head- first.' Despite his already queasy stomach, Jim popped the insect into his mouth, chewed and swallowed.

Dasher laughed, then noticed the green tinge in his friend's face. He figured the last thing Jim needed right then was a fistfight. Dasher decided he had better do something to put a stop to this, before it went any further. Fights between Australian and American soldiers were nothing new, they happened, all the time, but were something both sides seriously condemned. While most of these fights came and went with no huge issue, they could lead to disaster. The fights could be small, fast and even comical, at times, or they could be deadly.

An example of a typically nonlethal fight between Australian and American troops, was an incident in Vung Tau in 1966, when an Australian Army Small Ship, named HMAS *John Monash,* was tied up with a group of much larger American vessels. At the time, American ships were mostly dry (alcohol free) while the *John Monash,* had beer on board. The Americans would sometimes jump, from one vessel to the other, so they could come aboard and have a few drinks with their Aussie mates. As hard as it is to believe, during the 1960s, the US Navy still had segregation laws, while the Australian Defence Force, obviously, did not. On one occasion, a young Aboriginal digger was sitting in the other rank's (OR's) mess with his mates, enjoying a beer. When the Americans entered, they demanded that the young man be removed. That did not go down well with the Australians and the ensuing punch-up saw several US sailors pitched into the Dinh River.

Although, that incident, on board the *John Monash*, was benign, some incidents were anything but. The worst of which was the infamous 'Battle of Brisbane', during World War II. Before that horrific event, tensions between Australian and US servicepeople had been high, for some time. America military personnel were not only stationed in Australia, during the war, but spent a lot of their leave time there, as well. After years of intermingling, a fair amount of jealousy had arisen from the Australians towards the American troops, who were better dressed and better paid than they were. The Americans were also extremely popular with Australian women, which caused no end of problems. It was a situation which saw thousands of highly trained, fit young men, from two different countries, who had too much free time on their hands, intermingling and drinking together, every day. This was all during an incredibly stressful and uncertain time for the world and the situation created a tinderbox that was just waiting for a spark.

That spark eventually ignited, and the tinderbox exploded into flames, just before 1900 on 26 November 1942. A rather intoxicated Private Stein, of the US 404th Signal Company, staggered out of a pub in Brisbane and stopped to talk with three Australians. A US Military Police officer (MP) asked Stein for his leave pass and identification. The MP arrested Stein, before he had a chance to produce his ID, however, and the Australians took exception to this. They began swearing at the MP and a fight ensued. Soon, more MPs arrived, and nearby Australian servicemen and civilians, who witnessed the fight, joined in. Soon, an all-out riot was underway and sporadic fights were breaking out, all over Brisbane. The mayhem escalated and lasted two days. Many people were injured and, at the height of the fighting, an American serviceman, Gunner Edward Webster, was killed.

Some twenty-three years later, Dasher Wheatley was standing in front of three American majors and a lieutenant colonel who seemed hell-bent on repeating those events. Normally, Dasher would have been more than happy to oblige, but he was no fool. He was currently standing in an American base, and he knew, all too well, that if he were to get into a bar fight here, any ensuing court martials were unlikely to go against the four American officers. It would be Dasher and his now, extremely ill-looking mate, Jim Lowe, who would wind up behind bars.

Thinking on his feet, Dasher blew out a long breath and picked up the frog, which was still sitting on the table beside his beer. He turned to Lowe and said, 'No, no, no, you've got it all wrong, Skipper. Ya don't eat grasshoppers head-first, you eat them arsehole-first. You chew them down backwards. It's frogs you eat headfirst, like this!' The Americans all gasped and stepped back in shock, as Wheatley, holding the frog around the waist, put it headfirst into his mouth and bit clean through the little creature's abdomen. Blood squirted down his chin and the front of his shirt, along with the contents of the frog's stomach. Dasher flashed a bloody grin at the Americans, as he chewed, swallowed, and said, 'See, like that, Sirs.'

The lieutenant colonel turned away and vomited on the floor and the other three officers exited the bar, in a hurry. Thankfully, due to of Wheatley's quick and extremely out-of-the-box thinking, the altercation was over, and a fight had been avoided. 'You're one of a kind, Dash.' Jim said, trying not to retch up his freshly eaten meal.

Dasher smiled. 'Bugger me, Skipper, they left before the good part. Why does the US Army always bug out before the fighting starts?' He wiped his chin with a napkin and dropped what remained of the frog onto the table with a wet splat. Everyone in the bar was staring at him, in horror. Dasher waved a hand theatrically and said, 'Gents, this has been a wonderful evening, but we'll be on our way. Now that I've had my dessert, I'm off to bed. Big day tomorrow.'

Chapter 17

TENACITY

The following morning, the unit moved back to Quang Tri. On the drive north, Dasher and Jim Sharp were in high spirits, happy to be returning to their 'home away from home' at the Military Assistance Command Vietnam headquarters. Both men wore Hawaiian shirts and sat in the back of a jeep, being driven, as always, by Tam. They sang and joked and eventually, made it back to base, without incident. The next few weeks saw the team conduct numerous patrols with ARVN, most were west of Highway Number One, as they continued to harass the Vietcong along the Ho Chi Minh Trail.

On one of these week-long operations, Dasher and Jim Lowe were out the front of their patrol, their new radio operator between them, when dasher heard a sharp crack and whizzing sound. It was the unmistakable sound of sniper fire and a bullet zipping past his head. He heard a yell to his left and swore, as he turned to see the young radio operator fall to the ground screaming. He had been hit in the leg by a round, that Dasher was sure had been meant for him. Wheatley called for a medic and went to work eliminating the sniper. It did not take long and when he returned, he saw that the medic had treated and dressed the radio operator's wound.

Dasher was relieved, he liked the kid and did not want to lose another good radio operator. The young man was worryingly pale and complained he was feeling queasy and light-headed, obviously, from blood loss. There was no way he could walk. Dasher nodded, told the young man he understood, picked him up, put him on his back and started carrying him. Jim Lowe took the radio and strapped it to his back.

The radio, used by the ARVN in 1966, was the AN/PRC-25, affectionately known as the 'Prick 25'. It was the most widely used radio set by the US troops in the Vietnam war and was replaced by the PRC-77 in 1967. Carried in a backpack, the radio had a telephone-like receiver attached to the pack with a long cord and a thick antenna protruding from the top of the radio, to a considerable height. Considered to be a lightweight field radio, the Prick 25 weighed around 12 to 13 kilograms, when loaded into a pack with all the accessories it required, probably a lot more, when the weight of the backpack was taken into consideration. Adding this extra weight to the already heavy kit, Lowe was carrying, made life difficult for the marine, but he endured. It was nothing compared to the load Dasher was now carrying.

Wheatley carried the wounded man for over a kilometre, through the jungle, to an area that Hahn had order to be cleared to make a helicopter landing zone (LZ). When he arrived, Wheatley was exhausted. The day was hot and humid and the footing, through the jungle, had been treacherous and steep. As it turned out, however, the newly cleared LZ was useless, because there were no evac helicopters available, pretty much anywhere in South Vietnam, on that day. Lieutenant Lowe had tried his best to call one in, only to learn that they were apparently all tied up with a more pressing job. As luck would have it, US Senator Ted Kennedy had arrived in Vietnam, on a spur-of-the-moment visit. Kennedy had wanted to do a quick trip around the country, so he could see the war firsthand. With such an important VIP visiting, bringing with him his enormous entourage and media pool, every available aircraft in the area had been soaked up, to keep this one, very important man safe.

Chapter 17

Dasher sitting in grass with his radio operator

Lowe was furious. He had been carrying the wounded man's heavy radio, for over an hour and even he, with all his considerable contacts, could not get their comrade the hospital care he needed. Dasher knew that if something was not done, and quickly, the young man was going to die from blood loss and shock. The area, they were operating in, was crawling with Vietcong and, here in this LZ, they were horribly exposed. The term 'sitting ducks' came to Dasher's mind and he decided something had to be done. So, the Australian picked up the South-Vietnamese soldier again and set out.

He carried the man, for over three hours, through some of the most brutal terrain imaginable. This type of thing was typical of Dasher Wheatley. No one, who knew him, would have been the least bit surprised that Dasher would do that, nor that he would refuse to let anyone else help him. As far as Dasher was concerned, the bloke was his radio operator, his responsibility. End of story.

Eventually, after Wheatley had carried the man over the top of yet another ridgeline, he had to stop and rest. It had been nothing short of a superhuman display of strength, stamina, tenacity and compassion. The effort had left the Australian so exhausted that those around him were sure he was about to collapse, but he never did. Perhaps, predictably, it was Jim Lowe who finally convinced Dasher to relent and let someone else help. It is unlikely that anyone else would have been able to. So, Wheatley carried the radio, and the big American hoisted the wounded soldier onto his back, and they set out, once more. The terrain did not get any easier, as they moved for another hour, towards a rising slop in the jungle, where they thought they could clean a new LZ and land a Huey.

Dasher stayed close to Jim and the wounded radio operator, keeping a close eye on his friend. The marine had been pushing his limits for almost half an hour, as the heat and humidity of the day grew worse and now, he looked like he was beginning to falter. Dasher had to put his hand on Lowe's shoulder, a few times, to keep him steady, but eventually, the burden proved too much. Jim Lowe collapsed, falling backwards to the ground, and landing on top of the wounded man. The radio operator screamed in agony and Dasher heard an audible crack, as the kid's leg broke. He now had one leg with a gunshot wound and one that was broken. If the man had been in a bad state before, his condition was desperate now.

Dasher managed to bring Jim back around and tried the radio again for a medivac. This time he was successful, the dust-off chopper was on its way. There was only a short distance left to go, to reach the slope they were going to clear for an LZ. Wheatley managed to get the young man there in one piece, but he was exhausted, to the point of complete collapse, by the time he carried the young man up the steep slope and lowered him gently to the ground. The Huey eventually came in, rotors hammering and thumping the air, as it touched down. Dasher loaded the radio operator onboard and sent him on his way. The young man made a full recovery. By the time Dasher and the rest of 1/1 made it back to Quang Tri, their radio man was out of hospital and hobbling on crutches. This made Dasher Wheatley happy.

Over the years, many great men have been awarded medals for distinguished acts of determination and benevolence like Dasher's that day. One can find examples of deeds, during both world wars, where diggers were awarded a Distinguished Conduct Medal (DCM) for carrying wounded mates for hours, through dangerous landscapes and under all types of duress. Few of those men would claim to have done so under worse conditions or more difficult terrain than Dasher had. To suggest that Wheatley should have been written up for another award is by no means far-fetched, in fact, it seems obvious. As was the lot for the diggers in Vietnam, however, he was not written up for any award and received nothing. As with his other missing awards, at the time of writing this book, Kevin Wheatley has never been officially recognised for his actions, on that day. If he were still alive today, however, it is extremely doubtful that he would care.

Chapter 18

THE FORT OF DEATH.

In the northern autumn of 1965, Gunny Sharp finally completed his field tour and was sent to Hue, to take up a desk job. He would eventually make it back to the States, where he became a drill instructor and the first black mayor of the city of Flint, Michigan. Dasher and the boys gave him an emotional farewell. He was one of the finest infantrymen Wheatley had ever worked with and was going to be deeply missed. The hole he left in 1/1 was going to be impossible to fill.

At about the same time, the South-Vietnamese military, in its infinite wisdom, set-up a fort, about 25 kilometres west of Quang Tri, called the Boa Cam fort. The small, rectangular fortification was placed about 200 metres south of the Quang Tri River, on top of a hill. It housed four 105-mm Howitzer artillery guns and was designed to extend artillery cover for the units working out of Quang Tri. It was manned by local troops and was, in Dasher's opinion, a poorly defended camp in an extremely dangerous position that was begging to be overrun. And overrun it was, with no survivors.

Once again, long after the proverbial horse had bolted, Wheatley and the rest of 1/1 were sent west to clear the area and get the fort operational again. They were to set-up a temporary home in the poorly placed fort and run operations, out of there, until told otherwise. Operations which were designed to 'pacify' the Vietcong in the area. Of all the crazy, bullshit ideas the ARVN commanders had come up with, Dasher thought, this one took the cake. It was bound to end in disaster and Wheatley was determined to lead from the front, advise as stringently as he could, and bring home as many of his men alive as possible, if possible.

They made it to the wrecked fort in one piece and quickly set-up shop. The men spent the first couple of nights sleeping on cots in a large open tent, while underground sleeping bunkers were constructed. They worked themselves to the bone, digging trenches, expanding the fort, and strengthening whatever petty defences it had. Dasher laboured frantically, trying to get ready for the inevitable attack he knew would arrive, at any moment. The last time the Vietcong had attacked the fort, they had killed every man inside and he knew they were going to try and do it again. Sure enough, late on the second night, when Dasher was writing a letter home to his wife Edna, he heard the familiar thunk-thunk-thunk of mortars being dropped into tubes and launched into the steamy night air. The inevitable sound of incoming 82-mm mortar rounds quickly followed, along with Jim Lowe screaming, 'Incoming!'

Dasher dropped his letter and rolled out of his bunk, SLR in hand. He ran and dove into the closest foxhole he could find, just as explosions erupted all around him. Men swore and shouted, the earth quivered and shook, the noise was horrific. The 82-mm rounds were deadly, but seemed paltry to Dasher, compared to the huge American artillery shells that had been dropped on him, a few weeks earlier. In all, about 30 rounds hit the fort, that night, but somehow, the team suffered no casualties. This attack was to set the scene for what was to come. The next day, the men redoubled their efforts to improve Boa Cam fort's defences and Dasher and Lowe put a call through to MACV Quang Tri Sector command, voicing their deep concern over the situation.

Dasher knew they would never be able to defend the fort, with what equipment and people they had. It was just a matter of time, until they, like the poor souls who had occupied the fort before them, would be overrun and slaughtered, to a man. If they were going to hold the place, they needed concrete bunkers, barbed wire, artillery and air support, machine guns, and more men. To make matters worse, while Dasher and the other advisers 'advised' Major Hahn that he should be aggressively patrolling the area, by day, and setting-up ambushes, by night, Hahn preferred to sleep, during the day and play cards, at night. The major would frequently return to Quang Tri, for days on end and leave his men to fend for themselves, something that became a blessing in disguise. The advisers' suggestion, to scale-up daytime patrolling and plan nightly ambushes, was noted by Hahn, and dutifully ignored. Dasher absolutely hated the place. He was prepared to work and fight as hard as any man, but this mission was impossible and spiralling quickly towards disaster.

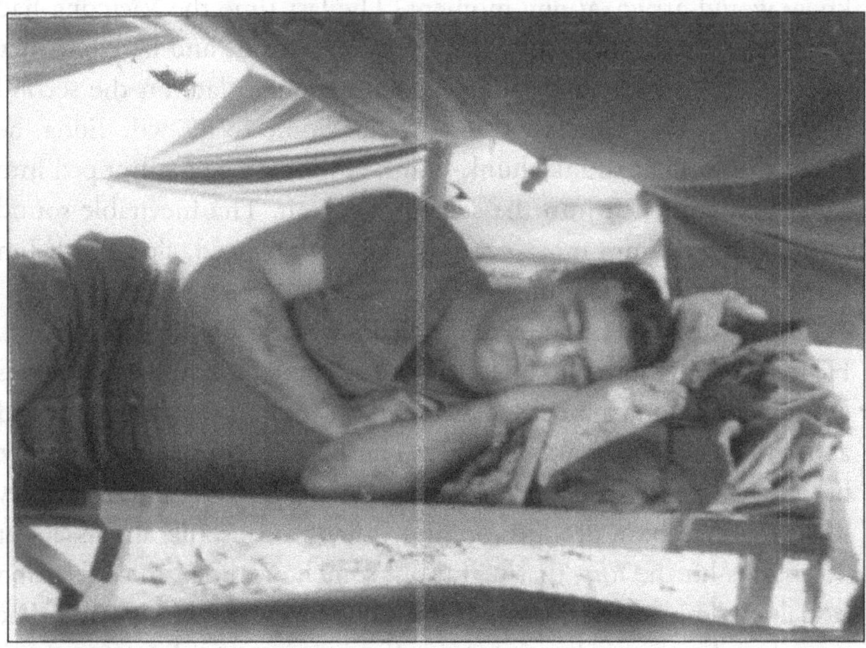

Wheatley taking a nap at the Bao Cam fort

The men worked on, living with constant fear and frequent shelling. They dwelt in wet and mouldy sandbag-lined trenches, which were soon overrun with huge rats. Dasher wondered if this was anything like the poor sods in World War I had to deal with on the Western

Front. Eventually, the advisers did manage to organise a platoon to patrol during daylight. Jim Lowe convinced an artillery captain mate of his, back at Quang Tri, to use the area surrounding the fort as target practice. At least, that way, they would have a steady barrage of artillery falling 360 degrees around the fort, from time to time. This acted like a ring of steel around them, and no matter how unreliable and infrequent that ring may have been, Dasher was glad when it was there. The shelling would give any local enemy second thoughts about setting-up an ambush, as they would have no idea when the next barrage would begin or who was calling it in.

Dasher figured that if the men of 1/1 only slept about once a week, kept the artillery barrages going, continued to patrol as aggressively as they could, built-up the base's defences, as quickly as possible and caught a truckload of luck, they just might make it out of the place alive. Mortar fire came in, every night, without fail. The team eventually managed to start setting-up nightly ambushes near the river and, every now and then, one of their mines would be set off in the middle of the night, causing their men to panic and spend tons of ammunition firing indiscriminately into the jungle. This was ammunition they could not afford to waste, and they were spending it in blind hope of hitting whatever had triggered the mines. Be it animal or human.

After the first week, Dasher had to almost physically restrain Lieutenant Lowe, who, he thought, might now be close to actively 'fragging' Major Hahn. The big marine's patience had run out and he had become convinced the little major was going to get them all killed. Fragging was the term given for the deliberate killing of a fellow soldier, usually a superior officer or non-commissioned officer, by one of his men. It was often done because the troops believed that the officer-in-charge was so incompetent that if he was not immediately removed, many other men would die, as a result of his poor leadership or stupidity. The word was coined, because these murders were normally carried out with a fragmentation grenade. It was easy to kill a person with a hand grenade in a war zone and make it look like an accident. Although fragging was not uncommon in

Vietnam, it is believed as many as 900 officers might have been killed this way, Dasher knew Jim Lowe would never actually do it. The American just needed to vent and frankly, Wheatley did not blame him.

Life at the Boa Cam fort of death was not all bad, though. On one of the team's now, almost nightly ambushes, they managed to catch a large column of, at least, 60 enemy soldiers by surprise. As the column moved past, Dasher, who was crouching low in the bush beside the small track, was about to give the order to attack, but hesitated, when he noticed something odd. It was hard to tell, in the dark, but something was different about the uniforms these people were wearing. They were enemy soldiers, their weapons gave that away, but their clothes appeared lighter in colour and better quality than those the Vietcong normally wore. Also, their AK-47s looked new or close enough to it and the way they moved suggested these men were professionally trained infantrymen, not just militia, like the Vietcong fighters they normally came up against, in this area.

Dismissing the questions that were beginning to form in his mind, Wheatley gave the order to attack, and his team detonated their mines and booby traps. Every one of Dasher's men emptied their magazines into the wall of humans in front of them, with devastating results. In perfect guerrilla style, Dasher and Jim Lowe led their men back to the fort, before the enemy had managed to even fire a single shot, in return. From there, a grinning Jim Lowe called in the artillery and fired the Howitzers, at the fort, back towards the position they had just vacated. Oddly enough, there was no mortar attack on the fort that night. Dasher and Jim took advantage of the rare quiet, that evening, to try and get some much-needed rest.

'Did you notice the uniforms?' Wheatley asked, as they were settling in.

Jim nodded. The two men were sitting in a bunker at the west side of the fort, keeping a careful eye on the jungle for any sign of an attack. 'Yep, and the weapons. I don't think they were VC, Dash, at least, not ordinary Quang Tri province VC.'

'NVA?'

Chapter 18

'Hope not.' Jim said. 'Looked like it, though. We better get back out there at first light and try and find out. Trying to fight VC from this shithole is stupid enough, taking on the NVA would be a different kind of stupid altogether.'

Dasher agreed. The Vietcong was an extremely dangerous enemy to fight, but the truth of it was, they were mostly farmers and local militia troops doing what they could, with inadequate weapons, little to no training and poor communications. The NVA, on the other hand, otherwise known as the PAVN or the People's Army of Vietnam, was a professionally trained, well-equipped, regimented military force, with literally hundreds of years of fighting experience. Dasher said, 'Typical.'

Jim said, 'And goddamn son of a bitch, Hahn's nowhere to be seen.'

'Just goes to show,' said Dasher, absently cleaning his already immaculate SLR. 'You don't need a long neck to be a goose.'

Lowe laughed and said, 'Never a truer word, Dash. Let's get some sleep.'

Chapter 19

TORTURE BY EMPATHY

They retired for the night and by dawn, the mystery of the unusually slick looking troops was answered. Just as the sun was starting to push misty light through the surrounding jungle, an enemy soldier, wearing a grey uniform, walked straight up to the front gate, hands on head, and turned himself in. He was quickly handcuffed and brought in. As it turned out, he was a PAVN artillery officer. He told the interpreters that, the night before, he was being escorted by local VC forces and some PAVN infantry to stake-out the Boa Cam fort and determine how best to destroy the place with artillery. He told them that the artillery was being brought in, via the Ho Chi Minh Trail. He had been among those hit in the ambush, the previous night, and wound up being left behind and getting lost.

Dasher and his men had just captured the first PAVN officer for the entire Vietnam war. No small accomplishment. Major Tieu Ta Hahn soon arrived, fresh from an enjoyable night at Quang Tri and set about interrogating the officer. Dasher stood by and listened, but left when he saw the electric generator and bucket of water roll out. The Vietnamese did not belong to the Geneva Convention and did not adhere to its rules. Subjecting prisoners of war (POWs) to mistreatment and torture was common, as many VC, PAVN and indeed, American servicepeople discovered.

Chapter 19

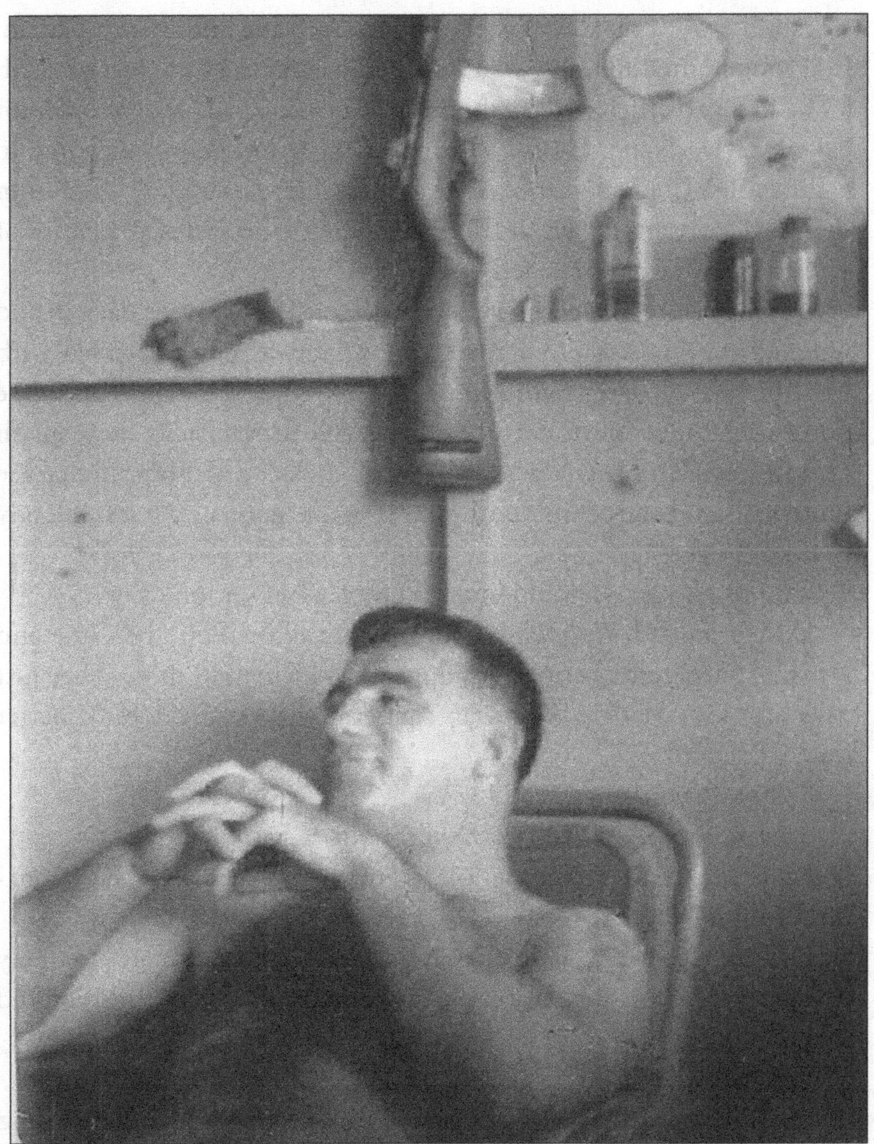

Dasher at the Bao Cam fort

As Dasher and Lowe moved around the fort, checking the defences against the counterattack they were sure was coming, they heard a lot of chatter about what had happened. Major Hahn had not wasted any time letting everyone back at Quang Tri MACV headquarters know that *he* had captured the first PAVN officer of the war. The news spread like wildfire, all the way to Hue, Da Nang and finally, Saigon. Everyone wanted to know what was going on at the little fort of death and, in short order, a joint interrogation team was flying up from Saigon to Da Nang. Dasher heard that their new guest was going to get the full VIP prisoner-of-war treatment. He was to be airlifted from their little fort and taken to Da Nang, where the enthusiastic team of interrogators would be eagerly awaiting him.

After checking the perimeter, a few times, Dasher went back in and watched the interrogation, for a while. He was not impressed with what he saw. He later found Jim Lowe and said, 'Damn! Vietnamese don't even know how to torture a bloke. A little electricity here, splash of water over the head there, couple of sticks of bamboo under the fingernails and they think he'll talk. If you're gonna do a job, bloody well do it right.'

'You think you could do better?' Lowe asked sardonically.

Dasher scoffed, 'Yep. They get the bloke all fired up, then stop and give him a cigarette. Seriously, Skipper, he's lovin' it in there. They just gave him his first-ever American cigarette. Anyway, it doesn't matter now, I fixed it.'

'What do you mean, you fixed it?'

'I fixed it, Skipper. Took care of the situation myself.'

Lowe looked at Dasher seriously and asked carefully, 'Dash, what did you do?'

Dasher gave his friend his widest grin. 'Like I said, mate, I bloody well fixed it. Those dickheads left the room, so I snuck inside and did the job properly.'

'Dasher, what did you do?'

'Nothin' bad, Skipper, I just gave the bloke a pack of cigarettes and a beer or two.'

Jim blinked, 'You gave him a beer?'

Dasher nodded, 'Or two. I had a little chat with the bloke. He reckons he'd been out there in the bush for three months and hadn't had a beer, the whole time. I thought, fuck me dead, that's not right. I reckon I'd turn meself in too, if that was me! So, I gave him a quick beer or two. Poor bugger.'

Chapter 19

It is entirely possible that Kevin 'Dasher' Wheatley is the only person in the world, who would have sat down with the first PAVN POW in history, an officer at that, and decide to start drinking beer with him in the middle of the morning, right under his commanding officer's nose. It was classic Wheatley behaviour and as it turned out, Dasher's idea of a 'quick beer or two' was vastly different to other people's. When the chopper came in to take the now-famous POW back to Da Nang, he was so drunk he could not remember his own name, let alone, disclose any useful intelligence. In fact, he was so intoxicated, that when the furious Americans loaded him into the Huey, he vomited all over himself and the two marines sitting either side of him. The Americans were ropable, and the brass wanted names and explanations ASAP.

Jim Lowe received a call from a livid colonel, demanding to speak to the 'smart-arse Aussie' who had drugged his prisoner. Jim smoothly explained that he had been out checking fortifications and gun positions when the incident had occurred, so was unable to either confirm or deny that it had even been the 'smart-arse Aussie' who had 'drugged' the prisoner. Which was kind of true, but his story did not work. Lowe was promptly ordered back to Quang Tri Headquarters to explain why he could not keep a leash on that 'damn Australian'. Jim Lowe states in his book that he did explain to the MACV colonel that, technically, Dasher Wheatley did not work for him, so there was nothing he could do. He told the officer that the 'damn Australian' was an independent adviser who reported only to the Australian major at the Quang Tri compound and not to the Americans. Jim told him that Dasher could basically do what he wanted and did so, all of time, and that he was the best and most effective soldier he had ever come across.

Wheatley was never punished for the 'drugging' of the POW and neither was Lowe, but they were, according to Jim's book, 'in the MACV doghouse' for a time, but they did not care about that. While the brass at Quang Tri smouldered and raged about that 'crazy damn Aussie', they continued to sleep in warm beds, eat hot meals and enjoy freshly pressed laundry, every day. At the same time, Dasher and Jim stayed at the fort of death and continued running patrols, conducting ambushes, being shot at and mortared daily, eating rice and cold fish and sharing their beds with hordes of rats and fleas. With hindsight and perspective, it is easy to see who, among them, should have been complaining.

Out on patrol, a few days later, Dasher led his men into a small hamlet. As they walked through town, an old woman ran out and screamed in Vietnamese, that she needed a doctor. Dasher told the woman he was not a doctor, but that Jim was. They were Caucasian and to the woman, that meant the same thing. The old woman pointed at the small shack, she had come out of and explained that her daughter was having trouble giving birth. She said the baby had breeched.

Dash walked over to Jim Lowe, put his arm around his shoulder and said, 'Congratulations, Skipper, you're a doctor today. We better go take a look.'

'A doctor?' Lowe asked, baffled. 'You told her I'm a doctor?'

'You're white, Skipper. Same thing.'

'Yeah, right.' Jim muttered. 'I'm a neurosurgeon and you're an obstetrician.'

Dasher laughed, 'You've done this before, right?'

'Done what?'

'Delivered a baby.'

Jim gasped and said, 'No, of course not!'

Undeterred by his mate's horror, Dasher ushered Lowe into the hut. He saw right away that the baby was breeching, so said to Jim, 'Right-o, Skipper, roll up your sleeves and get in there.'

'Me?' Jim was suddenly very pale and wide eyed. 'Why me?'

'You grew up on a farm,' Dasher reminded him.

'What the hell has that got to do with anything?'

'Well, I grew up in the city, mate, I don't know how to do this.'

'Dash, growing up on a farm doesn't make me a doctor.'

'Yeah, it does.' Dasher said, perfectly seriously. 'You told me once, you used to deliver calves on the farm, when you were a kid. And sometimes, they tried to come out backwards.'

Chapter 19

'Dash, that's cows, this is a person.'

Wheatley shook his head and pushed Jim towards the screaming woman. 'Same thing, mate. If you can deliver a cow, you can deliver a person.'

Seeing no other option, Lowe reluctantly washed his hands and managed to get the baby turned and Dasher grinned widely, as the child was safely delivered. Jim Lowe was an instant hero to the people of the hamlet. They were invited to stay the night as honoured guests and were fed a beautiful meal, inside the hamlet chief's hut. Occasionally, there were nice encounters, like this, in Vietnam, moments that showed the marvellous ability of humans to care and look out for each other. They were a stark and welcome contrast to the horrors one normally associates with war. The local people were hard-working, tough people, with kind and generous hearts. Dasher found that very endearing, probably because he was the same. Especially when it came to kids.

As they were leaving the hamlet, Dasher saw a group of children mingling nearby. He waved them over and threw them some salt-water taffy which he always kept handy. He still loved to trade cigarettes and other valuable supplies for sweets and toys, so he could hand them out to kids he came across on his travels. On this occasion, as he was handing-out the treats, he noticed two incredibly sad little faces, holding back, at the rear of the group. The two children were dirty and wore ragged clothes, which left them almost naked, and they were obviously malnourished. Dasher did not want to scare them away, so he waited and followed them back to a shack, where they lived, around the corner. The state of the home and the apparent poverty of the family was too much for him to bear. He hurried off to a local store and bought food for the family, clothes for the kids and even soap, which was awfully expensive in Vietnam, at that time.

When Dasher returned to his men, he wore his usual cheeky grin, as he said to Lowe, 'Let's go, Skipper.'

Jim had witnessed everything Dasher had just done. He said to his friend, 'Dash, what you just did was nice, but we can't feed and clothe every needy kid in this godforsaken country.'

Dasher shrugged, 'Not trying to, Skipper. As long as I've got something in my pocket to give, I will. I can't pass these little blokes by, not when they're in a state like that.'

They headed out and Jim considered his friend, for a long moment, then finally said, 'Dash, if I ever make it out of here and my wife and I have a son, someday, I'm going to call him Dasher.'

Wheatley stared at the American for a moment, then said, 'Shit, that'd make me his godfather.'

Jim laughed, 'If you say so.'

'Anyway, Dasher is only me nickname, you know that right?'

'Well, my son's official name won't be Dasher, either. Dasher will be his nickname and that's all I'll ever call him.'

Dasher walked in silence, for a moment, then said, 'You know my name's Kevin, right?'

'Not to me, Dash, not to me.'

That was their final patrol out of the deadly little fort. They were moved back to Quang Tri, the following day. Dasher was immensely relieved to be back and for him, the time had come to move on. He had been made an offer to travel to a place, south of Da Nang, called Tra Bong, with a crack group of soldiers. The move would see him reunited with Butch Swanton and a few of his other Australian mates, who would form a special A Team unit. They would be working with Civilian Irregular Defence Group (CIDG) troops, down there and Dasher had learned there would be a greater Australian presence in the area. Dasher had enjoyed his time working with Jim Lowe and the other people at Quang Tri, but the long, hard experience, at the fort, had made him miss his mates and the company of other Australians. The new role was not going to be like being back at 1RAR, but he figured it would be an improvement.

Saying goodbye to Lowe was difficult, but Dasher told him he would stay in touch and that they would see each other again, soon. The two men had become close, over their time together and had saved each other's lives, on more than one occasion. Lieutenant Jim Lowe survived his time in Vietnam and eventually, rotated home. He had a son whose nickname was Dasher. That is all Jim ever called him and the name he goes by, to this day.

Chapter 20

THE A TEAM

Wheatley's work as an adviser for the Civilian Irregular Defence Group was going to be challenging, but he was certain it would be nothing he could not handle. The Civilian Irregular Defence Group (CIDG) was a program that was developed by the CIA in early 1961. The idea had been to build irregular South-Vietnamese military units from minority populations, like the mountain-dwelling Montagnard people. It was hoped that this would counter the expanding Vietcong influence in the Central Highland area and that some of these people might even be stopped from joining the Vietcong and team up with the Americans, instead.

US Army Special Forces, like the Green Berets, set-up area development centres, where they would train local villagers and farmers. Some of these people were only meant to act as village guards who could resist VC attacks, while others would receive greater training and form mobile strike forces. The Montagnard people were hardy, resourceful and resilient, but were initially difficult to motivate, because they had no real love of either the North or South. They did get along well with the American Special Forces people, who had been sent to train them, however, so the program was successful. In 1963, the Americans felt they could be getting more out of their new unit, so launched Operation Switchback. The idea of Switchback was to transfer control of the CIDG from the CIA to the Military Assistance Command, Vietnam (MACV). In other words, the CIA handed the Civilian Irregular Defence Group over to advisers, like Kevin Wheatley, who would mentor and train them in the field.

Wheatley talking with CIDG locals

The base at Tra Bong was not as comfortable as the compound at Quang Tri had been, but it would do. Dasher moved in with the other 'A Team' members and was happy to catch up with some old mates. The other Australians at Tra Bong with Wheatley were, Warrant Officer Scott, Warrant Officer Palmer, Warrant Officer Hoyne, Warrant Officer Dowsett, Warrant Officer Anstee and Captain Fazekas. There were also a few Americans there, at the time, Second Lieutenant Bussey, Staff Sergeant Harris, Staff Sergeant Sershen and Staff Sergeant Foshee.

Another bloke, waiting for Dasher, when he arrived at the base, was Warrant Officer Ronald 'Butch' Swanton. The two mates greeted each other warmly and Dasher considered his new home. He figured it was well defended, but could be made better with some careful planning and hard work. Fortunately, the officer at the base, who would be Wheatley's direct superior, was an experienced Australian officer named Captain Felix Fazekas. Fazekas had arrived in Vietnam, that September and had taken over command of the AATTV at Tra Bong, soon after. The captain had set to work improving the base's defences, straight away.

Butch Swanton with another advisor at Tra Bong

Captain Fazekas was well known within the Australian Army and held in high regard by all that knew him. Fazekas even managed to earn praise from the man, who would become Australia's Governor-General, Sir Peter Cosgrove. In his book, *My Story*, General Cosgrove exemplifies this characteristic perfectly, when he writes:

> Another great character was Major Felix Fazekas. Felix was an extraordinary man. A Hungarian by birth, he had as a teenager been a member of the Hungarian Military Forces under German control during the last year of World War II. On emigrating to Australia, he joined the Australian Army and was highly regarded and widely admired for his professionalism and courage during his service with the Australian Army Training Team – Vietnam, for which he was awarded the Military Cross. The Training Team mentored and accompanied South-Vietnamese Army units on combat operations. He was a bit older than the average major, craggy, crew-cut and tough as nails, with a thick Hungarian accent to boot. He was battalion operations officer and part of his additional duties in getting the battalion ready to go to Malaysia was to act as our teacher in the Bahasa language. We are probably the only group of Aussies who speak Bahasa with guttural Hungarian intonation!

The South-Vietnamese officer, Fazekas reported to at Tra Bong, was the commander of the Vietnamese Special Forces, Second Lieutenant Quang. Quang was still young and inexperienced, for someone with so much responsibility, but appeared capable enough. The second lieutenant was, perhaps, more open to advice, while planning an operation than Hahn had been. Dasher quickly worked out that, once a patrol was on the way, however, the second lieutenant was far less likely to listen and would, sometimes, change plans halfway through an operation, regardless of what his advisers were telling him.

Once Fazekas had arrived at Tra Bong, he had immediately gone to work expanding patrols and strengthening the defences. The experienced Australian captain noted right away that the bunkers in the centre of the camp were crucial and needed to be fortified. Fazekas was wise enough not to fully trust the local forces working with him. He worried that if the Tra Bong base was overrun, he may not be able to rely on his Vietnamese troops to stick around and fight to the end. He decided that having defendable bunkers, deep within the base, was essential for the safety of his Australian and American troops, who he knew would stay and fight it out, should a large attack happen. Vietnam was a complicated war and Fazekas was no fool. He understood that, in war, prevention was always better than cure.

One terrifying lesson at Tra Bong, which confirmed the captain's distrust in his South-Vietnamese soldiers, came at dawn, one morning, when he was conducting a perimeter inspection. Fazekas had discovered that the M18 Claymore mines, which had been carefully planted around the perimeter, had been turned around, so that they faced inward towards the camp. This would mean that if someone, inside the base, were to approach the mines, they would be triggered and fire back on the base's defenders. The M18 Claymore mine was a command-detonated and directional explosive device used in Vietnam. It was fired by remote-control or by tripwire and, like a high-powered shotgun, expelled a blast of metal balls in whatever direction it was aimed. Pointing these lethal devices the wrong way, was not a mistake that highly trained special forces people would likely make, let alone do it with so many mines. Almost all of them as it turned out.

Claymore Mine used in Vietnam

The captain had the mines turned back around and concreted into position, so they could no longer be tampered with. For good measure, he had the camp's external barbed wire doubled into two lines and added 44-gallon drums, filled with a highly flammable petrol mixture, to the line. Should an attack occur, these could be set alight and rolled down the hill towards the attackers. Nothing was left to chance. Still not convinced his people were safe, Fazekas had the men build a third perimeter of barbed wire, this one was to be placed deep inside the base and encircle the bunkers where the advisors slept. This would be their final fallback position, should the worst happen.

This work took-up most of Dasher's time and, together with the regular patrols, he and Butch found themselves constantly busy and perpetually tired. Dasher was happy to do the work, but he knew the internal bunker area was already extremely well built and that it would be unlikely that any VC unit could fully overrun it. Still, like Fazekas, Dasher was no fool and was more than happy to err on the side of over-engineering, when it came to base defences. His time, at the fort of death, had reinforced that. Inside the defences, the command bunker was dug in deep. It had thick, reinforced concrete walls and a roof, strong enough to withstand a direct hit from mortar shells and even, artillery. Within the bunkers, the men placed machine guns, ammunition, radios, batteries, canned food and bottles of fresh water. There was enough there to last for days, should they be cut- off from outside help, which would no doubt arrive quickly from the American Marine base at Chu Lai, or some other special forces unit from Da Nang.

Dasher went on several patrols with his new unit and managed to escape any major incidents. The new team was a good fit for him, and he was finding working with Swanton and the other Australians extremely enjoyable. The CIDG troops were keen to learn, even if they were a little unreliable. During those first few weeks at Tra Bong, Dasher and Butch became even closer. The nature of their job forced them to work closely and so far, this had been a joy for Wheatley. Other than Fazekas and the few other Australian and Americans advisers, he had come to know and trust, there was no one else Dasher knew he could completely rely on. Dasher knew that, come what may, Butch Swanton would always have his back, and that his mate would never abandon him in a fight. Dasher would do likewise.

Chapter 20

Defences at Tra Bong

There was an American sergeant at Tra Bong, named Theodore Sershen, who Dasher had also been working with. Like most of the US Special Forces, Wheatley had encountered, he found Sershen to be smart, reliable and brave. The American typically stayed with Fazekas, while on patrols and had a good relationship with the CIDG men, who were always happy to follow him. With these people at his side, and the other advisers in the A Team, Dasher felt confident that they could handle most situations. Providing they could keep the CIDG men together, when the bullets started flying, that was. Those men were tested on a few occasions and although, they all knew how to fight, they tended to want to fall back sooner than they should. Wheatley had about the same amount of faith in the men from CIDG as he had had for the blokes he had worked with up north in the ARVN.

In late October, Wheatley came up for leave, once again, and considered his options. He thought hard about going to Honk Kong, or even Tokyo, but was not really excited about either idea. He had enjoyed his last stint of R&R overseas, but had been finding life with the AATTV lonely and he was still missing battalion life. So,

Wheatley came up with another idea. He knew that his old battalion, 1RAR was in country and set up at Bien Hoa, to the south. He decided that it might be fun to head down there and pay the boys a visit. For the men of 1RAR, this was welcome news. Dasher was their idol and they had been missing him, at least as much as he had been missing them.

The A Team at Tra Bong with Dasher

The day Dasher Wheatley came swaggering into camp, to catch up with the blokes from 1RAR, was a happy one. He was welcomed with open arms and for a few wonderful days, the beer flowed, the sausages sizzled and the stories flew back and forth. The base, where 1RAR had set up, was vastly different to what Dasher had been used to. The boys here had truckloads of VB, real red meat, newspapers from Australia, a semi-reliable mail service and their own Australian medical team. It was a 'home away from home'. While he was there, Wheatley slept on a stretcher in one of the four, 10-man tents the Australians had set up. The four large tents housed all the men from B Company platoon, with one set aside as the platoon HQ. This tent housed Dasher's old boss, the Platoon Commander and Regimental Sergeant Major, John

McKay MM. Dasher stayed in McKay's tent and the World War II veteran was thrilled to have him. The two men spent a lot of time talking into the small hours of the night.

The boys loved having Wheatley there and Dasher made the most of the barbeque. The men from 1RAR served up steak, which had been flown in from Guam by the Americans and made sure the VB was cold. Dasher told them stories about his exploits in the north and the medals he was supposed to be receiving. He learned, in turn, that 1RAR had suffered their fair share of losses, since arriving in Vietnam. McKay told Dasher about one particularly tragic event, which had occurred, not long after the battalion had landed in country. There had been an accidental grenade explosion in C Company that had shocked the entire battalion to its core. The company had just finished an operation and were returning to their lines in American trucks. As one 1RAR soldier jumped off the side of the truck, the retaining pin on one of his grenades, which he had stashed in his webbing, caught on the side of the truck and the grenade exploded. Three Australians were killed in the blast and seven more were seriously wounded. The American truck driver was also gravely wounded, but survived. An American signaller, who was sitting beside him, was not so lucky.

During the days that followed, Dasher would lounge around the camp, writing letters, reading and sleeping. When the men returned to camp from their day's work, he would lead them in a rowdy and thoroughly enjoyable drinking session. At the end of his week of leave, Dasher said goodbye to his old mates and left, making his way back to Tra Bong and the lonely work that awaited him there. Sadly, for the men of 1RAR, it would be a final farewell because, although, they could not have known it, at the time, none of them would ever see Dasher Wheatley alive again.

Chapter 21

THE FINAL PATROL

Dasher had not long returned to Tra Bong, from his break, visiting his mates at 1RAR, when Captain Fazekas announced in his thick Hungarian accent that they were going out on a two-day patrol. They were to head out as a single company, with the commander of the Vietnamese Special Forces A Team, Second Lieutenant Quang, in charge. As was typical, within this CIDG company would be three platoons, which would include a reconnaissance platoon and a weapons platoon.

Like so many other operations in the area, the idea was to search for and destroy a Vietcong force, which was believed to be operating close by. The target would be a village, called Vinh Tuy in the northern part of the search area, which was suspected to be supporting the Vietcong. The search area was a triangle-shaped region which was walled, on the west, by the Nui Hon Doat Mountain and on the east, by the Chap Toi Mountain. The northern border of the search area was a road that ran east to west. This mission was typical of the work the A Team had been doing out of Tra Bong, save for the fact that it was to be conducted further out than they would have normally patrolled. They would be operating more than ten kilometres away from base and would have no direct artillery support. This was not ideal, but also not unusual for special forces units.

Chapter 21

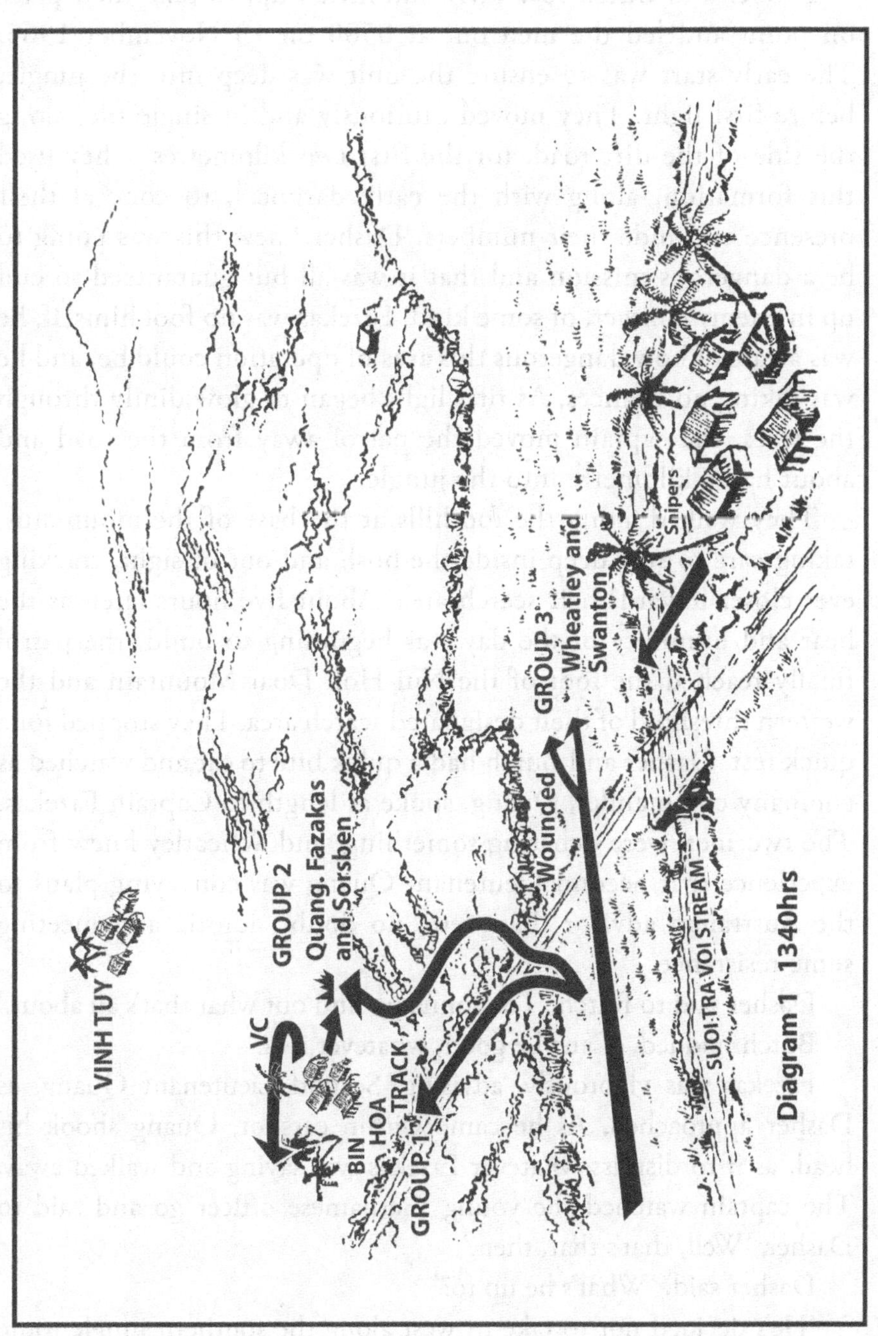

Diagram 1 1340hrs

Dasher and Butch rose early and kitted up, to take their place on point and led the men out at 0500 on 13 November 1965. The early start was to ensure the unit was deep into the jungle, before first light. They moved cautiously and in single file, along the side of the dirt road, for the first two kilometres. They used this formation, along with the early darkness, to conceal their presence and hide their numbers. Dasher knew this was going to be a dangerous mission and that it was all but guaranteed to end up in enemy contact, of some kind. Fazekas was no fool himself, he was aware of how dangerous this area of operation could be, and he was taking no chances. As first light began to glow dimly through the trees, the captain moved the patrol away from the road and about half a kilometre into the jungle.

They walked along the foothills at the base of the mountains, taking care to stay deep inside the bush and out of sight, tracking ever closer toward their search area. About five hours later, as the heat and humidity of the day was beginning to build, the patrol finally reached the foot of the Nui Hon Doat Mountain and the western threshold of their designated search area. They stopped for a quick rest. Dasher and Butch had a quick bite to eat and watched as company commander, Quang, spoke at length to Captain Fazekas. The two men were debating something, and Wheatley knew from experience that Second Lieutenant Quang was conveying plans to the Australian advisor that were, no doubt, idiotic and meeting some resistance.

Dasher said to Butch, 'I'm gonna go find out what that's all about.'

Butch nodded, 'Can't be good, whatever it is.'

Fazekas was vigorously 'advising' Second Lieutenant Quang, as Dasher approached. As he came within earshot, Quang shook his head, as if to dismiss whatever Fazekas was saying and walked away. The captain watched the young Vietnamese officer go and said to Dasher, 'Well, that's that, then.'

Dasher said, 'What's he up to?'

'He's decided not to take us west along the southern jungle route we laid out this morning.'

Chapter 21

Dasher pulled out his map, opened it and said, 'Then, where?'

Fazekas pointed to the open map, his accented voice was deep and calm. 'He wants to go that way, around to the north, then move south-east along eastern edge of the mountain. It is longer way around, but the jungle is not so thick that way. He wants to stay on edge of the bush, so we can move faster. It will be easier, but he is asking for trouble.'

Wheatley looked at the map and muttered under his breath, 'It's gonna be light green out that way, Skipper.'

The captain nodded. 'Light green' was a term Australian soldiers used in Vietnam for parts of their maps which indicated areas with little or no foliage. These areas offered little to no cover and were far more likely to be mined and booby trapped and were, therefore, to be avoided, whenever possible. 'He is going to get us spotted.' Fazekas complained.

'We don't have to agree, Skipper,' said Dasher, folding the map and putting it away, 'we just have to do as we're told.'

Fazekas laughed. 'You just summed-up army life, in one sentence, Dash. Go tell Butch and Sershen what we are doing. It will be a long day.'

Dasher agreed and moved off to inform the others of the change in plans. He was used to this sort of thing and had learned, long ago, that it was best to accept the things you cannot change and concentrate on the things you could. After all, there was only so much an advisor could do. At the end of the day, the South-Vietnamese were in charge and while the Australians could always 'advise' their Vietnamese comrades, when they thought they were making a mistake, they could not make them take that advice. Wheatley knew he was most effective when he understood the plan, no matter how foolish it might be, and when he was doing his best to operate intelligently, within the confines of that plan.

And so it was, that at about 1000 on 13 November 1965, Dasher's unit set off, once again. This time they headed north to sweep around the Nui Hon Doat Mountain. As the day aged and they probed forward, Second Lieutenant Quang instructed Wheatley and the point men to lead the troops along the edge of the jungle and around the northernmost point of the mountain. Dasher's frustration was rising, as Quang had been ignoring constant advise from Fazekas, to move the men back into the scrub and out of sight. They continued to move, almost completely, in the open and were inevitably spotted by a group of farmers, who were working a field, to their north. The locals were less than a hundred metres away and could not have missed the large patrol of Civilian Irregular Defence Group soldiers, moving along the edge of the jungle, if they tried. Dasher swore under his breath and stopped beside Butch. They could only watch, as the farmers, trying to appear casual, downed tools and moved away towards a group of huts, to their north.

'Bloody hell.' Butch said, taking a drink of water from his canteen. 'So much for the element of surprise.'

Dasher nodded and looked back to see Fazekas glaring at Quang. The young CIDG commander was watching the farmers move away, with a forced grin on his face, trying to look unconcerned. Fazekas said nothing, his thunderous expression conveyed his thoughts clearly enough. Dasher took a deep breath and forced down the anger, he felt rising inside him. They were working in an area where the Vietcong enjoyed a powerful influence over the local people. He knew, as he watched the farmers move away, that they were, even now, heading off to inform the VC of their presence, or that they, themselves, were members of the Vietcong and were going to collect their weapons and comrades.

Worst of all, there was nothing Dasher could do about it, save raise his weapon and kill every one of them, before they had the chance to get away. That, however, was not an option. Killing unarmed farmers, out of fear of what you suspected they were about to do, was obviously wrong, Dasher would never have even considered it, even though he was aware that not doing so was likely to get him and other people in his unit killed. Such was the unwinnable nature of the Vietnam war. As it would turn out, the Australian's fears were warranted.

A few hours later, the company arrived at what was to be the starting point of their search- and-destroy mission. It was about 1300 and they had come fully around the Nui Hon Doat mountain and were closing in on the Suoi Tra Voi stream and the road that crossed it. Captain

Chapter 21

Fazekas still looked concerned, and Dasher thought he was probably still upset that Quang had managed to get them spotted. Looking at the officer's dark expression, Wheatley was starting to worry that the captain had just received some more unwelcome news. He asked, 'What's up, Skipper? The plan changed again?'

Fazekas shook his head and pointed at the stream. 'We follow creek towards road, then split up. Three platoons, as outlined in briefing.'

Dasher nodded, 'I'm pretty sure they know we're here.' He took out his map and opened it, quickly finding their location.

'Not much we can do about that, we just get it done.' The captain's voice was still calm, but his Hungarian accent was beginning to become more prominent, which Dasher took to mean that he was trying to keep his temper in check. He was not the only one. Pointing to Dasher's map, Fazekas said. 'We make three platoons, I take Sershen and go with Quang in one, I want to keep eye on him. We take the mortar and a 30-cal machine gun and push north into centre of the search area. The second platoon will move north-west along main track towards Binh Hoa, see what they can flush out. You and Butch go with third platoon, take a 30-cal and move north-east. Follow the Suoi Tra Voi stream and cross the road here.' He pointed to the map. 'Push east towards Chap Toi Mountain. Once you have cleared out that rice paddy, move north. We will wait for you, south of Vinh Tuy village. We go in together. Stay in touch.'

Dasher moved to issue instructions to the men and in a short time, the three platoons had been formed and were moving out. Dasher, as was his *modus operandi*, took the lead with the forward scout. Butch and the platoon radio operator stayed with him at the front, until they moved into a wide rice paddy. They had been travelling for about twenty minutes, when Dasher heard AK-47 fire, from the north, followed by a short burst of M-2 Carbine fire. He called for the radio and contacted Fazekas.

'Yeah, all good, Dash', the captain said. Found some huts up here, with a few VC waiting inside. They bugged out, we're all good.'

Dasher acknowledged the update and said to Butch, 'They know we're here, mate. Tell the boys to stay awake.'

Butch nodded an affirmative and they continued, soon coming to the Binh Hoa track which cut through the rice paddy, from north to south. Dasher stopped and pulled out his map, he could see that, on the other side of the track, the rice paddy was walled by thick jungle, to the north and by the Suio Tra Voi stream, to the south. He guessed it was between two and three-hundred-metres wide and offered little, if any, cover. It was going to be a highly dangerous environment to work in, but his hands were tied. He had orders to clear it, so clear it he would, even though, he suspected that if an attack were to come, this would be the place for it. To Butch, he said, 'It's all light green out there, mate. Make sure the boys are ready. We'll use an open formation, once we reach the other side of the track and sweep through quickly. Tell 'em to keep their heads down.'

'No worries, Dash.' Butch said, then added. 'We'd better watch that village, to the south, other side of the stream there. If they hit us, they'll either come from there or from the jungle to the north.'

Dasher agreed, then led the men across the dirt track and into the rice fields, on the other side. On Swanton's order, the platoon spread out into an open formation and moved in an eastward direction. They had only travelled a short distance from the road, when Dasher saw movement, about twenty metres to his left. He turned to see three black-pyjama-wearing men jump up from the ground with AK-47s in hand. 'Contact!' He yelled and dropped to the ground. The men behind him followed suit, as a short volley of AK-47 fire passed harmlessly overhead. Dasher and Swanton raised their weapons and saw the three Vietcong soldiers, who had just fired at them, run for the jungle, to the north.

'Shit!' Butch yelled and signalled for two CIDG men to give chase, 'Get those pricks!' He shouted and the two young men took off running, firing as they went. The three Vietcong soldiers ahead dropped their weapons and fell to their knees, hands on head. The CIDG soldiers quickly caught them and immediately started to search them and bind their hands.

'Hold your positions!' Dasher shouted, 'Stay low, watch those trees. They'll be more of them out there.' Just then, the radio operator appeared at Dasher's side, telling him that Captain Fazekas wanted to know what was happening. Dasher, crouching low and methodically scanning the village to his south, took the radio. Not only did he have to move through this open area, in search of an enemy he knew was here, but he now had to do it, with prisoners.

Captain Felix Fazekas wiped sweat from his brow, as he watched the hut fall. He stepped back, as a plume of dust rose, with the collapsing of the small dwelling. He looked around to see the other members of his platoon taking to other huts with machetes and shovels, destroying the shelters, so they could not be used by the enemy. It was hot work, and the captain was tired. The Australian's mood was dark, he was still on edge, after they had been spotted by the farmers earlier and having just been attacked, when they had stumbled across these huts.

When the platoon had moved towards the huts, they had been greeted by small arms fire, but the force that had attacked them was disorganised and ineffective. The enemy had quickly fallen back, as Fazekas, and Sergeant Sershen, had organised their platoon to return fire and assault the huts. Fazekas could not say, for certain, that the ambush had been set up, after the Vietcong had been tipped off by the farmers, who had spotted them earlier, but he would have bet a month's pay that it had. As he watched the huts fall, the sound of distant gunfire came crashing through the jungle from the south. It was clearly Vietcong AK-47 gunfire and the answering crack of M-2 Carbines told him Dasher and Butch's men had engaged the enemy, somewhere off to his south-east.

Fazekas swore and called for a radio. A young South-Vietnamese, Civil Irregular Defence Group soldier appeared at his side, seconds later. His young, sweat-drenched face was worried, dust from the collapsed huts clung to the sweat on his brow. Fazekas took the radio receiver and called Wheatley. 'Dasher, report.'

Dasher's voice came back, 'Found some locals, Skipper, they're just saying g'day. The CIDG boys are rounding a few up. We can handle it.'

Captain Fazekas nodded, as if Wheatley could see him, 'Keep me posted, Dash.' He handed the receiver back to the young Vietnamese soldier.

The team finished up with the huts and moved out. As they pressed north, through the jungle, Fazekas heard the distinct sound of Chinese-made sniper rifles and more M-2 carbine fire, coming from his south and Fazekas was beginning to worry. Wheatley and Swanton were fine soldiers, as good or better than any he had ever seen, but their platoon, like his own, was made up of Civil Irregular Defence Group soldiers. They were capable fighters, but had a terrible reputation for running during the heat of battle. The temptation was for Fazekas to try to convince Quang to move back to where Wheatley and Swanton were, but he knew the young officer would want to push on. He had to trust that the Australian advisors, to his south, had everything in hand. So, reluctantly, Fazekas continued to move north. Whatever was happening to his south, Dasher and Butch would just have to handle it, on their own.

Chapter 22

CONTACT

Dasher ducked instinctively, as the crack of a VC sniper rifle sounded from his west. It had come from the direction of the road they had just crossed. He heard a scream to his left and saw one of the two CIDG men, who had been ushering the arrested VC soldiers, drop. He ordered his men to the ground, as more sniper fire came from the road behind. He could hear rounds whizzing overhead and smacking into the mud around his troops. He stayed low, Swanton beside him, and aimed his SLR over the knee-high rice, and scanned the road to his west. He caught a faint flash of nozzle flare, always difficult to spot during the day, and found a target, laying prone on the track. Months of hunting snipers with the marines out of Quang Tri had honed his skills and he quickly killed the sniper.

'Nice shot, Dash.' Swanton said.

'I fucken hate snipers!'

'Yeah, me too, mate.' More sniper fire was coming from the road and Butch nodded to where the CIDG soldier, who had been hit by the sniper, was now screaming in pain. 'Looks like that bloke's in a bad way. I'm gonna go see what I can do.'

'No worries, Butch.'

Dasher called for those around him to give cover fire and the snipers on the road were momentarily silenced, as Swanton jumped to his feet and took off in the direction of the wounded man. By the time the CIDG soldiers in Dasher's platoon finished firing, Butch had made it across to help the soldier. Dasher turned and saw a familiar face, a few metres behind him. It was a CIDG private, named Vo Trong Chan. He was the platoon's medic. 'Go with Butch,' Dasher ordered, just as the sniper fire from the road returned, only this time, it was accompanied by a volley of AK-47 shots. The young CIDG medic looked frightened and hesitated a moment. Dasher said, 'We fire, you run. Got it!' It was not a question. Dasher started firing towards the road to give the young man cover and the men around him joined in. 'Run, Private!'

To his credit, Private Vo Trong Chan got up, as ordered, and sprinted through the mud, towards where Butch was now giving aid to the fallen soldier. As the young CIDG medic made it across to Butch, and Dasher's men stopped to reload, the three prisoners, they had captured earlier, sprung to their feet and ran towards the road, their hands still tied behind their backs. Dasher ignored them and ordered his men to get down, as a fresh burst of AK-47 fire erupted from the road. It was hard to tell how many people were firing at them, but Wheatley thought it was no more than five or six. He knew that he could lead his men over there and take them all out, if his men would follow him. Butch would need cover to get the wounded man out and Dasher figured the best way to give him that cover would be to kill the people shooting at him.

Dasher started shouting orders to his men, getting them ready to attack the road. Just as he was about to give the command to move, heavy machine-gun fire exploded from the south. He turned to look and in the few split-seconds, before he dropped to the ground for cover, took in the enormity of what he now faced. He could see at least two heavy machine guns, firing from within the village, on the other side of the stream. There were figures moving around the huts, all wearing the telltale black pyjamas of the Vietcong and carrying AK-47s. He swore, as he realised, in an instant, that the situation had changed and that he would soon lose control, if he did not think fast. The incoming rounds came in a wave and Dasher had to lay down on his stomach, to get below it.

Chapter 22

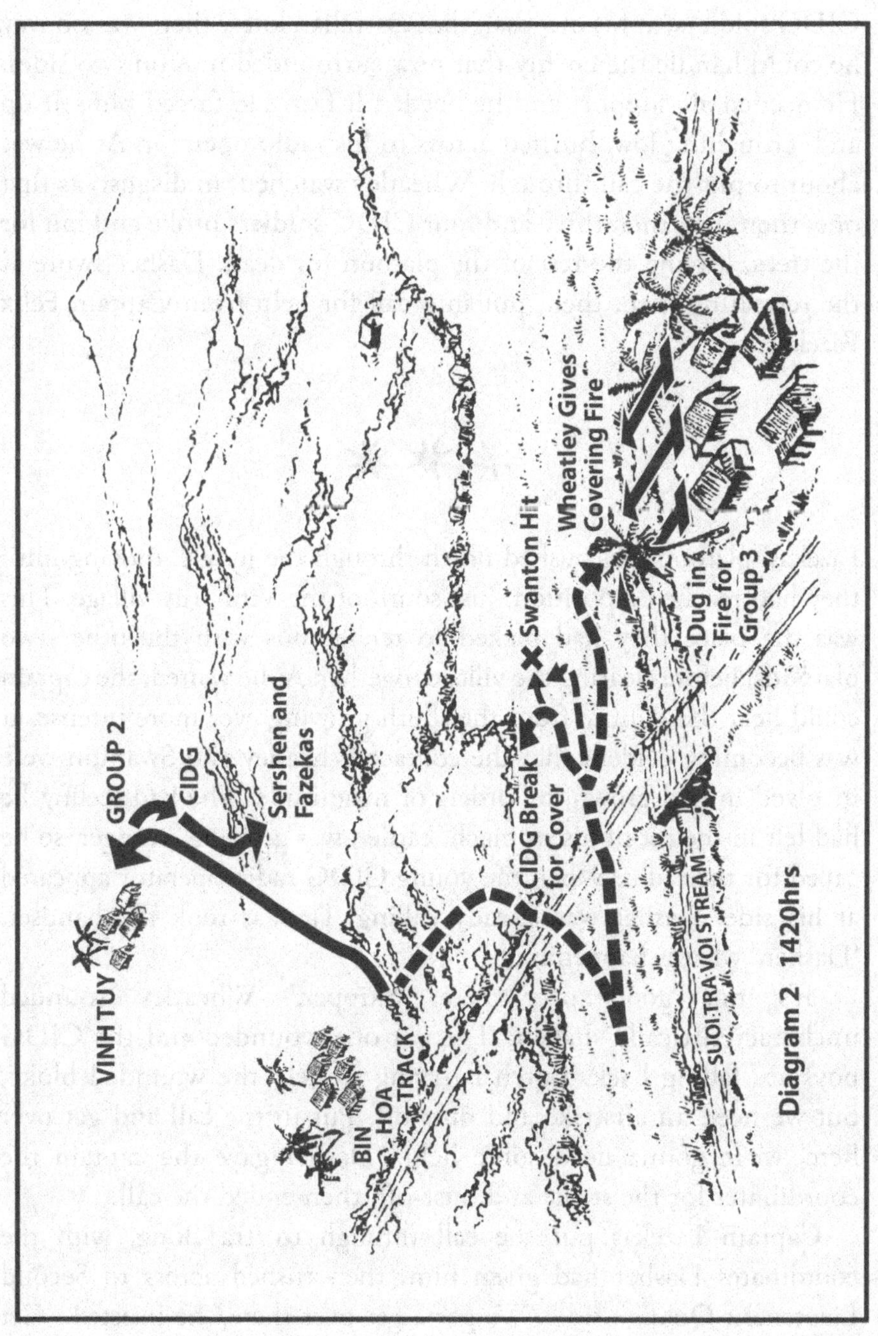

VINH TUY
GROUP 2
CIDG
Sershen and Fazekas
BIN HOA
TRACK
CIDG Break for Cover
Swanton Hit
Wheatley Gives Covering Fire
Dug in Fire for Group 3
SUOI TRA VOI STREAM
Diagram 2 1420hrs

Pinned down, with only one platoon of frightened and unreliable CIDG soldiers, at his disposal, the Australian knew there was no way he could handle the enemy that now surrounded him on two sides. He needed air support and he needed it fast. He forced himself up and, crouching low, hurried across to his radio operator. As he was about to put the call through, Wheatley watched, in disgust, as first one, then two, then three and four CIDG soldiers broke and ran for the trees, leaving the rest of the platoon for dead. Dasher swore at the retreating men, then, put in a call for help from Captain Felix Fazekas.

Fazekas' platoon had pushed north through the jungle, moving until they had reached a position, just south of the Vinh Tuy village. This was the place they had picked to rendezvous with the other two platoons, before clearing the village together. As he waited, the captain could hear the gunfire from the south growing ever more intense. It was becoming evident that the contact Wheatley and Swanton were involved in had grown, by orders of magnitude. The bad feeling he had felt in the pit of his stomach, earlier, was growing stronger, so he called for the radio. When the young CIDG radio operator appeared at his side, Dasher was already calling. Fazekas took the handset, 'Dasher,' what is happening?'

'It's not good over here, Skipper.' Wheatley sounded uncharacteristically shaken. 'I've got one wounded and the CIDG boys are falling back. Butch is trying to help the wounded bloke, but we need an airstrike and dust-off. Put in the call and get over here, we're gonna need some help.' Dasher gave the captain the coordinates for the strike and dust-off, then ended the call.

Captain Fazekas put the call through to Tra Bong, with the coordinates Dasher had given him, then rushed across to Second Lieutenant Quang's side. 'We gotta get over there,' he insisted. 'Get your men ready, we go help that platoon.'

Chapter 22

Quang's young face was pale, and he shook his head, 'No, we wait. Dasher ok, we wait.'

'What?' Fazekas forced his rising temper down, even as the distant gunfire became more intense. 'We need to get over there,' the Australian insisted, his accented voice growing louder. 'You need to bring other platoon in, we all need to go back and lend support. It sounds like Wheatley ran into a larger force than he can handle.'

Quang shook his head again, his young face growing stern. 'No, we stay.'

Fazekas swore. The next few minutes were not his finest, as he found himself in the midst of a shouting match with the commander of the Vietnamese Special Forces A Team. Quang stood his ground. The argument only stopped when Wheatley's voice returned over the radio, this time, he sounded desperate. Fazekas turned and hurried to the radio operator. As he picked up the receiver, he heard Wheatley shouting, '...enemy might be company strength... requesting immediate... surrounded... airstrike... company strength...' The distant roar of the battle, coming through the trees and over the radio, made it impossible to fully understand him. '...wounded... CIDG falling back...' Dasher yelled.

Frustrated, Fazekas shouted, 'You pricks stay here and hide, I'm going back to help! Anyone who wants to grow a pair, come with me!'

The American, Staff Sergeant Theodore Sershen, immediately stood up and said, 'I'm coming.'

Fazekas nodded his thanks to the American and said, 'Let's move.'

And so it was, that, without bothering to turn back to see who was following, Captain Fazekas headed out to help his mate. Wheatley had claimed on the radio that he thought the enemy was at company strength. That could mean more than 100 men. The Australian's platoon could be outnumbered, as much as four to one. Given the way the Vietcong operated, Dasher's people would most likely be surrounded and in the open. That is how ambushes went down out here. If the Vietcong did not have you over a barrel, they rarely attacked in those types of numbers. Patrolling this far out meant there was no artillery support and Dasher had said his men were abandoning him. Fazekas knew the situation was going to become desperate, very quickly, but what really alarmed the captain, the thing that had sent a cold shiver down his spine, was the tone of Dasher's voice.

Fazekas knew what type of soldier Warrant Officer Wheatley was, he had fought with men like him before. Dasher had a reputation for being able to deal with all manner of terrifying situation, with a calmness that had become something of a trademark. The man was a living legend. To hear Wheatley sound so rattled was shocking. Fazekas doubled his pace.

Dasher Wheatley fired at a Vietcong soldier, who was running across the front of the huts in the village. The man dropped to the ground and Wheatley reloaded his SLR. They had now been in this contact for over half an hour, and things were deteriorating quickly. Most of his men had retreated into the trees, to the north and while the handful of people, who remained, had been doing their best to help, they too were starting to bug out, one by one. Dasher knew it was only a matter of time, before he would be fighting alone. Just then, as if to confirm that fear, the platoon radio operator stood up and started to sprint away, to the north.

Wheatley immediately gave chase and brought the frightened man to the ground, with a tackle his old football mates would have been proud of. To lose the radio now would mean certain death for all of them, so a fuming Wheatley forcefully relieved the CIDG soldier of the radio, swearing at the man ferociously, as he did so. He pulled the heavy radio onto his own back, secured it in place, then continued to fight. He had already neutralised the few targets that were back on the road, to his west, but the number of VC, within the village, was growing by the minute and he was quickly losing control.

Over and again, the Australian warrant officer rallied what was left of his troops and urged them to follow his lead, to keep pouring as much fire into the targets, across the stream, as they could.

Chapter 22

Dasher had spotted an enemy-occupied weapons pit, just forward of the huts in the village. The pits were a short distance from the other side of the stream, and it was from there that the machine guns had been wreaking havoc on Dasher's platoon. In return, Wheatley had urged his dwindling troops to continue hammering that position as much as they could and, up until then, he had been somewhat successful at suppressing the machine guns. This had given Swanton, at least, some chance to move the wounded man he was trying to help, but Dasher knew he could not keep it up. Where was his airstrike?

Dasher continued to fire, while behind him, some forty metres to his north, Butch Swanton was desperately trying to carry the wounded CIDG soldier back to the jungle. The tree line was, at least, two hundred metres away and the muddy ground was sticky and difficult, so there was little to no chance he would make it, unless Dasher could knock out those machine guns. Wheatley had seen men commit brave and selfless acts, during his time in Vietnam and he was certainly no stranger to putting his own life on the line himself. He fully understood how much guts and determination it took. However, the actions he was witnessing by Warrant Officer Swanton, at that moment, were equal to, or above, any he had seen in his life.

Every time Butch stood up and tried to carry the wounded man, heavy machine-gun fire forced him back down. The Australian advisor was now hunched over, dragging the man through the mud, as withering machine-gun fire made the wet soil around him boil, like soup on a stove. Wheatley had no idea how his friend was still alive, in fact, he had been convinced, on at least two occasions, that the incoming fire was going to cut him down, yet somehow, Butch persisted. Dasher was now certain that, if Swanton did not stop trying to help the man, he was going to be killed. It was an absolute certainty. This realisation inspired and infuriated Dasher.

As he watched the last of his men quit the field and run away, Wheatley howled in rage, stood up and poured as much fire into the forward pits as he could. The machine guns stopped firing, but the small arms fire from around the huts continued. He stood in the open, deliberately placing himself between the enemy and Swanton and the wounded CIDG soldier, to make himself a target and draw the enemy fire. The tactic was working. Every VC soldier, within the village, stopped firing at Butch and turned their attention to Dasher and that was fine by him. He was a one-man wall, shielding his mate behind him, by soaking up all the enemy fire. Two more black-clad men dropped, as the magazine in his SLR emptied. Dasher knelt, found a M-2 carbine one of his men had dropped and emptied that into the village, before getting back down to reload his SLR.

And so, the terrific dance of death, between the two Australian soldiers and, what was likely, a company of over one hundred Vietcong combatants began. Dasher would spring to his feet, unload as much fire into the enemy position as he could, drop back down, reload and repeat. In return, the enemy across the stream would fire at Dasher as he stood up, then swing their attention back towards Butch, when Wheatley was forced down to reload. It was a terrifying stalemate, with only one inevitable outcome and eventually that outcome arrived.

At about 1420, some 40 minutes after the initial contact, Dasher rose and fired again. He ignored the hundreds of rounds that buzzed past his head and peppered the ground around him. The fire from his beloved SLR was so swift and accurate that the enemy were finding it difficult to hit him. His dark eyes darted, from target to target, as his lightning-fast hands moved in unison with his weapon and for a time, digger and rifle were one terrible machine that delivered swift 7.62-mm punishment to anyone who dared step into the open and fire back. More VC died, but Dasher's SLR emptied again and the machine guns, within the forward pits, opened up instantly. This time, Dasher did not drop to reload, but instead, spun around when he heard a horrible shriek of pain. He turned, just in time, to see Butch drop the wounded man he had been somehow carrying over one shoulder and fall to the ground, a bloody mist expelling from the Australian's chest. Dasher ran.

Chapter 22

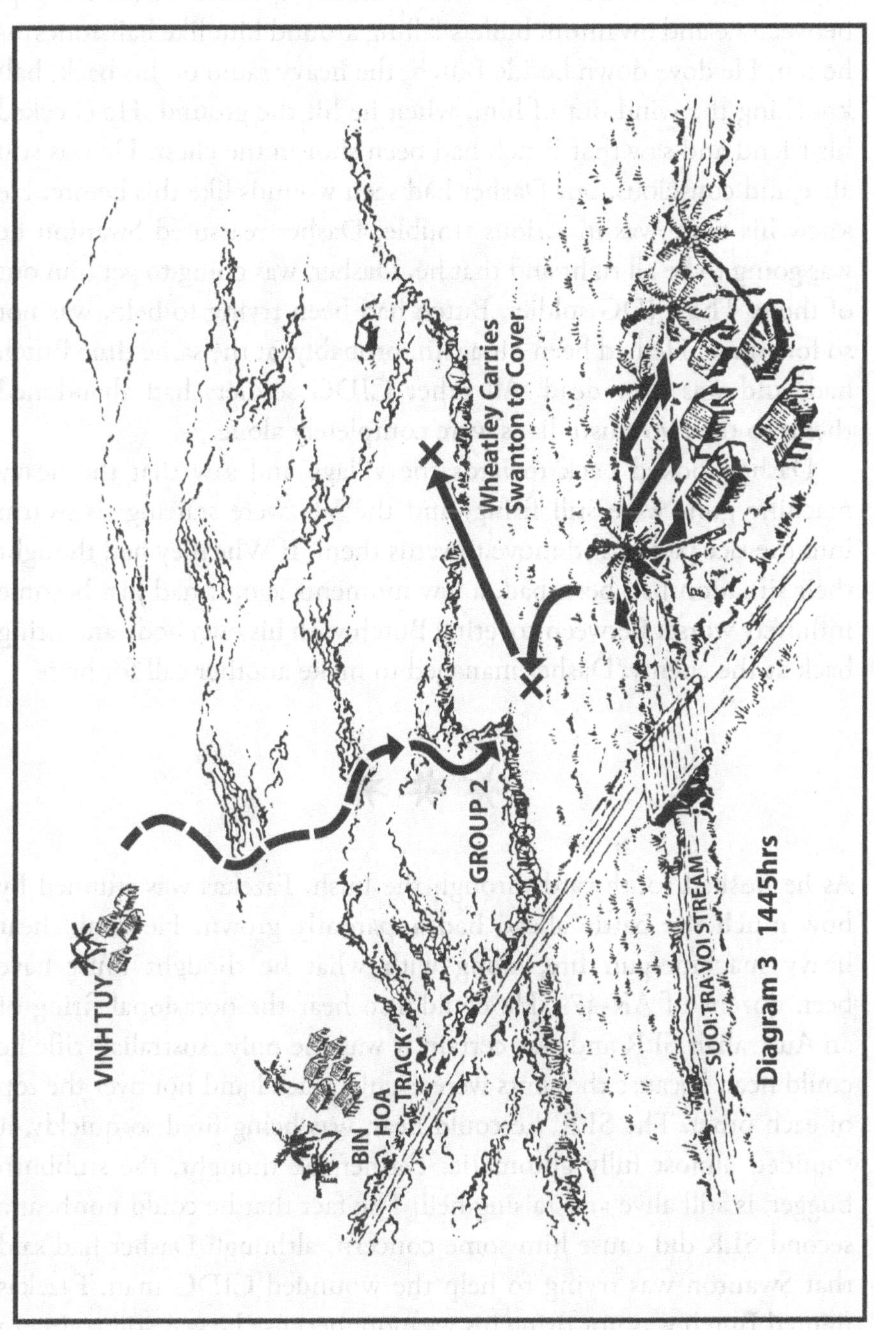

VINH TUY
BIN HOA TRACK
GROUP 2
Wheatley Carries Swanton to Cover
SUOI TRA VOI STREAM
Diagram 3 1445hrs

Convinced his mate was dead, Wheatley sprinted across the gap, between he and Swanton, bullets falling around him like hailstones, as he ran. He dove down beside Butch, the heavy radio on his back, half knocking the wind out of him, when he hit the ground. He checked his friend and saw that Butch had been shot in the chest. He was still alive and conscious, but Dasher had seen wounds like this before. He knew his mate was in serious trouble. Dasher reassured Swanton he was going to be all right and that he, Dasher, was going to get him out of there. The CIDG soldier, Butch had been trying to help, was not so fortunate. He had been hit again, probably, at the same time Butch had, and was now dead. All other CIDG soldiers had abandoned them, so the two Australians were completely alone.

Dasher looked back towards the village and saw that the heavy machine guns were still firing, and the VC were starting to swarm into the rice paddy and move towards them. If Wheatley had thought their situation had been bad, a few moments ago, it had just become infinitely worse. Between covering Butch with his own body and firing back at the enemy, Dasher managed to make another call for help.

As he pushed southward through the bush, Fazekas was stunned by how much the battle ahead had apparently grown. He could hear heavy machine-gun fire, along with what he thought must have been dozens of AK-47s. He could also hear the occasional firing of an Australian SLR and was certain it was the only Australian rifle he could hear, because the shots were evenly spaced and not over the top of each other. The SLR, he could hear, was being fired so quickly, it sounded almost fully automatic. Dasher, he thought, the stubborn bugger, is still alive and raising hell. The fact that he could not hear a second SLR did cause him some concern, although Dasher had said that Swanton was trying to help the wounded CIDG man. Fazekas figured Butch was not firing his weapon, because he was still trying to help his wounded comrade. Either that or he had been killed.

Chapter 22

As he moved towards the ferocious sound of battle, Fazekas was please to find that the young American soldier, Sershen, had been joined by at least half of the platoon, about fifteen men. Maybe, he thought, all was not lost. Second Lieutenant Quang, however, had not followed, but thankfully, the platoon radio operator had.

'Captain,' Sershen's accented voice called. Fazekas turned to see the American had stopped and was talking with someone on the radio. The captain hurried across and, as he neared, he could hear Dasher's voice. Over the sound of battle, he could not make out what Wheatley was saying, until he made it to beside Sershen, when he heard, 'God, somebody help us! Somebody do something!' Then Dasher was gone.

'Shit!' The captain took the receiver and tried to get Wheatley back, but to no avail. In the distance he could hear the single SLR firing again and breathed a sigh of relief. Dasher was still alive and obviously, too busy to talk. To Sershen he said, 'What he say?'

The American was pale. 'Multiple casualties, the platoon has abandoned them, and Swanton's been hit.'

'Bad?'

The American nodded, 'Chest wound. Dasher's... Dasher's trying, but it's just the two of them.'

Fazekas immediately radioed Tra Bong and again requested the medivac and airstrike for his mate. Even, as he put this request through, however, the captain's considerable combat experience and twisting stomach told him, it was too late. If there was help nearby, it would have arrived by now and the tone of Dasher's voice, as he had cried for help, had been uncharacteristically panicked. A lump formed in Fazekas' throat and cold rage built within him. He pondered for a moment what it would take to kill Dasher Wheatley. He thought to himself, the man's bulletproof, isn't he? Fearing the worst, Fazekas took off at a run, his men close behind. As it would turn out, the Australian advisor's darkest fears were soon to be realised. Warrant Office Second Class, Kevin 'Dasher' Wheatley was never heard from again.

Chapter 23

MATESHIP PERSONIFIED

Dasher fired as quickly as his semiautomatic rifle would allow. There were people moving all over the ground between him and the village and the machine guns were still working hard to put him down. His last magazine emptied, so he started to work through Swanton's ammunition. Butch was clearly in terrific pain, but was doing what he could to pull-out clips and hand them to Wheatley, who crouched as low as he could, as he reloaded.

Just as Dasher was about to raise and fire again, he heard a familiar voice behind him say, 'I here, I help. You hurt bad?' To Wheatley's surprise, Private Vo Trong Chan, the platoon medic who Dasher had sent to help Butch, had suddenly appeared at Swanton's side. The South-Vietnamese medic was on all fours examining the Australian's wounds.

Between gasps of pain, Swanton said, 'It's bad. My chest, I can't breathe.'

'Ok, I fix.'

Dasher said, 'You're a bloody champion, son! Look after him.' Then he rose again and unloaded another magazine, forcing the closing enemy to the ground and even managing to make a few turn and run. As he crouched to reload again, he saw Private Vo Trong Chan frantically trying to bandage Swanton, but chest wounds were notoriously difficult to bandage in the field. Dasher saw the worry on the medic's young face and did his best to keep the enemy at bay, while he worked.

Eventually, the medic said, 'Sir, I do all I can. We go now. Your friend die!'

Dasher stopped firing and turned his burning eyes towards the medic. To Butch, he said, 'Swanton, you still breathin'?'

'Yeah,' Swanton managed through clenched teeth. 'I've had it Dash, you better go.'

Another fresh burst of machine-gun fire swept across the ground, in front of Dasher, throwing-up mud and soil. Both he and the medic lay over the top of Swanton to shield him, causing the Australian to cry out in pain. Dasher examined his friend, as he covered him and started to swear. The bandages the medic had applied had done nothing to stop the bleeding and, it was obvious, Butch was finding it hard to breathe. Dasher searched the cloudy sky above, trying to will a helicopter and airstrike into existence, but to no avail, the sky remained empty. What he would give for artillery support, right now. But there was no artillery, and he knew now, that help was not coming or that, if it was, it would be too late. Swanton's lips were beginning to turn blue, his eyes were moving in and out of focus. He was dying.

Vo Trong Chang yelled over the deafening gunfire, 'Sir, we must go now! Your friend die and we go now!'

'You go,' Wheatley said, reloading his weapon and repositioning the heavy radio on his back. 'I'll take care of this bloke.' Without waiting for a reply, Dasher rose to one knee and opened fire towards the machine gun in the forward pits, ignoring the tumult of bullets passing within inches of his head. The machine gun stopped firing and Dasher yelled at the medic, 'Run!'

He fired, until his clip emptied and, without bothering to get down, dropped it out, slammed in a fresh magazine and emptied that one, as well. Dasher had no idea why Private Vo Trong Chan had changed his mind and risked his life to come back to try and help, but he would be damned, if he was going to let these bastards shoot the kid, while he ran for cover. Wheatley's covering fire worked and, as his second clip emptied and he dropped to the ground to reload, he saw the CIDG medic disappear into the jungle, to the north.

Turning to Butch, Dasher said, 'Right-o mate, let's get you out of here.' Butch nodded and Dasher slung his SLR over one shoulder and, still carrying the heavy radio on his back, got his hands beneath Swanton's armpits and said, 'Sorry, mate, this might hurt a bit.' Dasher heaved and Butch cried out in agony.

With bullets hammering the ground around him and dozens of people focusing all their attention squarely on him, Wheatley began to half carry, half drag his mate, through the sticky mud, towards the jungle, some 200 metres away. As he carried his dying friend, he had to stop, every now and then, to shoot at the enemy in a desperate bid to suppress their fire and hold them back. The effort of all of this was enormous. His breath burned in his lungs like napalm, his legs screamed in protest, his back and arms throbbed with agony and his heart felt like it was going to explode. Dasher soon realised that what he was trying to do was not humanly possible. The weight of his friend, combined with difficult footing, the load of his gear and weapon, plus the bulky radio on his back, were too much for any human to manage alone. He needed help! There was no way he could carry all his gear and drag his mate to safety, before being overrun and killed.

Dasher understood he had to lighten his load, somehow, if he were to have any chance of getting Butch out and that the heaviest thing he was carrying, besides Butch, was the radio on his back. Wheatley was no fool, the fact that discarding the radio would cut him off from the outside world and condemn him to an almost certain death was not lost on him, but what choice did he have? Leaving the radio behind, in a situation like this, was almost as good as suicide, but something had to go and it was not going to be his weapon. Leaving your rifle behind was not something Australian soldiers would do, under any circumstances, so it had to be either the radio or Butch. To Dasher the choice was clear, drop Swanton and take the radio and live or drop the radio, take Butch and die.

Chapter 23

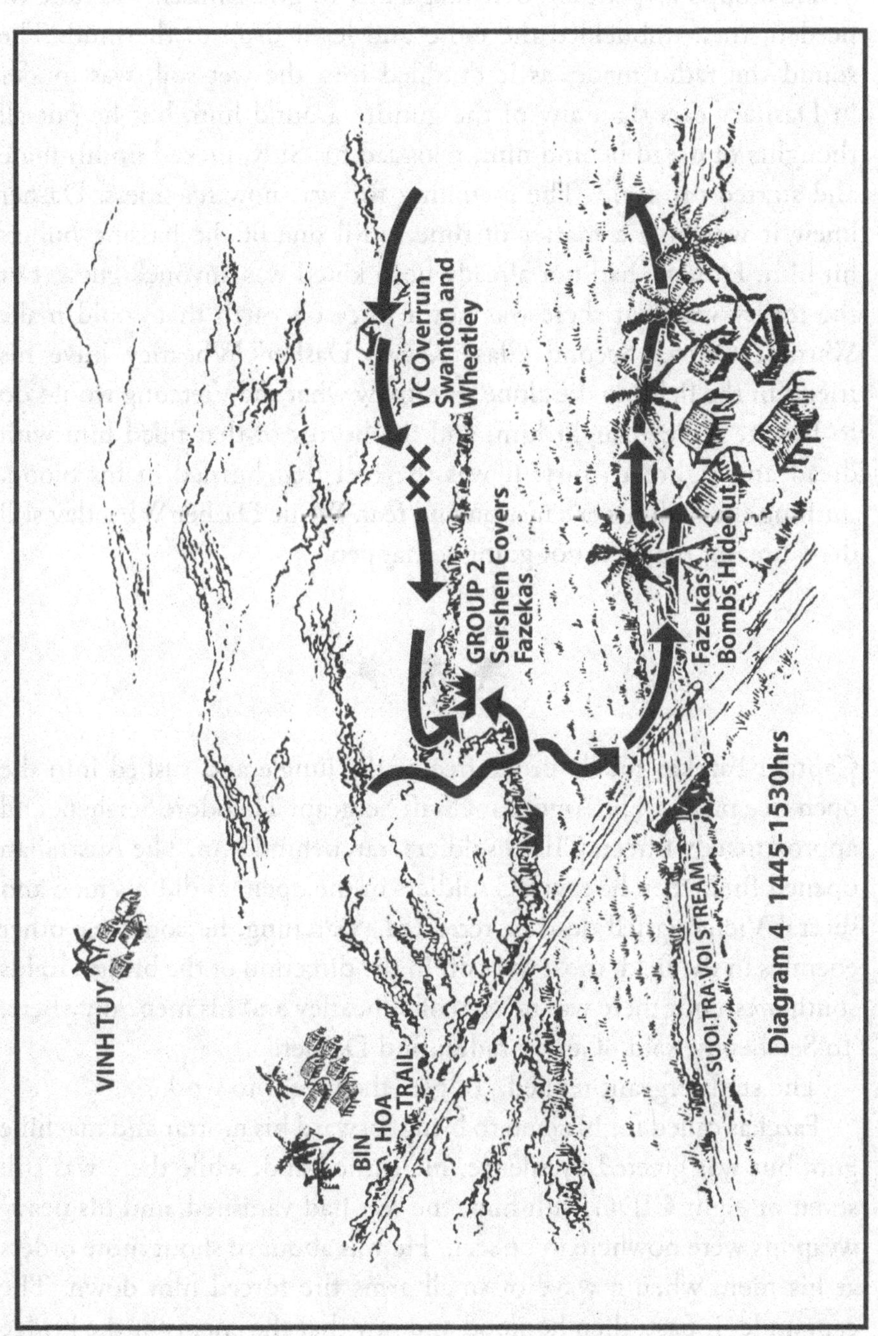

Diagram 4 1445-1530hrs

He stopped, spent another magazine, to give himself the time he needed, then unbuckled the radio and let it drop to the mud. The sound the radio made, as it thudded into the wet soil, was louder in Dasher's ears than any of the gunfire around him, but he put all thoughts of dread behind him, reloaded his SLR, picked up his mate and started off again. The incoming fire was now relentless. Dasher knew it was only a matter of time, until one of the passing bullets hit him. How he had not already been killed was anyone's guess, but the reality was that there was not a force on earth that could make Warrant Officer Second Class Kevin 'Dasher' Wheatley leave his friend in the field, to die alone. He knew what the Vietcong would do to Butch, if they caught him, and the horror of that filled him with dread and righteous fury. It was the fuel that burned in his blood, pushing through his exhaustion and fear. While Dasher Wheatley still drew breath, that was not going to happen.

Captain Fazekas finally broke free of the jungle and rushed into the open rice paddy. The American, Staff Sergeant Theodore Sershen, and approximately fifteen CIDG soldiers, ran behind him. The Australian opened fire, when he saw VC soldiers in the open, as did his men and several Vietcong fell dead or retreated. Searching, he could see other enemies in the field, most were off in the direction of the bridge, to his south-west, but there was no sign of Wheatley and his men, anywhere. To Sershen he said, 'Get on radio, find Dasher!'

The staff sergeant replied, 'Roger,' then went to work.

Fazekas called for his men to bring forward his mortar and machine gun, but was greeted by silence. He turned and, while there was still seven or eight CIDG with him, the rest had vanished, and his heavy weapons were nowhere to be seen. He was about to shout more orders at his men, when a wave of small arms fire forced him down. The captain let it pass, then he stood and saw that the enemy at the bridge had spotted him and were moving in. More were coming from the village across the stream, to his south. Undeterred, he engaged the people close to the bridge, two fell dead before the rest of his platoon joined in. More Vietcong died, and others began to run.

He shouted to Sershen, 'Wheatley?'

The American said, 'Nothing.'

Fazekas nodded and said, 'We need to push them back, clear that village.' He charged into the field, the American and seven CIDG soldiers following, as the Australian captain led a head-on charge, towards the bridge, to his southwest.

A few hundred metres to the east, Dasher's mighty struggle continued. Over and again, Wheatley had fallen, only to pick up his mate again and continue. He was now down to his final magazine and his last two hand grenades and was at the point of total exhaustion. Yet, he endured and was buoyed when he heard SLR and M-2 carbine fire from his west. He realised it had to be Fazekas's platoon engaging the VC and that help might had finally have arrived, but his heart sank, when he remembered he had discarded his radio and had no way of contacting them. For a moment, he thought of moving back in that direction, to find out if it was the captain, but a fresh wave of AK-47 fire, from his southwest, extinguished that idea.

'Is that Fazekas?' Butch asked, his voice was weak.

'Could be.' Dasher told him, 'Hang on.' Dasher raised his weapon and fired at a group of VC, who were closing in on him quickly. He had to spend his whole magazine to stop them, and he was now completely out of ammunition. It had, however, brought him enough time to make one final, desperate effort to reach the cover of the trees, which were, now, no more than twenty metres behind him. As he struggled to drag Swanton's limp body across the ground, he felt a hand on his shoulder and suddenly realised he was not alone. Startled he turned to see a young CIDG soldier had ran out of the trees to help. He could not believe his eyes, 'Private Dinh

Do!' Dasher greeted the young man with a huge smile. 'You're a ripper, mate, give me a hand.'

The private did and the two began to drag Butch towards the trees. As they did, another surge of small arms and machine-gun fire fell on them, tearing at the earth around them, but the two struggled on and quickly moved a groaning Swanton into the jungle. They laid him down in a hollow and, as Dasher struggled desperately to catch his breath, Private Dinh Do checked Butch's injuries. Dasher could see how bad Swanton was doing, his breathing was shallow, his face was white, and his lips were blue. Dasher knew his friend was just moments away from death and he saw about one dozen Vietcong running towards him from the rice paddy. He ignored them, although he still carried his trusty SLR, he had no rounds left. He figured he could use the SLR like a club, if he had to.

He hurried to Butch, knelt beside him and said, 'Still with me, Digger?'

Swanton nodded and said weakly, 'You need to go, mate.'

Dinh Do said, 'Sir – sir, VC coming, we go now! Your friend die now, we go.'

Dasher, breathing hard from effort, turned to regard the young man and for a moment, felt a flash of anger at the suggestion he should leave his mate. He realised, however, that the young private was right. If they stayed here, they would be dead in just a few moments and the young man had already risked his life to help drag Butch into cover. Without the CIDG private's help, Dasher knew he would not have been able to get Butch into the trees. Swallowing his anger, he said, 'Nah, mate, I'm staying with this bloke. You go.'

Dinh Do's jaw dropped open. 'Sir, he dead soon, we go now.'

'I'm staying.'

The expression on Dinh Do's face was incredulous. 'Sir, you have bullets?'

Dasher shook his head. 'Nah, mate, no bullets. Just these.' He knelt beside Swanton and removed two hand grenades. He put one hand protectively on his friend's chest and felt that Butch was trembling. He said with a grin, 'It's all right, mate, I'm not going anywhere.'

Butch nodded and Dinh Do said, 'Sir, we go! We die now!'

Chapter 23

'It's all right, Private,' Dasher said calmly. 'You take off. I can handle these blokes. The bastards aren't gettin' him.'

The private looked quickly towards the rice paddy and the group of VC soldiers charging towards them. Without a word, the young man nodded and ran into the jungle, leaving the two Australians to face their fate alone. Dasher squared his jaw and calmly pulled the pins on his grenades. Kneeling protectively above his mate and holding one grenade in each hand, Warrant Officer Second Class Kevin 'Dasher' Wheatley, stretched out his arms, knuckles white, as he held the live explosives in his fists, and faced the charging enemy. He would never give them another inch.

Warrant Officer Second Class Ronald 'Butch' Swanton, looked up at his mate, kneeling above him. The pain that had rattled him, since being shot, was mercifully fading, but it was being replaced by a cold numbness, which had moved its way steadily up his legs and was now creeping towards his bleeding chest. He knew he was about to die, if not at the hands of the closing enemy, then, by the spreading paralysis, which was creeping up his body and coming for his heart. But as he looked up at Dasher, Butch was calm.

Moments ago, his thoughts had been totally engulfed by fear, anger and dread. Shortly after being shot, Butch had been overcome by the shocking realisation that his life was going to end and that he would meet that end, far from home and family. That realisation had hammered him into a deep depression, unlike anything he had ever felt. It had been an absolute loneliness and fear, so overpowering, he would have openly wept, had he the strength to do so. A deep, all-consuming longing for home had washed over him, like a black cloud that sucked the breath from his lungs and made him want to cry out for his mother. To be a child again, safe at home in the protecting arms of a parent he knew to be in control of such big things.

But he was not a child anymore, he was a man, a soldier, a digger. He was going to die in the field, like thousands before him and there was nothing he could do about it. He wondered if all those fallen heroes, who had gone before, had felt the same fear and horror, as they had departed. He worried that his terror made him, somehow, unworthy of the name, digger, and the dignity of national remembrance. It did not.

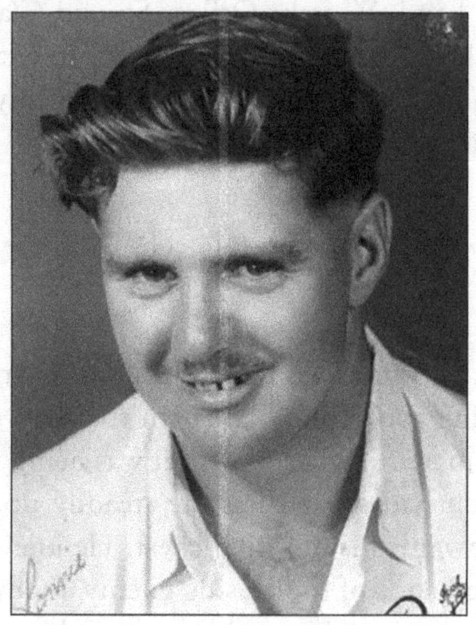

Butch Swanton

Now, however, those horrific feelings were gone, washed away by calm acceptance. He knew he was going to die, but he understood that his worst fears would not be realised. Butch knew, with total certainty, that his fate would not be to die alone in the mud, abandoned like an unwanted child in the dark. No, Ronald Swanton understood, without any doubt, that he was leaving this world, loved and protected. That simple realisation changed everything for Butch. It allowed him the dignity and courage he needed, to face his fate head-on. Moreover, this enlightening realisation was made ever clearer, because the man, who was presently hovering above him, was a man unlike any he had ever met. Dasher Wheatley was with him, and that simple truth liberated Butch. The knowledge that he was not alone comforted him, not just because it was an Australian digger who knelt protectively above him, but because that digger was Dasher bloody Wheatley.

Dasher had to know what was about to happen to them both. They were not only about to die, but they were going to be at the mercy of the dreaded Vietcong. The brutal torture, the VC inflicted on prisoners, did not bear thinking about. Tales of people, being slaughtered and skinned alive, were well known, and Butch knew that Dasher would have considered this already, but he was not about to flinch away from that fate. The knowledge that he might be taken by the enemy and spend his last moments in unthinkable agony had not cowered Dasher. Swanton knew from lived experience that there was no way, come what may, Wheatley would abandon him.

His friend's valour was brighter than any star in the heavens, it was stunning to behold. He had seen the man's loyalty and courage displayed, so many times, that it was beyond doubt. He had heard others tell of Dasher's courage, with stories from when Butch was not with him, and they were always the same. Dasher was Dasher and nothing could change that. He was a rock that held tight against even the fastest flowing river. Whether protecting mates while drinking at the pub, holding the line on the football field, carrying a wounded mate for hours through the jungle or charging head-on at the enemy to protect a tiny girl from certain death, Dasher's valour was absolute and completely unshakable. Butch was certain there had never been another man like him.

And so it was, that as Ronald 'Butch' Swanton felt the life drain out of him, he felt calm, loved and protected. He watched, as Wheatley used his last two grenades on the charging Vietcong, saw their bodies shatter and fly apart from the blasts. As the remaining VC closed in, to within one final metre, AK-47s raised for the kill, Butch snarled at them. Dasher leaned protectively over him, trying, even then, to cover his mate's body with his own and, in his last few seconds of life, as the Vietcong sighted them at point-blank range and pulled their triggers, Butch saw his mother's face. He could feel her warm embrace and smell her hair, as he imagined throwing his arms lovingly around her, for one final embrace. Then the AK-47s roared, and all went to white.

Chapter 24

AFTERMATH

Captain Fazekas charged across the rice field, his small group following behind. They fired, as they ran, killing any VC who got in their way and soon, the Australian led his men across the small stream and into the village. He moved about the huts, throwing grenades, and firing, as he went. His team of CIDG cleared hiding places and flushed out the Vietcong, who were working the machine guns in the forward pits. The Australian's attack was so furious and fast that the enemy dropped their weapons and supplies, as they fled for their lives.

Fazekas ordered Sershen to search for Wheatley and Swanton in the village, but to no avail. They were not there. The American stayed and continued to search the huts, as Fazekas moved back into the rice paddy, in a relentless effort to flush out more enemy and find his missing mates. As he ran through the rice field, Staff Sergeant Sershen covered the Australian from behind and, when two Vietcong suddenly appeared behind Fazekas, the American killed them both, before they had a chance to fire. Fazekas continued his forward assault and about fifteen Vietcong fighters emerged from the jungle, to his east. They spotted the Australian and formed up into a tight group to attack, but, once again, Sershen, who was at least 60 metres behind, intervened and saved the Australian's life.

Chapter 24

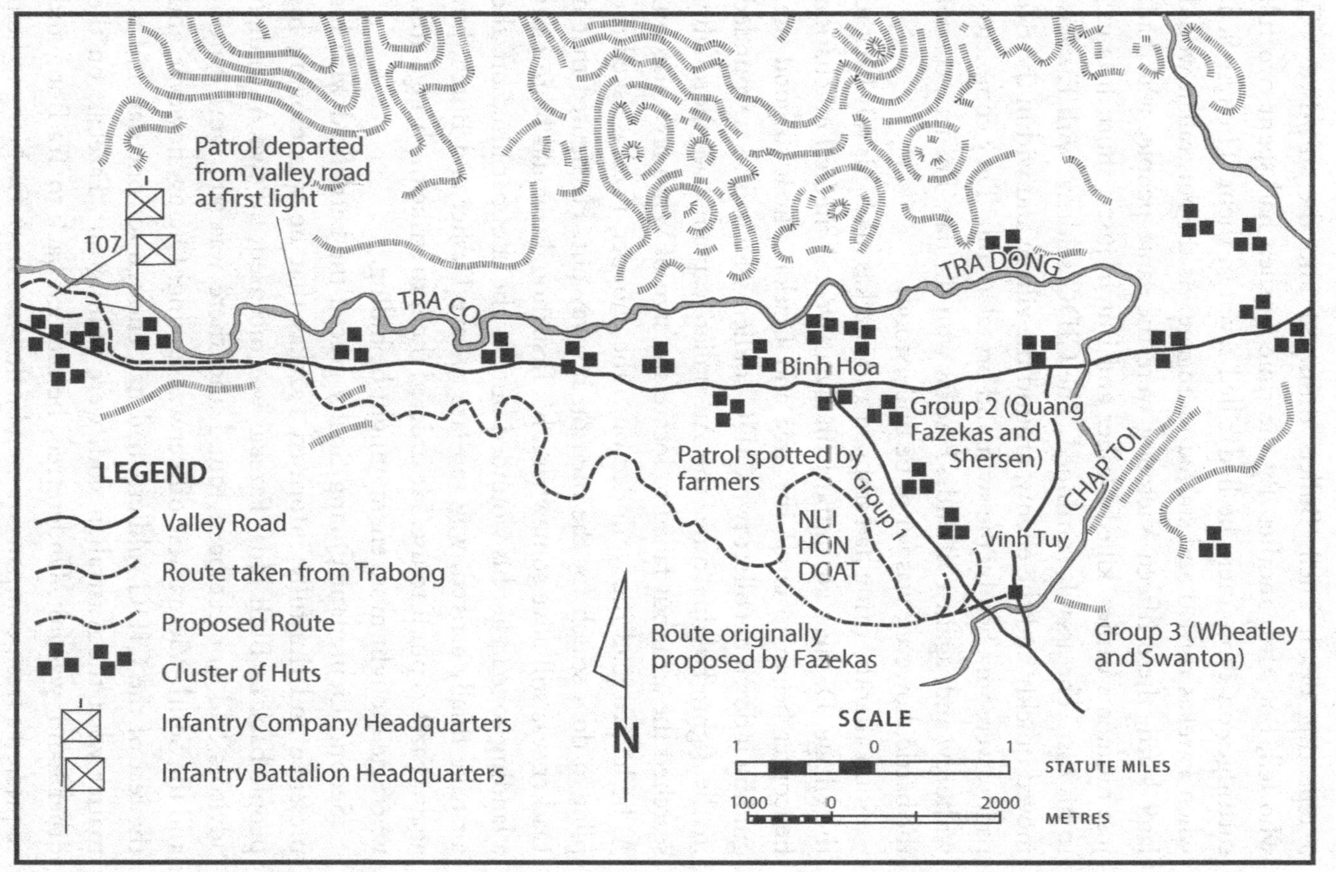

Patrol departed from valley road at first light
107
TRA CO
TRA DONG
Binh Hoa
Group 2 (Quang Fazekas and Shersen)
Patrol spotted by farmers
Group 1
NUI HON DOAT
CHAP TOI
Vinh Tuy
Route originally proposed by Fazekas
Group 3 (Wheatley and Swanton)
N
SCALE
1 0 1
STATUTE MILES
1000 0 2000
METRES
LEGEND
Valley Road
Route taken from Trabong
Proposed Route
Cluster of Huts
Infantry Company Headquarters
Infantry Battalion Headquarters

The chattering sound of the American's fully automatic rifle was a repeating death knell. Bullets thumped into the surprised VC, who fell, one after another. By the time Sershen had spent two full cartridges on those men, he had killed seven of them. The rest fled, when Fazekas turned and started to engage. As the Australian would later learn, these fifteen Vietcong were the same people, who had, just moments earlier, killed Dasher and Butch, just a short distance, to his east. The assault continued. The CIDG soldiers, with Fazekas, moved quickly and the enemy, around the village and within the rice paddy, were smashed by the swift and brutal assault. They completely withdrew and, against all odds, Fazekas won the day. The true cost of the battle, however, was yet to be understood.

Soon after the firing had stopped and Fazekas made his way back to the village, Dasher's air support finally arrived. A medical evacuation helicopter began to circle the area and Fazekas put it to good use, guiding it down to collect two CIDG soldiers who had been wounded in the fight. By this time, the Australian captain had thoroughly searched the area, but failed to locate any sign of Wheatley's platoon. As he helped load the wounded onto the chopper, Fazekas asked the pilot to do a search for the men on his way out. He figured that if Dasher was still alive somewhere, his first thought would be to clear a landing zone to get his wounded out. As the chopper lifted off, the airstrike finally arrived, way too late to save Dasher and Butch, but again, Fazekas put it to use. He ordered them to strike the bridge area, where he thought more enemy might be hiding.

Second Lieutenant Quang finally graced the battlefield with his presence and dutifully informed Fazekas that he was moving his people back to Binh Hoa. Fazekas was incensed, his two Australian advisors had not yet been found and there was still work to do, and the South-Vietnamese officer was leaving? Quang, however, and the rest of the CIDG soldiers, had had enough for one day and no matter what the Australian said, were pulling out. Fazekas, on the other hand, was not. Undeterred, he radioed back to Tra Bong and requested a fresh company of men be flown in from Da Nang to help him continue the search.

Chapter 24

Hours later, close to 1800, on the same day Dasher and Butch had died, choppers flew in with the fresh troops and put down in a landing zone, about one kilometre to Fazekas's north. The Commanding Officer of the Special Forces at Da Nang, Lieutenant Colonel Charles Ross, was with them. Fazekas led his new team back onto the battlefield, but it was now getting dark. They continued to search for the missing Australians and set-up defensive positions. At about 2230, the search was called off. It was simply too dark and too dangerous to continue. They set-up ambush positions in the night and killed two passing VC solders, but Wheatley and Swanton were not heard from. Throughout the night, members of Wheatley's team started to come in and were helping Fazekas put together the story of what had happened.

At dawn, the following morning, Fazekas was approached by Private Dinh Do, who told him that he had helped Dasher carry Swanton out of the rice paddy and into the trees. The young man was very emotional and led Fazekas directly to the place, where he had helped drag Swanton into cover. There, no more than fifty metres into the jungle, they found the bodies of the two Australians, in a hollow. Dasher and Butch were lying together, side by side, and they had both been shot through the head. Ronald Swanton had been 29 years old, Kevin Wheatley was just 28. Shattered, Fazekas called in a chopper and had his two mates' bodies airlifted to a marine base at Chu Lai.

Before the chopper had even put down, word had started to spread that the invincible Dasher Wheatley was dead. The news was met with disbelief, sorrow, and rage that his CIDG men had abandoned him. It rippled through and devastated the morale of three armies, those of Australia, the United States, and South Vietnam. So many people from all three armies had either known and loved Dasher, or they had heard about the man's extraordinary exploits and reputation. Hundreds of children, throughout South Vietnam, would keep a lookout for the smiling face of 'Ned Kelly', the friendly Australian they all loved, who would come and give them treats and soap, but that warm smile would never be seen again. Dasher still had soap and treats for them, in his pockets, when he was killed. Wheatley's death ignited a deep hatred of the local troops that would take a lot of work to heal. If it ever did.

Fazekas, Sershen and Din Doh at the scene, recovering Butch's and Dasher's bodies

Captain Felix Fazekas had Dasher's mates go through his private belongings back at Tra Bong and get them ready to be sent back to Edna and the family. While putting it all together, the diggers found a series of drafted cables he had intended to send back to his favourite pub in Sydney. The messages show how much Dasher had been looking forward to returning home. There were eleven of these messages, the first said simply, Ten days until Dasher Day, the second said, Nine days until Dasher Day, the third, Eight days until Dasher Day, and so on, until the final message which said, Roll out the barrel, the king is here!

Back home in Sydney, Edna Wheatley was at work, at her new job at the Campbelltown RSL. Edna had just started her shift, on what was her first day at the new job. A man, with a Scottish accent, came to her and told her she was to take off her apron and go downstairs. Edna was confused because she had just clocked on, but he insisted she follow him. She did and, when she got downstairs, Edna saw an army officer, with a cane swagger stick under his arm, standing beside a padre. She intuitively knew that Kevin was dead. Being given this news at work was tough and Edna was in shock, reeling from the news that the man she loved was gone and life, as she knew it, was over. Through all the white noise and immeasurable grief, one horror stood at the front of Edna's mind. She now had to dry her tears, go home, gather her children around her, look them in the eyes and shatter their lives.

Any parent will agree that the most overpowering instinct they have is to protect their children and shield them from pain and suffering, in any way they can. Edna knew that telling the kids that their father had been killed and that he would never be coming home, would likely cause them more pain and suffering than any other event they would ever experience, at least, until they had children of their own. Inflicting this pain on them went against every parental fibre she had, and she desperately did not want to do it, but she had to. There was no one else. She took a deep breath, straightened her back and the officer and the padre took Edna home, to break the hearts of her four little children.

When news reached Kevin's mother, Poppy, that she had lost another son to the military, she was utterly devastated. Separated from her son's body, by thousands of kilometres, she was desperate to get to him and hold him, one more time. Life would never be the same for her and the loss was so devastating, it would prove impossible to recover from.

News soon reached the men at 1RAR and the battalion, which had already suffered many horrible losses, were devastated, to a man. None were surprised that Dasher had stayed with Butch and done what he had, but many were finding it impossible to believe that Dasher Wheatley, *the* Dasher Wheatley, was dead. Most people, who knew the man, had believed he was invincible, that nothing could kill him. Many a fully grown and war-hardened man were reduced to open tears, when they learned that their champion had been killed and the heartbreaking way in which it had happened. Only a few days after Dasher's death, a letter arrived at their camp, written by Dasher Wheatley, himself, and addressed to the boys of 1RAR. He must had written and sent it, just days before his death. In it, he told them how much he had loved his few days there with them and that they should all keep their heads down and stay alive and he would see them all again. This letter is now on display at the 1RAR museum in Townsville.

For his gallantry and tenacity in leading the assault to clear the village and try to find Wheatley and Swanton, Captain Felix Fazekas was awarded the Military Cross. The Military Cross was a tier-three British military decoration which was awarded to officers, in recognition of acts of exemplary gallantry during active operations against the enemy. He was also awarded the American Silver Star. Captain Fazekas was eventually moved out of Tra Bong, and the base's new command had the extra barbed wire torn down and it was no longer the reliable fortress it had been. Fazekas would eventually be promoted to major and would survive the Vietnam War.

For their actions that day, the South-Vietnamese Government would posthumously award both Wheatley and Swanton the South-Vietnamese Military Merit Medal, which was the highest decoration the Republic of Vietnam could bestow on a military person, during the Vietnam War, for valour in the face of the enemy. They were also awarded the Republic of Vietnam Gallantry Cross with Palm, also known as the Vietnamese Gallantry Cross or Vietnam Cross of Gallantry. That medal was awarded, in recognition of deeds of valour or heroic conduct, while in combat with the enemy. Although it was obvious that Dasher was going to, once again, be put up for a gallantry award by the Australians, and that that award might even end up being the highest of all, the Victoria Cross, Swanton was not.

Butch Swanton had literally given his life, trying to carry a wounded comrade to safety, under withering, direct and deadly enemy fire. This is a deed, which has been carried out by other men, before and since, and one that has seen many people recognised with medals, up to, and including, the Victoria Cross. At the time of writing this book, however, Ronald Swanton has never been formally decorated, in any way, by the Australian Government, for giving his life for a fellow soldier. As with Dasher's missing awards, however, this is a mistake which could be corrected today, if only someone tried.

Chapter 25

BRING HIM HOME

There was a funeral service for Wheatley and Swanton at the Tan Son Nhut Chapel in Vietnam, which was later destroyed in a mortar attack in 1968. Jim Sharp flew up from Hue and attended the funeral, where he laid a wreath on the coffin. There are some heartbreaking photographs of the service, images of pallbearers carrying the coffins, draped with Australian flags and one of a South- Vietnamese general, pinning a gallantry medal to Wheatley's coffin. There were rumours that this was done out of frustration that the Australian Government would not allow the South-Vietnamese to award Dasher and Butch medals. The same rumours suggest that an American advisor did likewise, pinning his own Silver Star to Dasher's coffin, out of respect. This has never been verified and neither of these medals was ever presented to the family.

Today, a military funeral or ceremony, like the one for Butch and Dasher, that day, is called a ramp ceremony. This is a memorial service for a fallen soldier, which is usually held at the airport, prior to the departure of the aircraft, carrying the deceased's body home. The name, ramp ceremony, implies the moment when the pallbearers carry the coffin up the rear ramp of the aircraft and set it down inside. Today, a fallen soldier would receive a full military funeral, at the place of their family's choosing, back in Australia. Ramp ceremonies are hard on the soldiers left behind, it is a last goodbye to a fallen mate and the last chance for closure and reflection. The diggers are often buoyed, however, by the knowledge that their mate is being taken away, to be laid to rest at home, with family and loved ones.

South Vietnamese General, pinning Gallantry Award to Wheatley's coffin

For the people back home, burying a family member, who has been killed overseas, is obviously extremely difficult. The opportunity to do so, however, offers the family members a degree of closure that would, otherwise, be impossible to obtain. In some cases, they are grieving someone who left home, long ago, someone they did not have a chance to say goodbye to. Being involved in laying their loved ones to rest and completing the circle of life is crucial. The idea of denying a family this opportunity would seem outrageous and cruel, but leading up to 1965, Australia did not bring their fallen soldiers home. They were usually buried in overseas military cemeteries and the families never received the closure they needed. This led to some family members, including children, never being able to fully believe that their father had really died. Some people report living out most of their lives, expecting their father, son or brother, to walk through the door, at any given moment.

Jim Sharp laying a Wreath on Dasher's coffin

The Wheatley family were expecting Kevin's body to be brought home and were stunned when they were told that this was not going to happen. The only way to get him back would be for Edna to pay all the costs of flying him home, herself, plus all the funeral expenses. This was something that Edna, now without a husband and no longer able to pay her rent, could never afford. The minute Dasher had died, his pay had been stopped and Edna was on her own. There were no government or insurance payouts when a soldier was killed in action. For the Wheatleys, this was both financially and emotionally devastating and extremely confusing. The government of Australia had had no problem paying the costs of training Kevin, sending him to Vietnam and getting him killed, so why on earth did they have a problem bringing him home? If he had lived, the government would have flown Dasher back, when his tour was over, anyway, but now that he laid down his life for his mate and distinguished himself in the field, repeatedly, they refused.

The family begged and pleaded, as did Dasher's mates in Vietnam, but the Australian Government refused to budge. Kevin was going to have to be buried overseas, unless something could be done. Kevin's mother was inconsolable, she had now lost two sons to the Army and when she learned that she was going to be denied the chance to bury her own son, she was incensed and soon became frantic. The idea that Kevin would be buried, so far from home, was destroying her, but the Australian Government did not appear to care. They dug in their metaphorical heels, folded their figurative arms across their emblematic chests, and stuck their allegorical noses in the air.

Back in Vietnam, when the Americans found out that Dasher was not going to be sent back to his family, they were thunderstruck. Lieutenant Jim Lowe was totally distraught over the news that Dasher had been killed. When Lowe heard that the Australians were not going to pay to send their hero home, he was stunned and immediately commandeered a helicopter. Jim flew all over South Vietnam visiting advisers, both American and Australian, and had them donate a part of their pay to help raise money to send his friend back to his family. Dasher's death was already big news in

Australia and now that the media had caught wind of the fact that the government was not going to bring their hero home, they were running with it. The story was everywhere.

Kevin's mother after his death

The people of Australia were mortified and soon, there was a huge outcry, to bring Wheatley home. It is hard to overstate how big this story was. Dasher's death was part of a series of events that would create an enormous amount of pressure on the Australian Government, to change their longstanding policy of not returning war dead to their families. As it turned out, a large amount of this pressure came from

American servicemen, who had made friends with Australian soldiers in Vietnam. These proud American men had watched their Australian friends die and were infuriated, when they saw that they were not being sent back to their families. One notable case, like this, was Warrant Officer Second Class Scott, who was just the second member of the AATTV to be killed in action.

Father of two, Scott was killed when what had been a routine search of a village, near Tam Ky, went horribly wrong. An unexpected burst of enemy fire hit Scott and he died of his wounds, that afternoon. He had earlier made friends with American Master Sergeant Jordon. Scott had told the American that if he were to be killed, he wanted to be returned to his family. This would have seemed obvious to the American, as it was the policy of the United States military, at the time, to return fallen servicepeople home, no matter what it took. US forces will move heaven and earth to recover the body of a fallen comrade, even to the point of risking the lives of other servicepeople to do so. The idea that Australia, despite its wealth and highly capable military, would not even attempt to bring a fallen soldier home defied belief.

After Scott had been killed, Master Sergeant Jordon applied for leave, so he could accompany Scott's body to Australia, but soon learned about Australia's policy and that Scott was to be buried in Malaya. Outraged and wanting to ensure his friend's request, to be sent home, was honoured, Jordon spoke to an American general and asked if he could borrow an aircraft to fly Scott's body home himself. The American general, to his enormous credit, said 'yes', but this gesture of goodwill did not go down well with the Australians, who refused to allow it. The American general was, to say the least, appalled. Undeterred, Master Sergeant Jordon began a collection among other American advisors, who were all too willing to contribute their hard-earned money to the cause. This inspired the Australian soldiers to do likewise and soon the master sergeant had raised enough money, on his own, to pay to send Scott home. He soon found himself on a flight, escorting Scott's body back to Australia. Warrant Officer Second Class Scott was buried in the military section of Rookwood Cemetery in Sydney, at no expense to the Australian people.

Chapter 25

The media in Australia soon heard about this and ran the story. Australians are a proud and patriotic people and the policy of not returning the fallen was unknown to most. When Australians learned that American serviceman, disgusted by Australia's apparent lack of reverence for the fallen, had to step in, to send Warrant Officer Scott home, they were outraged and highly embarrassed. People did not like how this made Australia look to their 'big brother' nation, across the Pacific. Most Australians believed that this highly embarrassing incident would shame the Australian Government into changing its policy and start bringing its fallen home, with all the dignity and ceremony they deserved, but they were wrong. The Australian Government was totally unmoved and still refused to listen to the cries of the Australian people.

So it was that just a couple of months later, when Warrant Officers Wheatley and Swanton were killed in action, the Australian Government promptly turned its back on the families and refused to pay to bring them back. Not even rumours that the Queen was going to award Dasher the Victoria Cross changed their minds, so, as had been done a few months earlier with Scott, Dasher's mates set out to do it themselves.

Back home, one of Edna Wheatley's sisters, who was working with a solicitor, continued writing to the papers and did all she could to keep the story alive. Edna approached her RSL for help, the very place she worked, but to no avail. As Kevin had let his membership lapse, they told her that he was no longer a member and so no longer their concern. The RSL, at the time, did not believe that men should be returned home, anyway, and did not want Edna to make a fuss about it. The fact that she worked for the RSL was particularly embarrassing for them, so she was promptly told to keep her mouth shut and go away.

Soon, a journalist, Pat Burgess, weighed in on the argument. Pat had been in Vietnam as a war correspondent and had spent time with Dasher in country. The two men were friends and Pat felt strongly that Kevin should be brought home. He started writing scathing articles and the RSL became incensed, firing Edna for bringing them into disrepute. This was the way the RSL helped, when Dasher died, by directly trying to block efforts to bring him home and ensuring that his family, now, had no income, whatsoever. One can only imagine how angry this would have made Dasher, were he still alive.

Jim Lowe continued his collection for Dasher in Vietnam. In his book, *A Jarhead's Journey*, and in interviews he has done, since the war, Jim insists he raised enough money to bring Kevin home, with enough left over to go towards the children's future. None of that money ever found its way to Edna, however, and none of it was ever used to bring Kevin home. The family believes Jim is genuine and that he did manage to raise the money, but clearly, something broke down, somewhere along the line, because the cash never came through. It could be possible that it was caught up in army and government red tape, somehow, and was forgotten about or that it was misused. We will never know. It is probably a blessing that Jim Lowe died, still believing that the money, he worked so hard to collect, did help his friend, but in the end, his efforts had been for nought.

Back in Australia, *The Don Lane Show* got involved and started a fundraiser on television to raise money to help the family, who were now without an income. The fundraising was successful. A lot of Australians called in to support the Wheatleys, but the money was not going to arrive in time to bring Dasher home. Amidst all this, the Australian Government refused to budge. Eventually, it was reporter Pat Burgess who came to see Edna with some very welcome news. He told her that a group of businessmen had just set-up a company, called Pine Grove Funeral Homes. Pat said they were willing to pay for everything and, in the end, it was these four men who paid to bring the Australian hero home, covering all the costs of his flight and funeral.

When it finally happened, Kevin 'Dasher' Wheatley's funeral was massive and done with full military honours in Campbelltown, New South Wales. Edna and George attended the funeral, but the girls did not. As was the norm, in those days, it was felt that young children should never be subjected to funerals, so they missed out. As a result, they never received the appropriate closure and understanding that their father was truly gone, forever. George Wheatley can still remember the day, and the huge procession of people, who were standing to attention on either side of the road and saluting, as the coffin was wheeled past. For George, this moment was important. The years ahead were going to be extremely difficult, he needed to understand that his father was gone, forever.

Kevin Wheatley's funeral in Australia

On the other hand, Dasher's oldest daughter, Phyllis, went, for many years, still convinced that it had all been a mistake. She thought that her father was alive and going to return to her, someday. For years, whenever she saw another man, who looked like Dasher, walking towards her in the street, Phyllis mistakenly thought it was her father, finally coming home. The continuous cycle of hope and disappointment was devastating, and it was not until years later that she finally accepted that he was really gone.

The money raised by *The Don Lane Show* did come through, but Edna refused to spend it on herself. It was never going to be enough to buy a family home, so knowing how best to use it was difficult. In the end, the money was put into a trust, and she put it towards the children's education and used it to help them obtain home loans and other things, later in life. The outpouring of generosity and show of outrage, from the Australian people, should have showed the Australian Government just how wrong it was on the issue of bringing the fallen home, but it still could not grasp it. With hindsight, it appears that this should have been the easiest decision in political history, but somehow, it was not. If ever there was an example, of how disconnected politicians can become from the people, it is this.

It was not until 21 January 1966, that the Australian Government gave in to the enormous pressure it was still receiving over the Dasher Wheatley story and others like it. They finally announced that the bodies of servicepeople, who had died overseas, would be returned to Australia, fully paid for by the Commonwealth of Australia. This news was cheerfully received by the diggers, sailors and aircrew, fighting in South Vietnam. Coping with the many stresses, horrors and challenges of war is difficult, but, at least, this one had finally been removed. Since January 1966, Australia, like the United States, will stop at nothing to bring fallen servicepeople home. This is thanks, mainly, to the American and Australian soldiers in South Vietnam, the good people of Australia and the immovable legend that is Dasher Wheatley.

The total price of bringing Kevin Wheatley's body home, the sum that the Australian people apparently could not afford and that had caused such enormous political hurt was £300.

Chapter 26

THE VICTORIA CROSS

Rumours that Wheatley was going to be awarded the Victoria Cross started almost immediately after his death. The men at 1RAR had been told firsthand by reporter Don Simmons that Dasher was going to be put up for a VC and, frankly, none of them were surprised. Most of the men had decided, long ago, that, being who he was, Dasher was bound to end up with a Victoria Cross, one way or another. Once the blokes from 1RAR had been told how Wheatley had died, it was painfully obvious to them that a VC should be issued, as soon as possible.

Captain Fazekas compiled a comprehensive report and sworn statement, immediately after the action, which outlined, in detail, what had occurred and how Dasher and Butch had died. The Australians quickly collected sworn statements from the two CIDG men who had best witnessed Wheatley's final moments, Private Dinh Do and the medic, Private Vo Trong Chan. It was based on these statements, as well as official after-action reports, that a case for awarding Dasher a suitable gallantry award would be made.

Captain Fazekas's sworn statement was, as follows…

I was the senior adviser from the Australian Training Team Viet Nam(sic) which accompanied a Vietnamese Civil Irregular Defence Group on a search and destroy operation on 13th and

14th of November 1965. Also with them were Warrant Officer K. A. Wheatley and Warrant Officer R.J. Swanton. At about 1320 hours on 13th November 1965, Warrant Officer Wheatley reported contact with Viet Cong and subsequently reported that Warrant Officer Swanton had been hit in the chest and very seriously wounded, requesting medical evacuation which at that time was not possible.

Radio contact was then lost.

The next morning, we found the bodies and from there it could be judged that Warrant Officer Wheatley had dragged and carried Warrant Officer Swanton some 200 meters from the open area to a thicket where he had a last stand with grenades. The two Warrant Officers had been shot through the head several times from a close range. The estimated number of Viet Cong was originally a platoon in the fighting area, subsequently re-inforced(sic) with the remainder of the company.

CIDG Medic, Private Vo Trong Chan, swore the following…

I was with the Combat Reconnaissance Platoon on 13 November 1965 at 1340 hours when our element was engaged by VC (Viet Cong) at BS 456848.

At approximately 1435 hours one of the Australian advisers (WO Swanton), was hit in the abdomen by a round. I bandaged his wound and told the other Australian (WO Wheatley), that the wounded Australian was nearly dead. The VC (Viet Cong) firing was very heavy, and I asked the Australian (WO Wheatley), to run with the rest of the Combat Reconnaissance Platoon and leave the dying Australian.

He refused and started to half drag, half carry the wounded Australian from the open rice paddy where they were under heavy machine gun fire by this time. I saw him (WO Wheatley) drag him to a thicket about 200 meters away.

This was the last time I saw either of them.

Chapter 26

Private Ding Do testified the following…

> I was a member of the CIDG Combat Reconnaissance Platoon on 13 November 1965 at 1340 hours when our element was engaged by the VC (Viet Cong) at BS 456848. The fight increased as more VC (Viet Cong) converged in the area from the village at BS 455845. I saw WO Swanton carrying a wounded CIDG and he dropped the CIDG and I saw that he (WO Swanton) had been wounded in the stomach while carrying the wounded man. The other Australian (WO Wheatley) was returning heavy Viet Cong fire at this time.
>
> My platoon and the other platoon that was with us started to run away when I saw WO Wheatley half dragging, half carrying WO Swanton from the rice paddy to some heavy undergrowth. I helped him (WO Wheatley) in the last stages and asked him to run with us. He refused to leave his friend and he pulled the safety pins from the two grenades he had.
>
> I started to run when the VC (Viet Cong) were about ten metres away. Then I heard two grenades explode and several bursts of fire. This was the last time I saw the two Australian advisers alive. The next morning, I helped in the search and took Captain Fazekas to the position where I left them (WO Wheatley and WO Swanton) the previous day. They were both dead, shot through the head several times.

With these statements, the application for a suitable award began and it was clear that issuing a Victoria Cross, in this case, was vital. Dasher Wheatley was important to many people and his actions, openly and willingly, laying down his life, so that Butch Swanton did not have to die alone, mattered. Dasher had left a mark, as permanent as the tattoos on his own arms. He had missed out on awards, in the past, but the impact, his final actions were having on the people of Australia, was enormous. The story was in every newspaper and on every TV station. The sheer level of mateship, valour and dignity, Wheatley had displayed, had made the idea of not decorating him inconceivable. He had put the matter so far beyond dispute that, to do otherwise, was simply unfeasible. Wheatley was going to get something for what he had done, but what award should he receive? His actions had been so courageous and selfless that giving him anything less than the highest award for valour on earth, the Victoria Cross, appeared to be totally out of the question. But was it legal?

Debates over the Victoria Cross are common and are often led by people who are ignorant of how the award works. Many have claimed over, the years, that one VC, or another, was only awarded for political reasons and that the action, in question, had not been worthy. This thinking shows a stunning ignorance of the Victoria Cross and its history. Yes, each VC awarded is investigated and scrutinised, within an inch of its life and yes, each award must pass multiple levels of authority before being approved, but at the end of the day, even that is not enough. The final decision, on whether any Victoria Cross will be awarded, comes down to one person and one person alone, the Queen of England. Only the current sitting British monarch can award a VC, so no matter how much behind-the-scenes planning and plotting people think politicians might do, to get a VC over the line, none of it matters.

To imagine, for a moment, that the Queen of England cares about how one Australian politician or another is going in the polls is absurd. To think that she would jeopardise the institution of the Victoria Cross, to help an Australian politician get elected, is beyond laughable. Yet, for a Victoria Cross to be awarded for political reasons, as some people claim they often are, this is exactly what she would have to do. This applies as much to the Victoria Cross for Australia, issued today, as it did for those issued during the Crimean War, almost 170 years ago and everyone awarded, in between. It is up to the King or Queen of the day, and the Royal Family takes the Victoria Cross extremely seriously. There is no chance they would act in a way that may damage the Victoria Cross's standing as not only the pre-eminent award within the British Empire, but the highest and most revered decoration on the planet.

Sadly, tall-poppy syndrome is very real in Australia and VC recipients are far from immune. There are almost no examples of Victoria Crosses, which have been awarded throughout history, where at least one armchair general or one blowhard historian has not disputed its merit. These people, who were never there, at the time of the action, declare from the comfort of their office or living room that, 'in this case, a Victoria Cross was not warranted and was probably given for political reasons alone.' The arrogance of this is breathtaking.

However, over the almost-60 years, since Dasher's death, there are no examples of this, regarding his actions that day, not one. Indeed, many people who served with Dasher, as well as countless other career military people, will happily tell you that they and their colleagues have had many conversations about Victoria Cross recipients, over the years. These same people will insist that, in all their time within the military, they have never heard one single person, on the record or off, cast any doubt on the fact that Dasher Wheatley should have received a VC, for what he did that day. This is almost unheard of and shows how warranted the Victoria Cross was in Wheatley's case. It was by no means a given, however.

Perhaps, the most famous example of a deserving action that was not recognised with a Victoria Cross, was one that was witnessed by many people and said to be the most stunning, courageous, and remarkable act of valour in history. These were the actions of Australian soldier, Albert Jacka, at Pozières in 1916. Already a world-famous Victoria Cross recipient from Gallipoli, Jacka was fighting on the Western Front and had just been blown up, while sheltering in a bunker, when he committed an act of gallantry that is said to be one of the finest ever recorded. Jacka emerged from the bunker and saw that a group of about 80 Germans had captured around 50 Australian soldiers. Jacka charged and, despite, being shot seven times and being knocked off his feet by bullets and hand grenades three times, the Australian got back up and continued what became a one-man bayonet charge, against 80 highly trained and heavily armed German soldiers, all of whom were focused on nothing, other than trying to kill him.

Jacka slammed into the group and, with bayonet alone, killed about fifteen before they finally put him down. His actions had so dramatically inspired the 50 captured Australians that they turned on the Germans and attacked barehanded, defeating them totally. Fifty

Germans were captured, and the line was retaken. Jacka, somehow, survived this action, although, only just. After a stint in hospital, Jacka returned to the Western Front and committed at least two more similar acts, before the end of the war, one at Bullecourt which saw him receive a second Military Cross and one at Polygon Wood, where he received nothing.

Charles Bean, the official Australian war correspondent of World War I and the founder of the Australian War Memorial, described Jacka's attack at Pozières as, 'The most dramatic and effective act of individual audacity in the history of the AIF.' Despite this, and the many witnesses, who included high-ranking officers, who saw the whole thing, Jacka's recommendation for a VC was downgraded and he only received a Military Cross. The reasons for that were clear. The commanding officers, above him, hated Jacka and refused to give him another VC, no matter what he did. At his funeral, Jacka was described as Australia's greatest ever frontline soldier, and few would challenge that. Charles Bean said that anyone who knows the story, knows Jacka earned the Victoria Cross, three times.

This shows that, while politics alone cannot possibly see a person be awarded a Victoria Cross, it can and regularly does, stop people from receiving one. In Dasher's case, trying to block his VC would have been politically insane, but there was another glaring problem. The Victoria Cross was not normally awarded for actions in a war that did not involve the British and the British were not in Vietnam. This meant that no one was sure that Dasher could be awarded a Victoria Cross, no matter how much they wanted to give him one. In the end, the matter would not be resolved until a staggering 13 months after Dasher's death and would even see the Queen, herself, stepping in to personally change his citation. This was something that had never been done before and has not happened since and goes to show that when Dasher did something, he did not do it half-hearted.

So why does all this matter? What is the Victoria Cross and why does it mean so much to so many around the world? A lot of people are aware that the Victoria Cross is the highest award that Australia, or any other country within the Commonwealth, can award a member of its armed forces, for gallantry in the face of the enemy. In truth, however, the VC is much more than that. It is the highest award any person can receive for any reason. A good way to illustrate this is that when you are awarded a Victoria Cross, you get the postnominals VC, after your name. For example, Albert Jacka VC. There is no Knighthood, no PhD, no Grand Order or any other kind of decoration that is higher. Not even a Nobel Prize comes before a VC. It is always first and supersedes all other decorations and postnominals. The Victoria Cross is arguably the highest award that has ever existed, certainly, in modern times. The history of the Victoria Cross is as extraordinary and unique, as the people who receive it.

The Victoria Cross rose from the ashes of the Crimean War, a conflict which lasted from October 1853 to March 1856 and saw the United Kingdom and France fighting together against Russia. The Victoria Cross was to be the great leveller, a means by which a passionate Queen Victoria could remove restrictions of class and rank within the military, when considering decorations. This was something the United Kingdom had so far failed to do. Before the VC, the highest award, the UK could award, was the Order of the Bath, however, only senior officers could be admitted to the order. Junior officers and lower ranked men could only expect to receive a promotion in the field or a mention in the General's dispatches, at best.

There was growing awareness of this inequity, back home, mostly due to the reporting of war correspondents, such as William Howard Russell of *The Times*. While fighting alongside the French in the Crimean War, the British noticed their allies awarding something, called the French Legion of Honour, to men of all ranks and backgrounds. This was their most prestigious award and had been instituted by, none other than, Napoleon Bonaparte, in 1802. It was not reserved for officers or nobility, but was given to any person who deserved it. Queen Victoria had taken note of this, as had a Liberal Member of Parliament, Captain Thomas Scobell. In December 1854, Scobell made a famous speech to the House of Commons, where he declared that an order of merit should be awarded to persons serving in the Army or Navy for distinguished and prominent personal gallantry.

He suggested that every grade and individual, from the highest to the lowest, should be made admissible for this award.

About a month later, the Secretary of State for War, the Duke of Newcastle, added that it should be '… a new decoration, open to all ranks, for a single act of valour in the presence of the enemy.' Shortly after this, Lord Panmure, the new Secretary of State for War, took up the challenge and began working with Queen Victoria's husband, Prince Albert, to design this innovative decoration. The Queen, herself, took great interest in this new award. She kept personal diaries, every day, which show just how much she cared about her fighting forces. She wrote about the men, almost every day, both during and after the war. Queen Victoria felt strongly enough about the idea of the VC to intervene in the original design of the Cross. Initially, the words to be inscribed on the medal were 'For the Brave'. The Queen changed the inscription to 'For Valour' because she felt that the word 'valour' speaks to courage and boldness in battle, while 'brave' reflects courage or endurance in any situation. The Queen did not want anyone to think that she was suggesting that the only 'brave' men in her forces were those who had received the cross.

In 1855 Lord Panmure set out to commission a jeweller, to design and produce the Victoria Cross. Hancocks of London had only been in business for seven years, but had already gained a reputation for craftsmanship and excellence. They had obtained royal appointments with other monarchies in Europe for which they had received wide acclaim. This helped Queen Victoria finally choose Hancocks' founder, Charles Hancock, to make her new Victoria Cross. It was then decided that Hancocks should make the award from bronze, taken from captured cannons. Legend suggests that all Victoria Crosses are made from melted-down Russian cannons, which were captured during the Siege of Sevastopol during the Crimean War in 1854. This is incorrect, on several levels.

Firstly, the two 18-pound cannons, in question, were not melted down. They are still in one piece and are currently on display in Woolwich Barracks in England. Hancocks simply slices a piece from the 'cascabel', taken from one of the cannons and uses that piece to forge the crosses, whenever they need to. The cascabel is the part at the rear of a muzzle-loading cannon that is used to secure arresting ropes to help deal with the weapon's violent recoil.

Secondly, the cannons used are, in fact, Chinese, not Russian, and almost certainly were not captured in Sevastopol. Authors and experts have argued strongly that the cascabel, used today, is not the same metal as used in the past. It seems almost certain that although the cascabel has been used exclusively since some time during World War II, and at other times before, there have been periods where some other bronze was used. This suggests that there are some VCs, out there, which were made from metal from an unknown cannon. Whatever the case, what remains of the cascabel is held today, under strict security, at Ministry of Defence (MoD) Donnington, a British military base, situated to the north of Donnington in Telford, Shropshire.

What remains of the Cannon Cascabel

This lump of metal is of incalculable value, which is ironic, considering the metal it is made from has a monetary value of almost zero. The level of clearance and security, required to enter the vault where the metal is kept, is on par with that required to access areas where nuclear weapons are kept. Few people have ever seen it in person. For Hancocks, the task of re-using this cannon bronze has proven a nightmare. The gunmetal is so hard that the dies, which Hancocks used, kept cracking, forcing the jewellers to sand-cast the medals instead of striking them. As a result, the Crosses must be finished by hand and are much more detailed and tougher than they would have been if they had been die-stamped.

In the 1850s, Hancocks worked hard to produce a prototype cross for Queen Victoria's inspection. However, that first proof did not impress the Queen. Her Majesty said on examining the proof, 'The Cross looks very well in form, but the metal is ugly; it looks copper and not bronze and will look very heavy on a red coat.' So, Hancocks went back to the drawing board. Eventually, a new prototype Cross was made and delivered to Her Majesty, which she did approve of. Although this medal was die-struck in copper, she loved it so much that the only changes she made were to add some laurel leaves to the suspension bar and a little 'V' beneath it. That prototype remains in the royal collection at Windsor Castle and is one of the Royal Family's most treasured possessions.

In June 1857, the British Empire awarded the first Victoria Cross. It was decided that a pension of £10 a year should be paid to each recipient and Queen Victoria insisted to Lord Panmure that she would present every Victoria Cross, herself, at the ceremony. This was something of a surprise to Panmure, but set a precedent that stands, to this day. Even now, the VC is presented by the British monarch, wherever possible. Over the years, the Cross itself has changed little in appearance. In the early days, Victoria Crosses issued to navy personnel came with navy-blue ribbon, while those issued to army men had crimson. The blue ribbon was eventually abolished, in favour of crimson for all, after the Royal Air Force was formed in April 1918. That same navy-blue ribbon is now used for the George Cross. The George Cross is the civilian equivalent of the VC.

Chapter 26

The Prototype VC produced for the Queen in February 1856

Hancocks keep a book, called Victoria Cross Records, in which the details of every VC, issued since 1857, are written. Each entry contains the name of the awardee, the date and a secret code that describes marks made on the roundels and raised parts on the back of each Cross. This secret code etched into every VC is so it can be identified, if it is lost, stolen or goes up for sale. A number is given to each VC, in order of its issue. Whenever it comes time to make a new batch of Crosses, Hancocks contacts the Ministry of Defence.

Then, the Ministry of Defence shaves a slice of bronze off the lump of metal it holds at the Telford base, enough to do twelve medals, and delivers it to Hancocks, under extreme security. Once the batch of twelve medals is produced, Hancocks holds them unissued until the Ministry of Defence advises them that a Victoria Cross has been awarded. The Cross is then engraved with the recipient's name and the date of the action, then dispatched under tight security. The second a Victoria Cross is engraved, it goes from being an unremarkable bronze medal, worth almost nothing, to the most sought-after award on the planet. Today, a Victoria Cross, issued to an Australian, can sell at auction for as much as $1,500,000. There is nothing else like it in the world.

Since its inception, and until the time of writing, 1361 Victoria Crosses have been awarded to 1358 individual men. Three soldiers have been awarded it twice, two British servicemen and one New Zealander. Of those 1361 issued, only 101 have been to Australians. There were six Australian VCs awarded in the Boer War, 64 in World War I, two in North Russia, 21 in World War II, four in Vietnam and four in Afghanistan. The first Victoria Cross, ever awarded to an Australian, was to Brigadier General Sir Neville Howse VC KCB KCMG, dated 24 July 1900. Its number in the register is 479.

Throughout its history, the Victoria Cross has created a unique and powerful legacy. This legacy stems from both its unusual heritage and from the fact that it has become almost impossible to be awarded a VC. As the twentieth century progressed, and more people were sent to war than ever before, fewer VCs were granted. Since the end of World War II, only 11 Victoria Crosses have been awarded worldwide. When awarded a Victoria Cross, one becomes an international celebrity overnight. While the Cross is an incredible honour, the public recognition that comes with it can place considerable pressure on people who are already dealing with difficult memories of war and death.

Chapter 26

Victoria Cross Front

From 1975 onwards, Australia began to develop its own honours system. This system gradually replaced the imperial system of British honours, which ceased to be available to Australians in the late 1980s. In January 1991, the Australian Government instituted a group of awards, for bravery, gallantry, and conspicuous service, in the Australian honours system, with the Victoria Cross for Australia retained as the nation's pre-eminent award for valour. The fact that the Queen allowed Australia to do this is no small thing and something all Australians should be grateful for. To this day, she oversees every VC awarded, including the new Victoria Cross for Australia, which is still identical to the original, in every way. They come from the same vault and are engraved by the same hands as the Imperial VCs and undergo the same scrutiny before awarded.

Victoria Cross Back

Chapter 26

Like the Imperial VC, nominations for the Victoria Cross for Australia are rare. Each one needs to be supported by signed statements from at least three eyewitnesses and the nomination is considered by the Australian Operational Joint Force Commander and then, the Chief of Joint Operations. With these officers' support, the nomination is then forwarded to the Minister for Defence through the Chief of the Defence Force. It is then investigated and approved by the Australian Government and when the citation is finalised and signed by the Governor-General, it is forwarded to the Queen, who has the final say.

To this day, the Royal Family still regards the Victoria Cross with reverence. They are the last stop in the vetting process for the award, the ethical fortification that ensures the Cross is never tarnished by political objectives or other prejudices. It has been reported that the Queen holds a roundtable discussion with members of her family, about each citation. All this history would have been weighing on Queen Elizabeth's mind, when she was finally presented the Victoria Cross citation for a bloke named Kevin Wheatley.

Chapter 27

AN AUSTRALIA HERO

The final decision on what award Dasher should receive, and the time it took to get said award granted, was an unprecedented 13 months. During this agonising time, there was a considerable amount of correspondence between the British and Australian Governments over what should be done. The two nations were not simply arguing over whether it was legal to award a Victoria Cross for actions committed without the British being present, they were dealing with other issues, as well. There were serious problems with Wheatley's citation, and it is thought that it was this that caused most of the delay.

Drafting and completing the final citation proved to be no small feat, as it had to be changed several times. In the original draft, three of Wheatley's actions had been cited. The action, when he was killed in November, formed the spine of the citation, but it also included details of his deeds in May, when he had saved the little girl and the action in August, when he had led the uphill bayonet charge. It was decided that two of these actions, those from August and May, were superfluous and should be removed, as his gallantry and sacrifice on 13 November merited a Victoria Cross, on their own. It is now believed that this is the reason that Dasher did not receive those two awards, not because they were not warranted, but because they had been considered to have been already dealt with. Removing them from the VC citation undid this and no one ever took it upon themselves to reactivate them.

Regarding the legality of the Wheatley VC, one could argue that it should have been clear, in 1965, that it was legal, as there had been a precedent. On 14 January 1881, an army surgeon, named John Frederick McCrea, displayed outstanding acts of valour at Basutos in South Africa. McCrea was recommended for the VC and when the application was put to the War Office by the Colonial Office, the War Office was reluctant to approve it. They thought that, because McCrea's act of gallantry was performed within the Colonial Forces and in a battle which was not approved by the British Government, he might not be eligible. The Colonial Office argued successfully that this should not render McCrea ineligible for the award and the War Office relented and finally approved it. John McCrea's Victoria Cross was gazetted on 28 June 1881 and the cross was presented to him on 25 October 1881.

The time it took, to get Dasher Wheatley's citation completed, was extraordinary. Even though the original recommendation for the award had been signed by Brigadier Jackson on 31 December 1965, the amended citation was not sent to the Governor-General until 18 October 1966. It was cleared, signed, and forwarded to London, on the same day. As with all VC citations, the Queen took Dasher's case incredibly seriously. She left no stone unturned, as she considered if a Victoria Cross was indeed warranted. While reviewing the details of Dasher's actions on 13 November 1965, the Queen expressed concern about the wording that had been used in his citation and another 14-day delay ensued.

The Queen had taken exception to the fact that the citation stated that Wheatley had, 'discarded his rifle and radio'. She was fully aware that an Australian soldier would not discard his weapon, in any circumstances, so ordered that the words 'his rifle' be removed. Moreover, she felt that the wording did not make it clear that Dasher had used his grenades on the enemy and that he had been shot to death. She felt that it needed to be made unmistakably clear that the grenades were used against the enemy and not for the purpose of 'self-immolation'. She ordered that, as Wheatley had displayed such 'outstanding valour', the citation should leave no doubt in anyone's mind that his actions were 'of the exceptional quality required for a Victoria Cross'. This wonderful piece of clear thinking by Her Majesty, corrected a mistake that should never have happened in the first place. Her intervention extinguished any doubt that Dasher had died a hero and showed that he clearly deserved the highest recognition for his sacrifice. It was the first and only time in history that a monarch has directly intervened in the wording of a Victoria Cross citation.

The citation was amended, once more and sent back to London. On 15 November 1966, the Queen of England finally approved the awarding of the Victoria Cross to Kevin Wheatley. Kevin's final Victoria Cross citation was announced in the *London Gazette* on 15 December 1966 and read, as follows:

> The Queen has been graciously pleased on advice of Her Majesty's Australian Ministers to approve the Posthumous award of the VICTORIA CROSS to 29890 Warrant Officer Class II Kevin Arthur Wheatley, Australian Army; Training Team Vietnam.
>
> On 13 November 1965 at approximately 13:00 hours, a Vietnamese Civil Irregular Defence Group company commenced a search and destroy operation in the Tra Bong valley, 15 kilometres east of Tra Bong Special Forces camp in Quang Ngai Province. Accompanying the force were Captain F. Fazekas, senior Australian Adviser, with the centre platoon, and Warrant Officers K. A. Wheatley and R. J. Swanton with the right-hand platoon.
>
> At about 1340 hours, Warrant Officer Wheatley reported contact with Viet Cong elements. The Viet Cong resistance increased in strength until finally Warrant Officer Wheatley asked for assistance. Captain Fazekas immediately organised the centre platoon to help and personally led and fought towards the action area. While moving towards this area he received another radio message from Warrant Officer Wheatley to say

> that Warrant Officer Swanton had been hit in the chest, and requested an air strike and an aircraft, for the evacuation of casualties.
>
> At about this time the right platoon broke in the face of heavy Viet Cong fire and began to scatter. Although told by the Civil Irregular Defence Group medical assistant that Warrant Officer Swanton was dying, Warrant Officer Wheatley refused to abandon him. He discarded his radio to enable him to half drag, half carry Warrant Officer Swanton, under heavy machine-gun and automatic rifle fire, out of the open rice paddies into the comparative safety of a wooded area, some 200 metres away.
>
> He was assisted by a Civil Irregular Defence Group member, Private Dinh Do who, when the Viet Cong were only some ten metres away, urged him to leave his dying comrade. Again he refused, and was seen to pull the pins from two grenades and calmly awaited the Viet Cong, holding one grenade in each hand. Shortly afterwards, two grenade explosions were heard, followed by several bursts of small arms fire. The two bodies were found at first light next morning after the fighting had ceased, with Warrant Officer Wheatley lying beside Warrant Officer Swanton. Both had died of gunshot wounds.
>
> Warrant Officer Wheatley displayed magnificent courage in the face of an overwhelming Viet Cong force which was later estimated at more than a company. He had the clear choice of abandoning a wounded comrade and saving himself by escaping through the dense timber or of staying with Warrant Officer Swanton and thereby facing certain death. He deliberately chose the latter course. His acts of heroism, determination and unflinching loyalty in the face of the enemy will always stand as examples of the true meaning of valour.

Once the citation had been finalised, the palace sent the order through to Hancocks of London to remove a Victoria Cross from the vault and engrave it with Dasher's name and the date of his action. This was the first Victoria Cross issued, since the Korean War and the first to an Australian, since World War II. The Cross was inscribed and sent, under immense security and strict secrecy, to the Governor-General of Australia, Lord Casey. It arrived safely and the simple and ancient piece of carefully crafted bronze was finally ready to present to the Wheatleys.

The naming on Kevin's original Victoria Cross

By this time, Edna Wheatley still did not have a telephone. A member of her local mayor's office showed up at her front door and informed her that she was to get the family together and accompany him down to the mayor's office. He refused to tell her why, just that she needed to do as asked. Reluctantly, Edna did as she was told and when the family arrived at the mayor's office, they were greeted by a horde of media. This is how the Wheatley family was told that the Queen was going to award Kevin the Victoria Cross for the valour he had displayed in South Vietnam, over one year earlier. They could have been given this news in the comfort and privacy of their home, but the mayor obviously felt that the opportunity for some free publicity was too good to pass up.

Chapter 27

George Wheatley showing friends his father's South Vietnamese medals

At this stage, Edna did not know what the Victoria Cross was, although her eldest son George did. He had heard rumours that his dad might be going to receive the award and had done his research. Even, after learning what he could about the VC, however, there was no way he, nor the rest of the family, could have known how much it was going to affect their lives. The Wheatleys were invited to Canberra, where the Governor-General of Australia, Lord Casey, was going to present Kevin's posthumous Victoria Cross to his family. The children were excited, Edna was nervous. She struggled to scrape together enough money to buy the children new clothes and shoes for the big occasion. The girls were given matching hats and ensembles, with new stockings and slingbacks and George looked a million bucks. Other family members were there, as well, including Kevin's mother and his sister Florence. They boarded a plane together and touched down in Canberra, to a huge press of media and military representatives.

Wheatley family arriving in Canberra for the Victoria Cross investiture

As they walked across the tarmac, microphones and cameras were shoved in their faces, every step of the way, the young family quickly discovered that the Victoria Cross was something incredibly special and that their lives were never going to be the same again. They had all learned what Kevin had done, by then, how he had laid down his life for his mate. They knew that this made him a hero, but the scope of the fame that comes with a Victoria Cross was something none of them were prepared for. Colonel Russell McNamara, who had overseen the Training Team in Vietnam, was there on the day and took young George under his wing. It was going to fall on George to receive his dad's VC from the Governor-General and the enormity of what was happening was weighing heavily on the thirteen-year-old boy. Colonel McNamara stayed at his side and guided him throughout the day, later becoming a close family friend. George is the only child in history to have accepted a father's posthumous Victoria Cross.

Walking across the tarmac in Canberra with Colonel Russell McNamara

The family was taken to the Australian War Memorial and given a private tour of VC Corner, which is now known as The Hall of Valour. It is here that most of Australia's 101 Victoria Crosses are kept. At one stage, when the family was standing on the grass at the front of the AWM, the sprinklers suddenly came on and showered everyone standing nearby. The brief, but unscheduled, shower was greeted with peals of laughter and squeals of delight from the Wheatley children. It was a circuit-breaker from the growing nerves which had been building all day. After the tour of the memorial, the family was taken to Parliament House for lunch. Although receiving Kevin's Victoria Cross was a huge honour that the entire family received, with great pride, it would never fill the massive void left in their lives for the loss they had suffered. Today, any one of them will tell you that they would happily trade the VC for just one more day with Kevin, a final chance to see his smile and say goodbye.

The Wheatley children at the Pool of Reflection at the AWM

Word reached Dasher's mates that George had finally received his father's Victoria Cross. While they were all pleased to hear the news, it did little, to dull the hurt and the anger they were still feeling, over the way their mate had died. At the end of the day, Dasher had been abandoned, at his greatest moment of need and that fact was impossible to reconcile. The man had never asked anybody for anything and had always been first in line to help others, yet, when he had been the one in need, no one had been there for him. That hurt! Hatred for the local

CIDG troops was still palpable, especially among the men of 1RAR, who saw Dasher as their own. To them, Dasher had been sent away to the Training Team and had been killed, because the men he was trying to save abandoned him. They all knew that had 1RAR been there, that day, instead of the CIDG blokes, they would have stayed beside Dasher and never given an inch. They, as Captain Fazekas had done, would have smashed the Vietcong and Dasher and Butch would still be alive. They would have bloody well made sure of it. This was a sentiment, also felt by other members of the AATTV, Jim Lowe and every other US Marine who knew him. They were all deeply affected by Wheatley's death.

At the AWM with Colonel Russell McNamara

The Victoria Cross was welcomed by all. It had clearly been earned and not awarding it would have been an injustice none of them would have been able to move past, but it did not stop the pain. That is not what gallantry awards are for. They do not relieve the grief of families and friends, nor do they stop the nightmares of those who survive. In the minds of the men of 1RAR, the AATTV and everyone who had marched beside him, Dasher was always going to end up with a VC, anyway, one way or another. He was action plus, bulletproof, the perfect soldier, totally resilient and the ultimate professional. Dasher was never blasé or stupid about anything he did outside the wire, he was always calm and cool. He was a true battlefield commander, in the ilk of men like Albert Jacka and Harry Murray. His likes would never be seen again, and his nation was going to be all the poorer for his loss.

Signed photo from Governor General Lord Casey, presenting George Wheatly his father's Victoria Cross

Chapter 27

Today, Kevin 'Dasher' Wheatley VC is remembered in numerous ways. There is a Wheatley VC Memorial in Mawson Park, Campbelltown, New South Wales, the Wheatley VC Rest Area overlooking Lake George on the Federal Highway in New South Wales, and the Kevin Wheatley VC Memorial Wall at Dredges Cottage, Campbelltown, New South Wales. At Canungra Army Base in Queensland, the 'boozer' is called the Dasher Wheatley VC bar. There are numerous pictures of Dasher on the walls there, as well as plaques, bearing both his name and the letters AATTV, representing the unit he served with.

George, Lord Casey and the Wheatley Victoria Cross

The United States Army honour Dasher, to this day, by displaying his citation and photograph in the Hall of Heroes at the John F. Kennedy Centre for Military Assistance, Fort Bragg in North Carolina. In 1967, a trophy for an annual game, played by the Australian Services

Rugby Union Football team, was inaugurated in his name and a sports arena at Vung Tau, Vietnam, was named after him. Over the years, countless stories and poems have been written about Dasher, as well as a song, called 'Spirit of a Soldier'.

Governor General Lord Casey presenting George Wheatley a copy of They Dared Mightily

Chapter 28

LIFE GOES ON

The family stayed in Campbelltown for another two years and then, finally decided to move down the coast and try to escape the constant attention the Victoria Cross was bringing. Over the two years before they fled the city, there would be nasty incidents with war protesters, who tried to use Dasher's fame to gain publicity for themselves. Some protesters even went as far as to target the kids at school. On several occasions, the headmaster had to bring the children home, because they were being harassed at school and could not get out safely.

These malevolent protesters told the kids that their dad was a killer and a war criminal and verbally attacked them. This was extremely traumatic for the children, who were already trying to grieve the loss of their father. Hunting down defenceless children and telling them that their dead dad was a war criminal and a murderer is among the most deplorable and selfish acts, ever carried out by war protesters, in the history of Australia. The cruelty of this defies belief, yet, it happened repeatedly. Whenever there was a big story about the Vietnam War, reporters would show up at the family home and ask the Wheatleys what they thought of the war, including the children. Eventually, the attention became too much, and Edna decided to move the family to the south coast.

Life on the New South Wales south coast was a huge improvement. Nobody knew who they were, and the young family was able to blend into their new community and live like normal people. They moved into a rental house, across the road from the beach and tried their best to get ahead. Although, life was better there, it was still difficult for Edna, who was a single mother. There had been no life insurance, as was normal for a person killed in the line of duty and the Army does not do compassionate payouts, when they get someone killed. Not only did families of soldiers, who were killed in action during the Vietnam War, receive nothing, and have their source of income instantly removed, those living in married quarters were kicked out, immediately.

This was to happen to the family of Major Peter Badcoe, who was later awarded a posthumous Victoria Cross, for his actions in South Vietnam that had cost him his life. His wife and children, who had been living in military married quarters, at the time, were immediately kicked out. Their only source of income was cut off and they were told to move out the day after Peter had died. The Badcoes were given no financial support or any help to find a new place to live, but were, instead, turned out on the street and told to repay a portion of Peter's final pay cheque. As soldiers were paid two weeks in advance and Peter had been killed, before he had served those two weeks, the family had to give that money back and get out. Like the Badcoes, the Wheatleys were totally on their own.

By the mid-1990s Victoria Cross medals had become extremely valuable and Edna could no longer afford the insurance she had to pay to keep her husband's medals covered. While the Victoria Cross was in her home, the premiums were going to be impossible to pay and she would not be able to have the rest of the family's contents insured. At this stage, George had moved away and the girls spoke to their mother about the idea of selling the medals. At first, Edna was horrified by the thought of selling them, but there was no way she could afford to keep them. In those days, she kept the medals in a sock draw and if the house were to be broken into, they would have been found, stolen and never seen again. In the end, the decision was clear.

Chapter 28

Kevin loved Edna and all his children, and he was not interested in medals or awards, of any kind. Edna knew that, had he been able to talk to her, he would have insisted that she sell the medals and use the money to help his family. The idea that he would have wanted her to hold onto them, while she struggled to make ends meet, was ridiculous. The reason Kevin joined the Army, in the first place, was to look after his family by providing a wage. Clearly, if he thought selling the Cross would help them, he would have wanted it sold. Even had Edna tried to keep the medals, it was clear that there was no way she could pay the insurance premiums, which meant she would have been living with all her contents totally uninsured. The medals were too valuable to keep in the home and yet, Edna was still struggling to come to terms with the idea of letting them go. In the end, it took the advice from an old friend and former soldier, Donny Palmer, who finally convinced her to sell the medals. He knew it was what Dasher would have wanted.

Young family with picture of Dad

When Edna finally agreed to sell her husband's medals, she stipulated that no matter who purchased them, they must remain in Australia. This was an impressive piece of forward thinking by Edna and set the stage for a piece of national legislation, which would later be put in place, preventing any Victoria Cross issued to an Australian from leaving the country. The RSL, whose sole reason for existing is to help ex-servicepeople and their families, was outraged at the proposed sale. It did not bother trying to talk to the family and find out why they wanted to sell the medals, but, as it had done when the family had first tried to bring Kevin's body home, the RSL decided to interfere in something that was well beyond its authority. Led by then president, Bruce Ruxton, the RSL aggressively tried to block the sale of the medals and publicly attacked and vilified Edna in national newspapers and even on television.

News networks and papers, across Australia, carried the story that the Wheatley family intended to put Dasher's medals up for auction and it was not reported on kindly. At the time, dasher's daughter, Ellie, was starting a new teaching job in Sydney and was undergoing induction. As she arrived and began the induction, she was made aware of a large group of reporters, outside the building, who were trying to gain access. Ellie had no idea why they were there and, as they were in a government-run building, there was security present who were able to keep them out. During the induction meeting, Ellie could not help but notice the newspapers on her new boss's desk, each showing a photo of her father on the front page. The articles were talking about the upcoming sale of the medals, and some went as far as to accuse Edna of being a traitor and sellout. Ellie did her best to ignore all of this, but, during the meeting, her new boss was interrupted by a phone call.

When he answered the phone, a concerned look darkened his face and he said, 'I'm sorry, there is no one here by that name.' He hung up the phone then said to Ellie, 'Is there anything I should know about you before we sign your contract?'

Becoming more alarmed by the moment, Ellie said, 'No, why?'

He said, 'That was *A Current Affair* on the phone, they're asking for you.'

Chapter 28

'*A Current Affair?*' Ellie was confused, but as she looked again at the newspapers with her father's face on them, she began to piece things together. A terrible feeling washed over her that Ellie had not experienced since she was a little girl and being harassed by media and anti-war protesters. It was a feeling of being hunted. She could think of no other reason that people from the popular program, *A Current Affair*, would want to talk to her, other than the news that they were selling her father's medals.

Her boss said, 'Ellie, Derryn Hinch has been asking for you, by name and there is a group of journalists out the front. I'm beginning to suspect they're here for you. What have you done? Are you being investigated for something?'

Stunned, Ellie said, 'I haven't done anything.'

'Then, what's going on?'

Ellie pointed to the newspapers on her boss's desk and said, 'See that man on the front page. That's my dad. That's why they'll be here.'

There was a commotion from outside the office and Ellie saw photographers, through the window, trying to take her photo. The building's security officers were holding the media members back and Ellie had to be escorted out of the building and taken away by taxi. This was the new norm for the family, they were targeted and hounded by not just the media, but even members of the public, who were now calling them traitors. Edna was once physically attacked in the street in the Northern Territory, by a member of the public. All this pressure and hatred was coming as a direct result of the continuous attacks from the RSL. This overstepping of authority was unwarranted and highly inappropriate. It would cause enormous amounts of stress for Edna and the rest of the family, for many years to come. It did nothing to affect the outcome of the sale of Kevin's Victoria Cross and had little positive or lasting effect on the heritage of the VC, going forward.

All this ridicule did nothing to improve the lives of other Victoria Cross families, like the Wheatleys, either. Over the following decades, many more Victoria Cross families would find themselves in similar situations to the Wheatleys, being forced to sell their Victoria Crosses, for many varied and complicated reasons. It should be obvious to say that these are family decisions and no person, outside the family, has any right to tell them what they should or should not do with their medals. Yet, largely, because of the way the RSL acted, during this time, even today, families receive huge amounts of pushback when they attempt to sell their VCs. This pressure never helps and always comes from a place of ignorance, which shows how little people understand how much the Cross can complicate the lives of these families. For many, keeping their Victoria Cross is impossible.

Even at the time of the auction of Dasher's medals in 1993, the Americans had still not been permitted to award Wheatley's Silver Star for his actions on 18 August 1965. An application for the star had been blocked by the Australian Government, as late as 1981 and the idea of trying, once more, only to have the award denied again, was more than Edna could bear. A few years earlier, the medals had been mounted with an unissued Silver Star, as she had decided that she would never see her husband's real star. Edna needed them mounted, as she had to attend a ceremony at the Australian War Memorial, for the opening of VC Corner with Prince Charles. It was this unofficial Silver Star which was with the medals when they were sold and the same star that is on Wheatley's medals in the Hall of Valour, to this day.

In contrast to the RSL's interference and attacks, level heads eventually prevailed, and they started a fundraiser to raise money and help purchase the medals. Through the generosity of many good Australians, they raised a significant amount. Despite the difficult relationship they had built with Edna, the RSL would become extremely supportive of her, later in life. Over the years, they have gone to great lengths to help, as has Legacy, who have supported Edna, whenever she has needed it. They have been reliable advocates for the family over the journey, and Edna is very fond of the people from Legacy and the modern day RSL. She is deeply appreciative of the work they have done, not just for her, but for all war widows and families.

In the end, Kevin Wheatley's medals were purchased by media magnate, Kerry Stokes, with the aid of some of the money raised by the RSL. Mr Stokes was incredibly supportive of the Wheatley family and has since become a friend. He continues to support them, to this day, by attending remembrance events and unveilings in Dasher's name, whenever he can. Mr Stokes donated Dasher's medals to the Australian War Memorial in Canberra, where they remain on display there in the Hall of Valour, to this day. The struggle, to have Dasher's real Silver Star issued to the family, would continue for another 28 years and counting.

Chapter 29

THE SILVER STAR

During the 1970s, there was a fire in an archive building in the United States, where records of Kevin Wheatley's Silver Star action and his citation were kept. It is thought that Kevin's American records were destroyed in that fire, but the hard-working people in the US were able to verify and approve the award when Edna Wheatley applied for it again in 1981.

A letter to Edna, from the United States military, dated 26 May 1981, confirms that they tried to get the Silver Star presented, but the Australian Government had denied them permission. This had been due to Australia's policy of not allowing servicepeople to accept foreign awards. After this disappointment, the Wheatley family gave up and did not try again for another 37 years. In 2018, the family, with the aid of friends, pushed for the Silver Star again. The Americans approved the award, but still could not find a copy of Dasher's citation. The Wheatley family understandably felt that it would be improper to accept the Star, without a citation explaining what it had been awarded for. Without the details of Kevin's actions, it was just a piece of metal and ribbon.

It was going to take a lot of man-hours, to comb through American buildings full of military records, to try and find something they could base a new citation on, and that meant money. The Wheatleys asked the Australian government if they could put in a formal request to have the Americans do this. They were told in an email that they could, but the family would have to cover the costs. This was an expense the family could not cover, however, and one that the Australian government, perhaps, should have. A short time after this, George was emailed by a member of the Australian government, who told him he would not be permitted to accept his father's Silver Star. The email stated that the government had investigated the case and proven that the Silver Star had already been awarded. The extent of this investigation, as it would turn out, was to Google a picture of Dasher's medals, on the Australian War Memorial's website, where they saw that there was already a Silver Star attached.

By 2020, some very good people were asked to step in, and these were people in high positions. This group was spearheaded by Chris Hartley, a friend of the Wheatley family, who went to extraordinary lengths to help. Under Chris' guidance, it did not take long for these, high ranking people, to understand what was happening. They were unhappy that one of Australia's most famous and loved soldiers, had still not received an approved gallantry award from the 1960s, so took steps to open the way. The matter should have been simple, the Silver Star is an American decoration, and the American military would know if it had awarded a Silver Star to a Victoria Cross recipient or not. As the Americans were insisting the Silver Star had not been issued, and Australian policies no longer forbid foreign decorations from being awarded, there should have been no issue.

Using official Australian accounts of what had happened on 18 August 1965, the outline of a dummy citation was put together by volunteers. These volunteers included a hard-working member of Australian Honours and Awards. In 2020, Chris Hartley, was giving a talk to members of the US Navy and US Marine Corps, at The United States Naval Academy, at Annapolis, Maryland in the United States. Chris approached a US Marine Corps General about Wheatley's Silver Star, and the General told him that, by using the information which the volunteers had put together, he could write an official

Silver Star citation for Wheatley. It was soon announced, however, that as he was a Marine Corps General, and Dasher's Silver Star had been recommended by the United States Army, he was not legally permitted to do so.

Thanks to all this work, however, the Americans now had a clear understanding of what Kevin had done that day, and now that the Australian government was no longer objecting to it, they were free to hold an investiture. An investiture is a ceremony where someone is officially awarded a decoration and the Americans intended to make sure Dasher's Silver Star was handed over, with all the dignity it deserved. Although, it was unlikely there would be an official citation to accompany the Silver Star, the details of Dasher's actions could be read out and a certificate of some kind could be presented. This process had taken a staggering 55 years, the longest for any Silver Star to an Australian Vietnam veteran in history. The news was met with incredible relief and great appreciation from the Wheatley family. Some outstanding people had stuck their necks out to get this done, but frustratingly, the story of Dasher Wheatley's Silver Star had a few twists and turns still to come.

The original idea for the investiture was to fly to the United States and have the US President, himself, present the award. This was proving difficult to organise, however, despite the efforts of one American general who sat with the president on the Joint Chiefs of Staff. In early 2020, then President Donald Trump, was completely obsessed with the upcoming election. It was felt by those close to him that he would not pay attention long enough to get his head around the idea of presenting the Silver Star. There was even a possibility, that a high-ranking American Officer, could bring an entire US Naval fleet to Australia and present the Star on board an aircraft carrier, but the first pandemic in 100 years put a stop to that. The next obvious choice was to have the US Ambassador to Australia present the Star at the Australian Embassy in Canberra, as the embassy is considered American soil. Sadly, however, President Trump never bothered to appoint an ambassador to Australia, and the fast-approaching 2020 US election was creating so much turmoil in the United States that the investiture was not acted on until November.

Chapter 29

On 13 November 2020, the 55th anniversary of Kevin's death, the Australian War Memorial would hold a remembrance service for him. This event was to be attended by 30 family members of the Wheatley family who would lay wreaths and listened to Kevin's story be read out. The ceremony would also be attended by the Australian Governor-General, David Hurley AC DSC, Keith Payne VC AM, Kerry Stokes AC, Brendon Nelson AO, a representative of the United States military and many more. It would be the perfect opportunity for a high-ranking American to finally conduct the investiture and the Silver Star was mailed from the United States to Australia for the occasion. Mail, during the Covid-19 pandemic, was not as fast as normal, however, and the Silver Star did not arrive on time, so, once again, the Star was not awarded. President Trump lost the election, a few weeks later, and the ensuing chaos meant there was no way the investiture was going to happen in 2020. So, the family and its group of volunteers, went back to the drawing board.

It was understood that the new American President, Joe Biden, was going to appoint an ambassador to Australia, so the Americans decided to wait for that to happen. Once again, politics and Covid-19 worked their magic, and it took six months for a date to finally be set. President Biden announced he was putting Caroline Kennedy forward to be the new US Ambassador to Australia and a date of 4 August 2021 was locked in, to present Dasher's Silver Star. This was fantastic news and the idea that Caroline Kennedy might be the person to conduct the investiture was very exciting. Caroline had served as the United States Ambassador to Japan from 2013 to 2017. She is the only surviving child of former President John F. Kennedy and First Lady Jacqueline Kennedy Onassis.

It was a little ironic that it was Caroline's uncle, Ted Kennedy, who had flown into Vietnam, on that day in 1965 and soaked up all available aircraft, so that George Wheatley's dad, Dasher, had to carry his wounded radio operator through the jungle for five hours. George was looking forward to having a bit of a joke with Ms Kennedy about that, but even this ceremony was eventually called off. The highly infectious Delta variant of Covid-19 was spreading fast through New

South Wales. As state borders had been closed in June, it was going to be impossible to stage the ceremony. An email was sent out by the American Government to those invited, stating that this was regrettable, but that it would reschedule when things returned to normal.

Unbelievably, at the time of writing and some 56 years after the event, Kevin Wheatley's Silver Star has still not been issued. Thanks to the work of many wonderful people, however, there is no doubt that it will be. It is only a matter of time. Once the investiture has taken place, work can begin on trying to have Dasher's missing Australian awards issued, those from May and August 1965. That will almost certainly be more difficult than getting the Silver Star was, but most worthwhile things are difficult and awards like this matter.

Together in the USA: Phyllis Everill (third from left), Jim Lowe (second from right) Paul Everill (far right)

Although the Silver Star and other gallantry awards like it are extremely important ways of recognising valour and sacrifice, they do not heal all wounds. They do not replace dead husbands, fathers and sons and they do not make life easier for those who receive them. They do little to help the families of the fallen and can, sometimes, make things worse. This is understandable, however, as that was never their purpose. What they can do is inspire people to greatness and help keep alive the stories of all servicepeople.

Every decorated veteran has a story that defies belief, and telling these stories is a great way to help people learn about military history. It is easy to sell the story of a decorated veteran, they are always entertaining. For better or worse, we are naturally drawn to tales of violence, valour, hardship and greatness and it is by sharing these tales that we show people the broader picture of history behind them. We can introduce the reader to the stories of the people behind the decorated veterans, people whose stories are equally as important, but might have otherwise been forgotten. It is simple marketing that is vital to long-term remembrance. There is no award on earth, save, perhaps, the American Medal of Honour, that does this as well as the Victoria Cross.

When awarded a VC, a person is written into the history books and the nation's psyche forever. This can never be undone. We hold these people up as something remarkable and put them forward as examples the rest of us should aspire to, few more so than Kevin 'Dasher' Wheatley VC. As we read and learn, we, mere mortals, can only look on in awe and say, 'Good on ya, Digger, we will remember you. Lest we forget.'

EPILOGUE

Throughout the decades since Kevin's death, many people have gone to great lengths to remember and honour his sacrifice. This extends to his children, grandchildren and now his great-grandchildren. There is no doubt this would have meant the world to Dasher, especially if he were to have seen his great-grandson, Cohen, who when asked by his teachers to dress up as a hero from a book he had read for Book Day, decided to dress up as Kevin.

Kevin's Great Grandson, Cohen, dressed up as Dasher for Book Day

Epilogue

The following is a collection of thoughts from various people who knew Kevin Wheatley or who were in some way affected by his life and death. These short compositions are told, in their own words and are here to help us understand why Dasher's story is so important and how deeply his sacrifice touched people. With the help of these people and others like them, Dasher Wheatley will never be forgotten.

Warrant Officer (ret) Keith Payne VC AM, AATTV Vietnam

Losing Dasher was sad. Of cause, being an outstanding Australian, he knew Swanton well and he was not going to leave him. Butch was dying and he was still carrying him, so yeah, it was incredibly sad. It was sad to lose a character like Dasher. He was Dasher, he was a character; he had that bit of bushie in him, even though he came from the city.

He was outstanding in his own way because of his character. He was obviously a brave man, everything the bloke did was tactically sound; it was not just being stupid. I am sure Dasher knew that Butch was dying, but as far as Dasher was concerned, he was helping his mate. I can see that. Swanton had become his responsibility, you do your job. He wasn't going to leave him in a paddock, we don't do that.

Lieutenant (ret) Jim Lowe, United States Marine Corps Vietnam

I'm out in the field on November 14th and I get a radio message that Dasher and Swanton are dead. From what I understand, they were outmanned and outgunned. The other Aussie, Butch Swanton, got hit with machine-gun fire and Dasher told the rest of them, 'I'll stay here with Butch and hold them off, you guys retreat.' He stayed with Butch, he tried to get Butch evacuated but couldn't get a helicopter in. I think his last words over the radio were, 'My God, someone help us!' He stayed there and he took a bunch of Vietcong with him. He used his grenades, but they finally overran him.

I was asked to go down and identify the body, because I knew him, and they needed it verified. They knew if anyone could identify him, I could. So, I went down and identified the body. I went to the memorial service after, which I didn't remember doing, at first, until I looked at my letters to my wife and remembered that I did. I told my wife, if that had of happened here, we'd have had a helicopter out. We would have had help on the way. And I felt, I don't know, I felt kind of guilty. If I would have been there, I could have at least paid back some things.

The Aussies didn't automatically bring their dead people home. So, I got a helicopter and took up a collection. I was payroll officer at the time, so I was able to go all over Vietnam to see the advisors. By then I was pretty well known. I collected enough money to help send Dasher's body home. Dasher lived hard, and he fought hard, he was good people. It's like the bible says, anyone who lays down his life for a friend…

Senior Sergeant Tim Britten CV (Private 1RAR ret)

I can honestly say I always knew about Dasher Wheatley, along with the other VC recipients from Vietnam, Keith Payne, Ray Simpson and Peter Badcoe. I remember learning about them in my earliest school days and the resulting Anzac Day services. Through subsequent classroom discussions and teachings, I had instilled in me a deep admiration for the Australian soldier, none more so than our Victoria Cross recipients. Even though, their actions took place well before I was born, I looked up to them and learned about them. I wanted to be like them and wanted a chance to prove myself, to be tested, as they had been.

On becoming a young man, I followed my heroes into the Australian Regular Army and, like Dasher, found myself standing on the parade ground of the First Battalion Royal Australian Regiment. Dasher had served several years in this place and was promoted to sergeant and then warrant officer there, prior to his posting to the Training Team. I knew I was in a good place at 1RAR. The Battalion was proud of Dasher and what he had done, stories would often be retold of the many actions that saw him become legend.

I still find it hard to comprehend the sacrifice he made and the most incredible display of loyalty and mateship he exhibited. As his good mate lay dying on that battlefield, Dasher could have saved himself and probably, lived a long life to spend time with his wonderful wife Edna and his four children. He could have easily turned and run to safety, but he did not. He stayed with his mate and gave him the comfort he needed, to meet his end. This was the soldier's soldier, the Australian's Australian, and if I stop and really think about what he did, its almost too much to comprehend.

His was an act that defies normal human understanding, but that was Dasher, he was not a normal man. It is because of this action, and others like it, that Kevin 'Dasher' Wheatley became a legend. Not only within the military, to inspire others and be discussed over a beer in an army boozer, but a legend of humanity and mateship for everyone.

Getting to know and becoming mates with Dasher's son, George, is an honour I truly cherish. He is a great bloke and a good mate. He loves his mum, family and country, exactly what I'd expect of the son of such a great man.

George Wheatley (son of Kevin Wheatley VC)

I remember being in the backyard with my younger sisters Phyllis, Ellen and Leeanne. Mum had started her first day of work at her new job at the Campbelltown RSL. Suddenly, Mum came through the side gate, accompanied by an Army Chaplain and a RSM, both in uniform. Mum was visibly upset. I knew immediately something had happened to Dad.

Mum told us what had happened, that Dad was KIA . It was hard to fathom, it must have been incredibly difficult for Mum to give us that news. We all cried and hugged. I was stunned. I thought it couldn't be true. The last time I had seen Dad was before he went to Vietnam in February 1965. I thought of the letters I had from him and all the cherished memories. Through all the emotion of that day, and following days and even years, my thoughts often turn to the good memories of Dad.

Home was a happy place, even better, when he was home from the Army and not away on his training trips and that trip to PNG. I remember Dad bringing home Army ration packs and the days when he was home with us. We would play cricket and football in the backyard, my sisters played on the swing set, we had barbeques with Dad's mates, visits to see Grandma and Dad's sister, Aunty Florence. We lived next door to an orchard and Dad would practise his golf swing and I would retrieve the golf balls. Life would never be the same in so many ways.

Even before Vietnam, Dad had a huge reputation as a wild, humorous and caring man. After talking with Dad's mates, they all said they would have expected nothing less from Dad then what he did that day. It was in his nature, the courage, determination, love of his fellow human beings. After his death, the stories of Dad being recommended for a Victoria Cross came out and the media became more intense and started harassing Mum and us kids. I was the eldest, nearly 13 years old, but I was expected to grow up straight away. It was hard on all of us, especially mum. Whenever there was a story about Vietnam in the media, Dad and Butch came up. The Vietnam War was a war which was on nightly television, we saw Aussie heroes dying for their mates and country, all the time. Cameras and reporters came to our school, our home, Grandma's place, even my local footy field. Mum was our strength, through all of it. I think people have an illusion about the Victoria Cross, that it comes with fame and fortune. The fame come, sure enough, but not the fortune. There was no insurance money, no pay cheques and mum had to support us, on her own.

After I received Dad's Victoria Cross from Lord Casey, representing our family, Dad was no longer just our father. He was Kevin 'Dasher' Wheatley VC, and he belonged to the nation, as well. Everyone had a story about Dad, you would have thought the whole Army had served with him. Throughout school, whenever I was in trouble, I would be told that I was not living up to Dad's reputation. Who could have? From the moment the VC was announced, life would never be the same for us. I was barely a teenager, and I was looked on as the eldest son of a Victoria Cross recipient, not as George. I remember once being approached by a man who told me that his dad deserved a medal from Vietnam and got nothing, but my dad got the VC which was not fair. I asked him if his dad was alive, he replied 'yes'. I said, 'Mate, you've got more than me.'

Epilogue

One of my favourite descriptions of my dad was written by his commanding officer, Colonel A. V. Preece DSO MVO.

> How does one describe Dasher? On first meeting him there was no doubt here was a personality. He wore his cap at a rakish angle and had a slightly crooked smile. He was a friendly soul with an expression that suggested a devilish sense of humour with a large dose of the devil don't care, fuck you for the conventional. He only had to walk into a room or join a group to lighten it up. This cheerful disposition and potential for fun had an effect on everybody. And yet, to see this in him was only to see a part of the man and who he was. He was a very capable professional soldier and possessed in(sic) abundance of these qualities and more, which set him apart from the rest.
>
> If I were to summarise my recollection of Dasher, it is part humorous and practical joker, part delightful larrikin, part fine, professional soldier. A very likeable fellow but most of all a loyal caring mate. A man amongst men whose bravery and example will never be forgotten, especially by those who served with him.

After Dad's medals were sold, Kerry Stokes was on television and talking about Dad. I rang his office after the show, and he got back to me straight away. He told me that we make heroes out of sports stars and politicians, but it's people 'like your dad and especially your mum who are the real heroes'. He said that Dad was the type of bloke he would have loved to have a schooner with. That meant the world to meat the time.

I often wonder what drives people to do extraordinary deeds like Dad's. I thought of joining the Army myself, but was told that having a Victoria Cross in the family was an extremely hard heritage to carry into the service. Dad's legacy lives on through many memorials and many stories, some true, some not so true. I am sure Dad would be pleased his memory lives on, through his children, his grandchildren and great grandchildren. Kevin Arthur Wheatley VC 'DASHER' was a man I am proud to call my dad.

Phyllis Everill (eldest daughter to Dasher)

I struggled, for years, to acknowledge my dad was gone and never coming home. I wasn't allowed to go to his funeral, no closure, the seed to my denial. At 10 years old, I couldn't accept he wasn't going to just turn up and take us on another trip to Sydney and across the Harbour on the ferry to Manly. I looked for him everywhere, I guess, consumed by a multitude of feelings and thoughts, which were conflicted with mixed messages, my childhood view on what the adults around me were telling me, how I should think and feel. Denial, anger, sadness, hatred, guilt, and selfishness, long before understanding and pride of his actions on that day.

Life changed quite quickly and dramatically, after the news of Dad's death. I remember being escorted home from school by the principal to avoid waiting photographers, people talking and Mum, sad and very protective. It was such an emotional time for me, caught in my emotions and the emotions of others. Where's my dad, why is Mum so sad, why am I so jealous that my Nan is paying more attention to my sister.

I recall my first real memory of attending an Anzac Day service, getting up well before dawn and travelling to Rooty Hill, afterwards having hot soup at the old wooden club hall and listening to stories about mateship among soldiers. Dawn services are now always where I feel connected to Dad. I rarely miss them. Most of the time, I go silently with my husband in amongst the crowd. Some, though, have been extra special, at Currumbin in Queensland with Dad's mates, Donny Palmer and Ron Workman, with Teddy Kenna VC and members of 3RAR on Norfolk Island and in Canberra, where I marched carrying Dad's flag.

Over the years, growing up, becoming an adult, marrying and having family of my own, there have been a number of times that have triggered memories and feelings, some, of course, more special than others. The trip to Canberra to be presented with Dad's VC, all decked out in the latest fashion twinset, hat, slingback shoes and stockings, only to be caught in an unexpected sprinkler system watering the lawns still makes me laugh.

Epilogue

The rest area dedicated to Dad, located on the Federal Highway to Canberra, on the shores of Lake George, always gets a toilet stop or proud salute, as we pass. Even a chuckle, as one of Dad's mates once said to me, 'Dasher would be laughing and making jokes about having shit put on him now!'

My most endearing memories, though, come from connecting with some of Dad's oldest friends.

It was 1994, I was 39 years old and married with four children. I accompanied Mum to Norfolk Island, for a reunion with 3RAR and during that time, I asked Donny Palmer to tell me about my dad, I wanted to get to know him, not about what he did on that day, other things about him that made him the person he was. Donny laughed and together with Ron Workman said 'I guess you're old enough now to hear it all' and we stayed up late into the night, laughing and crying and telling stories. It was like my wake for Dad. I learnt a lot from that night and every other time we got together, from that day onwards. Donny has since passed and I miss him dearly.

Jump forward a few decades and my eldest son Ben meets and marries an American girl and settles in the US. With the help of the internet, he found Jim Lowe and his son Dasher. I made contact, hoping one day we'd meet. In the meantime, I was given a copy of his book *A Jarhead's Journey,* which had a few chapters dedicated to Dad. The cover photo on Jim's book was taken by Dad when they were out on patrol, another one of his larrikin tricks, where he asked Jim to toss him his camera, so he could capture him out of his usually neatly pressed uniform. In 2014, I was fortunate to finally meet, in person, along with my son Ben and husband Paul. We met at young Dasher's home near Chicago, it was the most memorable day. Jim shared many precious memories with us of his Aussie mate, who he held in such high regard. He very emotionally shared the incident of why his son is named Dasher. We all cried together at his heartfelt story.

'Here, look at my lovely family. They are here only because of your father.'

Jim gave me photos and signed my book with these heartfelt words.

> 'Your dad and family have a special place in the hearts of the Lowe family. Thank you so much for arranging our get-together. What a pleasant honour. Wishing you all the very best.'

With young Dasher, it felt like I was meeting my other brother, he was extremely proud of who he was named after. Sadly, Jim is gone now, too, he was a wonderful man.

Jim Lowe helped me contact Jim Sharp, another US marine, featured in Dad's life in Vietnam. I spent 4 days staying with Jim and his wife Tessie in their home in Phoenix. It was a very special time for us, more laughs, stories and photos shared from their time in Quang Tri together, I will always hold these in my heart. This was when I learnt how he and his wife made a trip to Australia to visit Dad's grave. Unfortunately, we didn't get to meet then, it was a time when my sister, whom he contacted, thought he was just another person claiming to be a close friend (which by the way often happened) and the call-out was ignored. Jim is not in the best of health now and his memory is failing, but I still have contact and facetime regularly, I feel blessed to have had the opportunity to get to know my dad and the impact he has had personally on the lives of those men that truly could call him his mate.

And to my lovely mother, who protected and nurtured us through her most difficult years, my brother and sisters and I are so grateful and proud, we love you and thank you for sharing your story too. Our heroes. Dad would be very proud, firstly, of his wife, who did such a damn good job of raising all his children, grandchildren and great grandchildren, as they are of him.

Ellen Roach (Daughter of Dasher Wheatley)

I was seven years, old when Dad was killed, so I can still remember clearly how life was when he was still with us. Dad was away a lot with his work in the Army. We lived in Campbelltown in Patterson Rd, and Dad caught the train to work and home, as we did not have a car. We would all have our baths in the afternoon, prior to Dad getting home and sit on our front steps and wait eagerly for Dad to arrive. His coming home was always such a happy and special time.

When Dad had days off, he used to take us kids on outings. Those outings were such a treat for us, as we led quite a simple life. I say simple, but it was a special family unit that was happy. It still makes me smile when I think about how Mum and Dad could make us feel like we had everything, and we did, we had two parents whose life was dedicated to us. I suppose, like all kids, I remember the times that made me happy, and they have stayed vivid memories, to this day.

When Dad took us on adventures on his days off, it always started with a ride on the train, as we did not have a car. Dad used to take us to Luna Park, and I can still remember entering through the park's big mouth and that Dad always bought me a Pink Pussy Cat ice cream. I have no memories of going on any rides just that ice cream he bought for me. I just loved them and still, today, smile at the memory. They don't make those ice creams anymore, but they were like a Splice and if I have a Splice today, it reminds me of those days. It warms my soul.

Dad used to visit his mate two doors up from us in Campbelltown, I only remember him as Mr Reading. The Readings had a real porch, not a landing with steps like we did, and Dad used to sit and chat to his mate. Dad would call out to me by the pet name he had for me. He called me, Little Pattie, after his favourite female singer, and I would run up to him, bursting with happiness and sit proudly on his lap, while he spoke with his friends. They were happy days, I felt so safe and loved.

Dad took us to Centennial Park in Sydney and took a photo of us, with our heads and hands in the stocks. We did not have a camera, so he must have used someone else's. I just love that photo. We often went to the Civic Hotel in Sydney, and we would go upstairs and sit in the publican Ma North's, lovely flat upstairs. We would have chips and soft drink, a luxury we never had at home. What a treat. We also went to slot cars in Liverpool and Dad went to the Crossroads Hotel. We loved the slot cars and our treats.

After Dad died, all that stopped, because it was just mum. She did such a good job, but it was incredibly hard for her. In the years before we moved away from Sydney to the south coast, mum suffered a lot. She lost her job at the RSL, because they didn't like the attention she was bringing, and the family was a constant target for war protesters and media. I don't know how she did it.

Leeanne Millward (Daughter of Dasher Wheatley)

My dad went to Vietnam two weeks before my fourth Birthday, so I have very few memories of him, except the gifts and letters which were coming in the mail. Those presents continued to arrive after I was told he had been killed in action, which was confusing at such at a young age.

In March 1966, when compulsory National Service began, the public started to protest our involvement in the Vietnam War. Later that year, Dad was to be posthumously awarded the Victoria Cross, which created conflict for me over being proud of his bravery and sacrifice, and not being able to tell people about it due to the continued opposition of our involvement there. It was the first War that was in our loungerooms on live TV. As I grew up and our government and the public finally recognised Vietnam Veterans for the sacrifice they had endured whilst serving their country, I finally felt able to publicly show pride for all the people who had been touched by this conflict.

I feel very much part of a community that has looked out for me over the years. Vietnam Veterans first and foremost, no matter what battalion they fought in or when they fought, have all been like one big family. Legacy was also a big part of growing up for me, it is where I first met kids like me who had lost their dads as well. Then meeting other members of the AATTV and their families at reunions has been some of my best experiences, where I felt I really belonged. Then in 1987 I was given the honour of carrying my dad's flag in the Vietnam Veterans Welcome Home Parade. On my way out, Colonel McNamara whispered in my ear, 'Your dad is marching beside you, Leeanne.' I cried most of the way. To lead the flags at the front of the march was my proudest moment.

Then in 1998, I moved to England with my family and found a whole new community when I attended my first Victoria Cross and

George Cross biannual reunion in London. I was honoured to sit with the Queen Mother and Sir Roden Cutler VC at table number one. In 2003 I was invited to be part of the Service of Dedication of the VC and GC Memorial in Westminster Abbey, where a stone is now in place in the nave next to the tomb of the forgotten soldier. We escorted a Victoria Cross and a George Cross on pillows down the aisle and presented them to the Queen. My three children have been able to join me at these and many other reunions and my mother came over to London for reunions twice as well. The numbers are getting smaller every year at the VC & GC reunions, so I'm grateful that we had 20 years in the UK and could experience them.

My other proud moment as a mother was watching my children march alongside the Chelsea Pensioners, one Anzac Day in London. Afterwards, we sat with them in the memorial service in Westminster Abbey. We have attended Dawn Service's on Anzac Day in Singapore and Remembrance Day in whatever country we have lived in and I'm sure we will continue to carry on this tradition for as long as we can.

I'm grateful to have been born here in Australia and have never had to experience the horrors of war firsthand, although through our travels we have visited places like the killing fields in Cambodia. I hope that one day we can all live together in harmony and no-one else will have to grow up without ever knowing their father due to another conflict of war.

Captain (ret) Robert Fazekas (son of Felix Fazekas MC)

On the 13th of November, every year, a candle would burn all day in the Fazekas household. This was a somewhat strange occurrence for a kid of five or six years of age and I remember asking Dad what it was for. The answer was a somewhat gruff and sombre, 'It's for remembering'. It was several years later, that I was old enough to read and begin to comprehend the actions of the A Team at Tra Bong, on that fateful day of 13 November 1965.

It was years later still, after I had joined the Army myself, that I had the opportunity to really talk with Dad about that day and hear firsthand about the legend of Dasher Wheatley. Most of what we discussed is well documented here in this book, and in other historical accounts, but what was clear from our discussions was that Dad was immensely proud to have served with both Butch and Dasher. Dad continued to light a candle every 13th of November, until his death in 1998.

Warrant Officer (ret) Bill William 1RAR Vietnam

I was in Vietnam on the 14th of November 1965 with 5 Platoon B Company 1RAR. That's Dasher's old unit. On that day, 6 Platoon had a visit from the reporter Don Simmons, who used to come out with 6 Platoon on operations. He travelled to Bien Hoa from Saigon because he wanted to speak to 6 Platoon, as a whole group. After they had gathered around the platoon headquarters tent, Don told them Dasher and Swanton had been killed, the previous day. The tragic news soon spread across the entire B Company and the battalion. There was total shock and disbelief on hearing of Dasher's death.

After we heard about what had happened and how they left Dasher and Swanton, the distrust of the South-Vietnamese soldiers became rampant in 1RAR. We started questioning what the bloody hell we were doing there. If they wouldn't fight to save our guys or to save Dasher and Swanton, why should we be fighting for them? After he died, we were all in a foul mood, because Wheatley was an extremely popular character in the regiment and well known. Not just the battalion, the regiment. There was so much anger, Dasher epitomised the rugged individualist, which the diggers liked to associate with Australian infantrymen. He was a rough, wild man and a good soldier and was left to die. We wanted blood. We knew he would have taken a bunch of the pricks with him, but you never expected him to die. Not Dasher. He was such a good soldier and such a loss for the Army. His death was felt at home, as well. Dasher drank at the Civic Hotel in the Heart of Sydney, at the weekends and the Railway Hotel in Liverpool, during the week. He was well known and loved, at both venues. These are the two hotels where the legend of Dasher the Larrikin was established and where he was seen at his playful best.

To understand why he was such a good soldier, you must understand the people who trained him. He was taught by people like Macca McKay MM. Macca was awarded the Military Medal fighting on the Kokoda Track with the 39th Battalion in 1942. He was in Malaya, as well as World War II. That is the sort of bloke you want out front leading you. He was the RSM when Wheatley was made up to sergeant from corporal. Dasher went to Malaya with him. You cannot even imagine how valuable that sort of experience is. That was the group of people he learned from, so losing Dasher was a real loss for the Australian Army, because not only was he so well loved, but because people like him were incredibly valuable.

A couple of weeks after that, Reg Hillier got killed. He was the only Northern Territory guy that got killed in Vietnam. He was best mates with Dasher. Reg Hillier was known as 'Cowboy' because he worked as a stockman in the Northern Territory before he joined the Army. He was a good-looking guy and liked Wheatley. They used to go to the Civic Hotel a lot together. That is when the morale of the battalion plummeted. It was almost too much to bear.

Captain (ret) Michael Von Burg MC OAM
1RAR / 5RAR Vietnam

On the night of the 14th November 1965, three of the Infantry Training Wing's NCOs, who knew that I was friendly with Dasher, sought me out. They wanted to tell me that Dasher had been killed in Vietnam with the Training Team, the day before. I was visibly shaken and upset, and the NCO, led by Sergeant Massingham, took me out to spend the night with the NCOs in their base camp, where I had the opportunity to have a few beers and talk about Dasher with many that knew him. The talk, although sombre, was more about the 'character' and the hilarious things he used to get up to, not about his death. This, of course, eased the pain of losing someone who you respected and liked, but it was still a dark cloud that stayed with me, for some time.

At this time, I still didn't know where I would be posted as a newly commissioned officer and when it was announced that I would be posted to 5RAR 'The Tiger Battalion', I was delighted, because many of the diggers and NCOs in that battalion were originally 1RAR. This meant I ended up in Vietnam, surrounded by people that I knew and the memories of 1RAR and Dasher made me feel comfortable, as a newly commissioned officer. But what Dasher's death instilled in me, at that time, was that, as a platoon commander, I would do everything possible to bring all of my blokes home. The thought of losing any of my blokes did not inhibit me in any way from doing my job, but it did influence my decision making. Fighting the fight as much as possible and on my terms normally worked.

When Dasher's VC announced in Dec 1966, I was in Vietnam as Commander of the Reconnaissance Platoon and many of my NCOs were ex 1RAR. We celebrated his award which was no surprise for many of us. Again, it was recalling the character and some of his antics that had us in stitches, but, at the same time, proud in his posthumous award and that we had all known him. Dasher oozed natural leadership qualities and had a way of getting you to do things with enthusiasm and determination.

I had never served with Dasher in a military role. It was all on the rugby field, socially and a few scraps that I had been involved in, but if he fought the war as he fought on the rugby field and in life, then he was always going to make his mark. In the end, he most certainly did, sadly costing him his life. Dasher was, at my young age, a mentor and confidante and in many ways, he has influenced my leadership style. Not all socially acceptable, but getting the job done and making a few friends, along the way. Although, Dasher was what some would call a rough diamond, everyone in the battalion loved him from the CO, Colonel 'Sandy' Pearson, down. He had a way of endearing himself without sucking up or not being himself. He was always himself in any company and that was one of the things that people respected.

I am incredibly grateful and thankful that I had the pleasure of meeting Dasher, at the start of my military career. It, in many ways, had a profound effect on me and the future performance of my duties. I feel grateful for his encouragement and guidance in me seeking a commission. His lasting memorable quote to me in encouraging me to go to Portsea was, 'Look at some of the lieutenants in this battalion. If they can do it, then so can you.'

Those words certainly motivated me at that time, but sadly, our time together was far too short, but it has not through time past diminished my enormous admiration and respect for a life cut tragically short, through the most extreme act of bravery. You would not expect anything less from Dasher. Trying to save a mate!

Warrant Officer (ret) Ray O'Brien 1RAR / 4RAR Vietnam

I remember when Dasher came to visit us, just before he died. Everyone was talking about it. He hung around for about five or six days. Then, one morning, not long after he left, Donnie Simmons came and paid us a visit. Donnie was a reporter working out of Saigon. He came along and he said can I speak to the boys. We are thinking what the bloody hell is he here so early for? It's only about 0800 and it would have taken him awhile to come from Saigon. He got the platoon on parade, and he said, 'I have got bad news for everyone'.

He said 'Dash was killed yesterday' with another warrant officer. He said, 'according to the report in Saigon yesterday, he will get the Victoria Cross'. And we were like, 'Ya got to be joking, Dash the VC?' And he goes, 'Yeah, it was heroic.'

We could not believe he was dead. Blokes started crying and cracking up. Donnie Simmons just left us there for a minute. He told us he had to get back to Saigon to write a story about something and off he went. Then, about three days later, a bloke named Terry gets a letter from Dash that he wrote after he paid us a visit. The letter said that he enjoyed seeing the old platoon and all his old mates again, and 'everyone keep safe and keep your head down. Make sure you get home safely'. It was a strange thing.

Lieutenant Colonel (ret) John Sullivan OAM 1RAR / 2RAR Vietnam

Butch Swanton was a wonderful bloke, both he and Dasher were highly regarded within the AATTV. The Team had a glorious record, there is no doubt about that. They had a well-deserved reputation, because of the conditions under which they lived and operated. They worked almost independently of authority and did a magnificent job. They were briefed by the South-Vietnamese about what their duties were and then, it was up to the individuals to get on with it. And they did. I guess there would be some clowns among them, here and there, but overall, they were a magnificent, bloody group.

They could suggest to the Vietnamese Command what should be done, but they had no executive authority at all. They were there to advise, not to be the director of any operation and that was extremely difficult and stressful. Butch and Dasher knew and trusted each other well enough to be remarkably effective operators. Their loss was devastating to all of us.

Warrant Officer (ret) Gordan Traill (5RAR Iraq)

Rugby is a huge part of Battalion life. When I joined the Australian Army, it was filled with mainly Vietnam Veterans. Those were the people who trained me and my mates. Wednesday was always a 'Sporties Day', everyone would go and watch Rugby. Afterwards you all went to the 'Sporties Bar' to talk about the game and have a few drinks. I vividly remember some of the veterans speaking of some of the greats of Battalion Rugby. Even then, Dasher Wheatley's name would always come up and he would be spoken of in reverence for deeds he did on the Rugby field and in the war.

Bill Charlton (ret) 1RAR Vietnam

What can I say about Dasher
That hasn't been said before?
He was the ideal soldier,
You needed for a war!

He was strong, he was brave.
Yes, both rugged and tough.
A real man's man
He loved to play rough.

Epilogue

Respected and feared
A real digger of note.
If they asked for a favourite.
He'd be getting my vote.

Filled with compassion.
He loved little kids.
Risked his life for them.
It was just how he lived

When his mate was wounded.
He didn't leave him to die.
Stuck with him to the end.
You don't have to ask why.

Some are born to greatness
Many are just brave men.
And then we have the legends.
Dasher Wheatley is among them

Yes he was awarded the VC
He deserved it too.
Dasher was a warrior
And he was true blue!

The End